STIMULATE YOUR CHILD
THROUGH THE YEARS WITHOUT GOING
BANKRUPT

REVISED

STIMULATE YOUR CHILD
THROUGH THE YEARS WITHOUT GOING
BANKRUPT

REVISED

MARIE TAYLOR COLTRANE

CITI OF BOOKS

Copyright © 2024 by Marie Taylor Coltrane

All rights reserved. No part of this publication may be reproduced, distributed, or transmitted in any form or by any means, including photocopying, recording, or other electronic or mechanical methods, without the prior written permission of the copyright owner and the publisher, except in the case of brief quotations embodied in critical reviews and certain other noncommercial uses permitted by copyright law. For permission requests,write to the publisher, addressed "Attention: Permissions Coordinator," at the address below.

CITIOFBOOKS, INC.
3736 Eubank NE Suite A1
Albuquerque, NM 871113579
www.citiofbooks.com
Hotline: 1 (877) 3892759
Fax: 1 (505) 9307244

Ordering Information:

Quantity sales. Special discounts are available on quantity purchases by corporations, associations, and others. For details, contact the publisher at the address above.

Printed in the United States of America.

ISBN13:	Softcover	979-8-89391-422-1
	eBook	979-8-89391-423-8

Library of Congress Control Number: 2024923097

Part 1: Age-Appropriate Activities 1

The Unborn 1
    Touch 1
    Hearing 2
    Sight 2
    Taste 3
    Smell 3
    Talk 3
    Music 4
    Read 5
    Don't Forget Yourself 6
    Older Siblings 7
    Other 8

Infants 8

Games and Activities to do with Your Infant 11
    One to Three Months 11
    Three to Six Months 18
    Six to Nine Months 24
    Nine to Twelve Months 31
    Twelve to Fifteen Months 35
    Fifteen to Eighteen Months 38
    Eighteen to Twenty-one Months 41
    Twenty-one to Twenty-four Months 50

Part 2: Toys, Games, and Activities that Cost Almost Nothing 53
Over 400 fun activities for you to do with your child

Art 53
Nature Arts, Crafts, and Activities 62
Crafts 68
Play Time 78
Food 101
Animals 102
Holidays 105

    Fireworks 105
    Valentines Day 106
    Spring 106
    St. Patrick's Day 107
    Easter 107
    Summer 108
    4th of July or Other Patriotic Holiday 108
    Fall 109
    Halloween 109
    Thanksgiving 111
    Winter 113
    Hanukkah 113
    Christmas 114
Gifts 117
Tips and Hints 118

Part 3: Rhyming Fun 122
Over 50 rhymes, songs, and finger plays

Part 4: Craft Recipes 185

Bubbles 185
Editable – Playdough, Clay, and Molding Dough 189
Non-Toxic – Playdough, Clay, and Molding Dough 194
Non-Editable – Playdough, Clay, and Molding Dough 206
Chalk 221
Paint – Non-Edible 224
Paint – Edible 232
Finger Paint – Non-Edible 234
Finger Paint – Edible 239
Flubber, Slime, Goop, Gak, and Silly Putty 242
Papier Mâché, Glue and Paste 250
Rice and Pasta 259
Sand and Salt 260
Other Recipes 262

More Helps

Materials for the Art Box and Sensory Play 271
Alternative Paint Brushes 274
More Age-Appropriate Activities 276
Images 280
Toddler Property Laws 298

Dedication:

I would like to dedicate this book to my children:
Donald (DG), Andrew, Naomimarie, Cynthia, Charity, and Hyrum
I would also like to dedicate this book to my future grandchildren and great grandchildren.

Acknowledgement:

I would like to acknowledge all the friends and family that have helped me with ideas and tips to help raise my children. Especially my husband, my mother, and my mother-in-law.

Age-Appropriate Activities

The Unborn

I just wanted to add a quick note about your unborn child, before we get into the fun part of having your baby home from the hospital.

As your child develops during pregnancy there are many ways to increase brain stimulation as well as bonding with him or her. Your partner, older siblings, grandparents, and others can also bond with them with your help.

This can help with their development and personality once they are born. The longer they are in the womb the more developed their senses are going to be. By the time they are ready to be born their senses are fully awakened and you will be able to help them fully develop them during the next few months.

Touch

This is the first of the senses to develop. Your baby will start to explore the sense of touch by clutching and unclutching their hand, kicking, playing with the umbilical cord, sucking their thumb, rubbing up against the womb, etc.

Most moms will be feeling their baby move by 24 weeks. Shortly after this point the movements become detectable by others on the outside. This is a great opportunity to pull dad, siblings or others into pregnancy.

A fun game to play with your unborn child is when the baby kicks you; press down on your belly. Then try pressing somewhere else on your belly the baby will then move to kick you there. Keep on doing this. Young children and daddies enjoy this game a lot. By bringing even the youngest child or oldest family member into the "game" you will begin to see the bonds appear.

Gently rub your belly. This will help the baby relax. Others can get into this activity as well. Studies have shown that babies can differentiate between mom's and dad's touch. You could also combine it with talking or reading to your baby. When you rub your belly, you can rub in some olive oil this helps prevent stretch marks.

Even if you are not artistic try using nontoxic paints, you can paint your belly using your fingers. Then take pictures of your belly and show your child and talk about how they were a part of creating that art. Have your partner do this as well either by creating art together or each of you do it separately. Do not use paintbrushes or other tools to create your art with as you could at times put more pressure on your belly than would be recommended.

Hearing

This is the sense that is the most developed before your baby is born. By 7 months their hearing is fully developed, and they can hear both things inside and outside of the womb. They can also react to what they hear.

Starting as early as 13 weeks their hearing starts to develop. They will start with hearing your heartbeat or your stomach rumbling. It will then develop to the point when they can hear external sounds such as your voice, music, loud noises. They will start to react to those sounds as early as 25 weeks. Some sounds will sooth them such as your voice, relaxing music, etc. Where other sounds could stimulate them or cause them to be upset.

Sight

Your babies' eyes will open between 25 to 28 weeks they will be able to tell the light from the dark. When you are exposed to a lot of light (sunlight) your babies heart rate will increase.

Your baby will turn away from a bright light aimed directly at your belly.

A fun game to play with them turning on and off the light talk about what we do during the light being on (playing, working, etc.) and what happens during the dark (sleep).

Taste

As you leave your first trimester your baby will have taste buds that they can use to taste the amniotic fluid. Through this they can taste different things that you eat.

Midway through the second trimester they can distinguish between some tastes such as sweet, salty, sour, and bitter.

If you vary what you eat during your pregnancy you will help them develop their taste. Make sure you are following any diet that your doctor or medical provider gives you but within that there will be many variations that you can try and that will give you the nutrition that you need as well as give your child different flavors to experiment with.

Unless told by a medical professional you do not need to dull down your palate you can still eat the spicy or flavorful foods that you love.

As you eat your food describe what you are eating the texture, the smells, and the taste. Talk to them about what you like and do not like.

Smell

During your final trimester your baby will be able to "smell" the food you eat through their tasting of the amniotic fluid.

They can also start to smell you which will help them after birth to bond with you as well as calm them the first time you hold them in your arms. This is how they will immediately start to recognize you.

Immediately after you give birth your breasts will start to smell like your amniotic fluid. This is why babies immediately start to seek them out to bring them comfort of the familiar.

Talk

Talk to your baby. This may seem a bit abstract for some, but it can be a lot of fun and leads itself into games later, consider reading to your baby or telling your baby what you are doing or how your day went. Your partner and older siblings should join you in talking to your baby. The baby will then learn to recognize their voices as well. Although your voice will be the most soothing for the baby. This is a fun soothing activity for both you and the baby.

Some things to keep in mind while talking to them: talk in a calm loving tone, this will help them relax. Even when talking with others, talk in that same calm loving voice. Have conversations with them. Use their name and nick name frequently while having your conversations with them. When talking with others call the other person by name so they can start to recognize and associate the sound of that person's name and the sound of their voice. Say "I love you" frequently to the baby. You can also give other complements like, " you are beautiful (hansom)" "thank you for not kicking so hard".

When babies get used to hearing certain voices while in the womb, these are the voices that they respond to and turn to outside of the womb. They respond best to their mother's voice because that is what they hear the most of, after that other voices depending on how often your baby hear those voices.

They can easily hear low pitched sounds like male voice, certain music instruments, waves crashing on the beach etc. These sounds will have a calming effect on them. Where the high pitched or sudden noises such as a door being slammed could stratal them.

Music

Music is another great way to stimulate their hearing. Some people buy fancy listening devices to use on their bellies, but just being in a room with music exposes the baby to the sounds. You can protect their ears by keeping the volume down (normal conversation volume) and not putting headphones or ear buds directly on your stomach. Also avoid loud environments such as concerts, clubs, parties, arguments, etc. as these, if exposed to them for long periods of time can damage their ears.

When I was pregnant with each of my 6 children I would often sing or hum songs for them. I loved singing church songs to them. After they were born when they were fussy, I would often rub their back, rock them back and forth, and sing or hum the same church songs. This almost always calmed them within a few minutes. Even when they did not calm all the way down, they did calm part way down so I could figure out what was wrong and take care of the issue.

It does not matter if you sing church songs, children's songs, rock and roll, country, or any other genre that you can think of, your baby loves your voice so sing, hum, read, talk, etc. to them. Repetition is great. If you sing the same songs, read the same stories, recite the same nursery rhymes your baby will learn the sounds associated with them and will find comfort in them.

With the push for classical music for babies and their brain development it's not a bad idea to add some in there, but flavor is also good. Remember, listening to your favorite music, the stuff that makes you want to dance and sing in your car, is the stuff that will help release endorphins (hormones that produce a feeling of wellbeing for you and baby) into your body. Listen to the same songs frequently, your baby will then learn to recognize them, and they will have a calming/soothing effect on them even after they are born.

Read

You can read to the baby each night before bed you can start to accustom them to a nightly routine. Try reading at the same time each evening. If you have older children reading to them will help your baby know when "bedtime" is. Reading to them will begin a love of books. While every child is different when you are consistent in your routine it will help them once they are born.

Some studies have shown that when you read to your baby it will help lay the foundation of speech and language patterns. Reading rhymes to your baby it helps develop their sound recognition it also helps them understand the rhythm of words and language. Some experts suggest that reading to the baby and throughout their childhood will help them develop a love for books.

Don't be afraid to use silly voice, speak in an accent, as well as using your regular voice. This will help them become accustomed to different ways of speaking. After they are born you can add silly faces. This will help make this time more memorable to both of you.

Don't Forget Yourself

There are many things that you can do during your pregnancy to take care of yourself and your baby. Here are a few suggestions of things that I found during my 6 pregnancies to work for me.

Give yourself time to reflect and meditate. As an expectant mother there are many thoughts that go through your mind such as yours and your baby's health and what the future will hold. Relaxing and resting from all these thoughts that come at you will help you deal with anything that comes your way.

Destress. There are many things that cause us stress during our lives. It could be work, family, friends, a bad day, bad news, or many other things. Take time each day to de-stress. This will help you relax, and your body needs the down time from all of the stress. Remember what happens to you happens to baby. If you are stressed, the baby is stressed. Everyone has different ways to reduce the stress in their lives, use what works for you and practice it every day.

Go for a walk. Most experts agree that women need to have some physical activity (unless they have told you bed rest). A walk is the perfect gentle activity you can go by yourself and use the time to reflect and meditate or use the time to spend with friends and family who are supporting you through this time. Exercising will help increase your blood circulation which will help deliver oxygen and nutrients to your baby. Exercising can also help you release some stress. With anything speak to your medical professional to make sure you are creating the correct balance in your life.

When you exercise it will rock your baby to sleep. You can create a routine of exercising at the same time each day and that could be your baby's bedtime. This will help them once they are born to get into the routine and they will already feel that that time is bedtime. Some ideas of exercise your can-do would-be yoga, stretching, walking, swimming, etc.

A nice relaxing warm bath is just the thing to relax your muscles and give you time to pamper yourself. Note do not make the water too warm or use a professional jacuzzi as the water temperature will cause your body temperature to increase and cause the baby distress.

Write in a diary or stories to the baby about what you are experiencing. You and your child will enjoy reading these entries once they are born. You can also research your family history and find stories about your ancestors that would entertain your baby. Be sure to read these to your baby as you read to them. Children of all ages are fascinated with true stories about people that they are connected to such as yourself, your partner, grandparents, siblings, and ancestors.

Talk to others who are pregnant now or who have gone through pregnancy in the past and you will find strength and insight listening to their stories and sharing your own experience with them.

Get enough sleep. Sometimes it may feel hard to get the sleep you need but try to listen to your body and sleep when you need to. Take naps during the day if you can.

Older Siblings

Older children often feel jealous or neglected when everyone is focused on the new arrival. They may revert to undesirable behavior just to get attention. You will need to help them understand that they are not forgotten and loved as well.

Use some of the activities in this book for special bonding time with them both before the baby is born as well as after. This will give them a creative outlet to express their feelings that they might not be able to articulate.

Talk to them about the changes that are happening and address any fears that they may have. Read stories and talk to them about babies and pregnancy.

Let them help with preparations for the baby's arrival. Such as taking them shopping for baby supplies and letting them help set up the baby's room. They can draw pictures and hang them on the wall.

Some parents feel that if they buy something for their baby, they also must buy something for their older child as well. While everyone likes gifts and wants to feel special, that way you do not always have to buy extra. For example, when you are about to go out and buy furniture for the baby's room go through the older child's room and talk about the bed and how you bought them that and then go through the other furniture as well. Take the child with you to get the new furniture and talk to them about how you are getting them a bed to sleep in etc.

Other

There is some research that suggests that babies can start to develop their language recognition while still in the womb. If you speak multiple languages (or trying to learn another one). Speak or sing to your child in both languages.

When you get an ultrasound try talking or singing to your baby. See what kind of reaction you get from them.

While you cannot teach them anything until they are born you can start to accustom them to specific sounds and sound patterns. This will make it a little easier when you are ready to start teaching them.

Infants

Playing with your baby is often instinctual. Don't get over wrought with how or when to play with your baby, most people will find that it will come naturally. Remember that the key is to have fun and enjoy your baby.

To decide what materials to provide for your infant, ask yourself these questions:
- What objects interest the baby most?
- Are there things the infant tried to do but couldn't because of the difficulty level?
- Will the materials be challenging enough to attract the baby's attention?
- Are the materials, equipment, and toys safe?

Babies are hard at work whenever they are awake, trying to learn all about the world. Learning takes place from the very beginning of an infant's life. Having a plan to help babies learn is an important part of caring for them. Infants, however, learn very differently from older children. Therefore, you should offer activities that are carefully tailored to their methods of learning. To help them learn, they need many different safe things to play with and inspect. Objects you have around your home offer many possibilities.

Your baby will learn a lot from playing, and it is also a great way for you to get to know each other.

Babies love repetition and you will undoubtedly get the most giggles when you repeat a familiar game or activity. Introduce a new game or activity when you are getting bored with the old ones.

Clap and make a fuss whenever baby learns a new trick or achieves a new goal.

There are always balls, blocks and other toys to play with.

Consider your baby to be a sponge. They are soaking up information and testing new skills all the time. The trick to being involved in this and being able to provide more opportunities for them is to be aware of their capabilities.

People often think that because their baby doesn't appear to do much besides eat and sleep that they are not open to any kind of stimulation besides a crib and a bottle. This couldn't be further from the truth. A baby is learning at a rate faster than either you or I could imagine. And while it is true that the kinds of activities and games suitable for a baby are not worthy of genius status as far as you or I are concerned, they still warrant the same amount of attention. They are just as worthy of initiation as things you might do with an older child.

Remember that baby has just spent nine months wrapped up in a warm and mobile environment. They have been accustomed to a certain degree of motion for quite some time and they will find it very soothing if you keep it going. This is why your baby may cry as soon as you put them down. So basic movement, swaying and rocking while you sing will provide a very satisfied baby!

Much of an infant's day involves care-giving activities such as feeding, diapering, and holding. Infants learn a great deal during these routines. You can foster language development by talking to infants as you change or feed them. You help them learn that they can affect others through your reactions to their facial expressions. When you smile and touch them softly, you are helping them learn to trust others and to feel good about themselves.

Playing with objects and people around them is another significant way that infants learn. When your baby is awake and alert, provide equipment, materials, and activities that encourage the baby to explore.

You will need to carefully watch your baby. Observe them as you care for them and while they are playing. Watch what they are doing with their mouths, their fingers, their bodies, and the things around them. Then plan activities that will help them practice these skills. Keep in mind that each baby is different from the other. Two infants the same age may be at different stages of development. Therefore, it is important to watch each child carefully. Please refer to the sections on activities for your infant by month and the section on rhymes that you can do with your baby.

Safety should be the main concern when determining what toys, material, and equipment to provide. Look the materials over carefully. Toys given to infants should be at least 1 5/8" in diameter. Provide toys and materials that are easily sanitized. Make sure they have no small pieces or sharp edges. Never use balloons as toys. Many children have died from suffocation after inhaling a piece of a popped balloon.

Wooden toys should be checked continually for any splintered corners or surfaces. Items that are made of small, easily swallowed pieces, such as a string of beads, should be tested often to make sure they will not come apart. Also, be aware of materials, such as paint or Styrofoam, which could flake off or crumble when they are mouthed or chewed.

The key to providing quality activities for infants is close observation as they interact naturally with their environment. By responding to their interests and abilities, and by monitoring the safety of the materials you have provided, you are creating a healthy and challenging environment that will promote physical, mental, social, and emotional growth.

Infants not only prefer to look at high contrast images, but that they can help increase concentration skills, stimulate the creation of synapses (brain cell connections), increase an infant's attention span, calm a baby (when they are bored), and enhance curiosity.

Games and Activities to do with your Infant

Although these games and activities are grouped by age, there are many overlaps - don't go strictly by the ages the games and activities are in. Do a game or activity until the baby has totally mastered the game or activity. If the baby becomes frustrated or bored with a game or activity, do something else for a while and then come back to it, then it will seem like a new game or activity.

Overall, just remember to keep it simple, but keep constantly interacting with your baby. Provide lots of things to stimulate all their senses and watch for cues as to when they get over stimulated. A baby's usual response to being over stimulated is to just go to sleep, but not before a bit of wailing!

One to Three Months

Hug your baby, rock, kiss, or hold them firmly. This can be your first activity with the baby, it helps with the bonding but also like most new moms you won't want to let your baby go.

After a bath, rub them firmly with the towel.

Have your baby hold objects with different textures in both hands. You might try objects like the following: Different textures of cloth, Yarn pom-pom, Metal objects, Plastic objects, Sponge, Dough, Sandpaper, Pot scrubber, Beans, macaroni, rice, Keys, Paper (wax paper, newspaper, tinfoil, etc.), Ice cubes, snow, Water, Grass, Flowers, Flour, sugar, cornmeal, or whatever else you can think of.

Sight is the least developed of the senses when your baby is born. They can only see things close up and bright light is not good for them. They cannot tell one color from the next. They also have no depth perception and only a narrow field of vision. Their vision will rapidly improve over the next few months then slow down until they are about 4 years old at that time they will have reached their optimum acuity.

Let your baby crawl, walk, or be on a variety of surfaces—carpet, linoleum, wood, grass, and sand, for example.

Use colored sheets and blankets.

Before they can roll over, sit and crawl, babies need opportunities to stretch and flex those upper torso muscles. Gather a few interesting objects or toys for your baby. Lay a blanket on the floor and place your baby on it, belly down, some babies don't like to lay and play on their tummies. For these babies, a rolled-up towel, blanket or a pillow placed underneath baby's chest and arms can make tummy time more tolerable. To begin the game, place an object or toy in front of baby, just beyond babies reach and encourage your baby to reach for it. Move it closer, if baby becomes too frustrated trying to reach it. After the baby obtains the object and has a chance to observe and play with it, place another toy or object, off to the right or left of baby, just outside of baby's reach. Repeat the reach and grab process a few times, or for as long as you are both content with playing, putting each new object just a little bit farther away than the last.

Hang a bright mobile on the baby's bed. A newborn keeps his head to the side and will not see toys hung over the middle of the bed, so attach a bright object to the side of the crib nine to twelve inches from his nose. Try to change the mobile in some way every week.

Take the baby from room to room with you.

Holding them in your arms while feeding them is the perfect way to help them focus on your face and help them recognize it.

For some quick, visual fun, draw a face or geometric design, with bright markers, onto a paper plate. Yarn can be glued on for hair to give it texture. (Babies particularly like eyes, so the more detail you can do on them the better) Glue a Popsicle stick low on the back for holding, and move the plate at different distances from baby, move it up and down, and side to side. By about 3 months babies can "track" objects with their eyes. See the images that are included in the book for some ideas.

When babies are first born, they don't have the visual range that adults have. The general rule of thumb is that they can see as far as their mother's face while they are nursing. So is it any wonder that they find faces so amusing.

When you are with your baby, get in as close as possible, as close as it takes for them to reach out a chubby hand and grab your nose. A face is very interesting, and a baby will delight in exploring it, especially if it is making all sorts of funny noises and shapes.

Have you ever caught your baby seemingly just staring off into space or looking at the ceiling or a wall? While you may at first be a little concerned that they are just vacantly staring, take comfort in the fact that they are just exploring within their visual capabilities. Not only is a baby's visual range limited at birth, the colors that they see are also limited. At first, they will only be able to see red, white and black. So, if you are sitting next to a big white wall with some black shadows then your baby is going to be absolutely fascinated. The same goes for nice white ceiling fans, bright red signs, Venetian blinds and many more other such things following this pattern.

Another common tool for amusing a baby is a mobile in their crib. These are successful for the same reason as your face. Make sure to hang it very low so that the baby will be able to see it. Many mobiles these days come with adjustable height so that you can adjust it with the baby's abilities.

When your baby is lying on their back, dangle a brightly colored toy or rattle about ten to twelve inches above their eyes. When the baby focuses on it, move the object in an arc or half-circle.

Hold them or sit them in an upright position occasionally so they can see how things look from that angle.

During the day, shift the crib to another part of the room. Put it by a window, if possible.

Talk to your baby. Tell them what you are doing for them, what you are cooking for dinner, what your feelings are about life, people, and politics, etc.

Use black and white images to stimulate their eyes. Use the ones included in this book or make your own.

Sing to them or say a nursery rhyme. See the list of rhymes that are included or make up your own.

When your baby makes a sound, imitate it. Show them your delight in his "speech" by smiling, hugging, or praising.

Let the baby hear noises around your house. You don't have to keep the house quiet. Let them listen to the radio, television, or stereo for a short time. Let them play with noise-making toys like rattles and musical animals.

Take some white paper or a paper plate and draw some bold black and red shapes on them. Your baby will delight in looking at them. You can also use the images included with this book.

Babies also love to feel things. To maximize this sense, provide lots of sensory and textural things for your baby to explore. Lay them on a blanket with a different texture. I am sure that you have probably seen in many stores, the various numbers of play surfaces and rugs for babies. Take advantage of them and let your baby explore the surfaces. As they grow, and can grasp and mouth objects, find some toys that have different textures and sensations.

Also expose your baby to as many auditory experiences as possible. Make the crib mobile a musical one, play soft music on the CD player and most importantly talk, and talk some more. Babies naturally prefer higher pitched voices so make sure you indulge them. This is why Mommy softly singing a lullaby will have them entertained for ages, and while babies are not likely to talk back to you any time soon, this is the preliminary steps to learning language skills.

Let your baby smell many things, such as soaps, lotions, perfumes, spices, and food.

When your doctor says your baby is old enough, gradually introduce a variety of foods to them.

Shake a rattle to your baby's left and then to the baby's right. Watch your baby follow the rattle or turn toward the sound. When a little older (six weeks) holds it beyond his head or over his tummy – now the baby will move its head to see it.

You are your baby's first and best "toy". Being with you is pleasurable--looking at your face, feeling your warmth and comfort, hearing your voice, and recognizing your scent are all opportunities for your baby to get to know you. So, play lots together and enjoy getting acquainted.

A few simple toys are all you need during these first months as your baby begins to focus and notice the world around them. A rattle, some plastic rings, and a hanging mobile--all begin to attract their attention.

After a few months, you'll be able to play more actively with your baby. Try dancing in a circle to your favorite music. Or move her gently through the air like an airplane. Find ways of moving together that you both enjoy.

Lie on your back and place your baby on their belly against your chest. Or place them on the bed with their face near the edge on their belly, and then crouch on the floor at face level with them. They love to look at your face! And these positions help them grow comfortable being on their belly and learn to raise their head.

Stand in front of your baby with another adult and take turns talking to them. Let them look back and forth between you so that they can learn to differentiate who is speaking.

Start a babbling exchange: Copy a sound your baby makes, and then give them a chance to respond. These are their first "conversations"!

Sit on the floor with your knees bent and your feet flat on the floor. Prop your baby against your thighs with his feet on your chest so that you're face-to-face. Look them in the face with your eyes wide open and smile, and then look away. Repeat for as long as they are interested.

Hold up a mirror and let them look at both of your faces. Babies find it fascinating to look at reflective surfaces, especially those that have faces in them.

While they are on a changing table or lying on a bed, experiment with different forms of touch to see if he likes firm pressure or a feather-light touch, to have their tummy rubbed gently or the thighs caressed. If you keep an eye on his facial expressions, it'll be easy for you to discover what they like and what they don't.

Stick out your tongue. Say "La-la-la", wiggle your tongue, etc. very young infants will imitate you.

Cluck your tongue or make tsk-tsk noises.

Hold your fingers 6 to 12 inches above the babies' face then slowly lower your hand until you touch their face. Try it with wiggly fingers or stationary fingers.

Hold your hand over baby's head. Wiggle your fingers all at once, then one at a time.

Place a mirror about 7 inches from your baby's eyes and let them watch the reflection of their own movements.

To soothe or cheer them, sing simple songs to her such as "Twinkle, Twinkle Little Star" or "Hush, Little Baby."

To help your baby relax, lie down on a bed next to them. Then try to match your breathing pattern with them.

Make a tape of your baby's sounds and play it back to them. Listening to their coos, goos, and cries will fascinate and relax them, even though they won't realize it's them who are making them.

With baby at your shoulder put your arm under the feet and let them push themselves up.

Hold a toy about six inches from their eyes and let them swipe at it with her hand.

Show baby pictures of faces – in magazines, books, on TV, etc.

Now that their fists are uncurling, play with their fingers, tickle their palm, and put their hand up to your face.

Crumple up a piece of paper in front of baby. Flatten and repeat.

Gently guide your baby's feet in a cycling motion. Soon they'll be doing it on their own, joyfully! It's a natural exercise in gaining muscle strength and control.

Sit on the floor with your knees bent and your feet flat on the floor. Prop your baby against your thighs with their feet on your belly and let them push against you and learn what their muscles can do.

Hold baby on your shoulder and tour the house telling baby the name of objects: i.e. bed, refrigerator, TV, etc. Let your baby touch the objects as you name them.

Lay baby down on his stomach in different rooms to give them different things to look at.

Take baby on a tour of your yard. Listen to birds or wind or airplanes. Show baby trees, flowers, and grass and let them touch them.

Follow baby's lead and imitate things he does – sighs, coughs, laughs, and smiles.

Babble at baby – totally nonsensical sounds.

Put a toy in front of your baby and encourage them to push up on his arms to look at it.

When baby starts to swipe at things, dangle a toy for them to swing at.

You will want to "Converse" with your baby by imitating their cooing and gurgling noises.

Put baby on your lap facing you and chant, "Never know when you're going" over and over until suddenly and (and holding on tightly to baby) you open your knees to let baby drop down a few inches. The surprise is how many times you chant before you "drop" baby. Your baby will giggle in anticipation.

Play with a puppet. A sock with a face drawn on it will do fine.

Three to Six Months

Watch how your baby reacts when things disappear. Does baby lean over to look for things they dropped? Does baby put a toy down and go right back to it later? These are signs that baby's memory is growing. Show baby a toy, then cover it -- slowly at first -- with a cloth or cup. See if your infant will try to pull the cover off. What happens if you cover only part of the toy? Try different toys, and different covers. Play peek-a-boo to help baby learn that you come back when you go away. Sometimes cover your face, and sometimes cover your baby's face. If your baby doesn't play these games now, wait a few weeks and try again.

If the baby enjoys kicking, dangle a rattle from your fingers so that when baby kicks it, he's rewarded with an exciting jangling noise.

Your baby becomes more playful now and enjoys looking around and taking in the scene. You are still your baby's favorite "toy" to touch and explore. Enjoy many playtimes together; sing and chat with your baby in your lap and on the floor.

Toys are used more now as your baby notices and is attracted to what you offer. Rattles, teething toys, items to swat, pull, and push, simple pop-up toys and a few soft, small stuffed animals all come in handy when spending time with your baby.

Let the manufacturers' age guidelines help you choose safe, appropriate items for your baby. Resist the temptation to rush ahead to the next age range, which may not be right for her.

Buy or make some simple mobiles to hang where your baby can see them and reach for them without pulling them down. This may engage her quite a while.

As your baby is more responsive, try your first rounds of peek-a-boo. Use your hands to cover your face for a brief second. "Peek-a-boo, I see you!" It's an all-time favorite!

Bubbles are an easy item to have on hand. Blow a few bubbles where your baby can reach out to grasp them. Keep an extra bottle of bubbles in your stroller bag for when it may come in handy!

Holding your baby goes a long way. Have some fun with it. Walk in a circle at different speeds. Add music. Add singing. Try stopping at the same places along the way to make a game of it.

When your baby is on her back, gently move her legs and arms back and forth for a "bicycle ride". Chat and sing with her to add to the fun.

Walk your baby around the house to visit the baby in the mirror. Babies love to see themselves and you. Talk to the baby in the mirror together. Watch and enjoy your baby's reaction! Take the baby round the room, pointing at things and naming items for them.

Show your baby their face in the mirror.

Look out of the window and tell them what you can see.

Let your baby make faces at you and pause sometimes when you're talking to them. They may make some noises back at you and you can show your delight and pleasure to encourage them.

Let the baby watch a ceiling fan (don't let them be in the draft). Chant something like "round and round and round it goes, where it stops nobody knows"

Show the baby their hands and feet, telling them what they are called. Touch other body parts telling baby what each is called.

Take a bright object, such as a red ball, and place it in front of your baby's eyes. Slowly move it to the left, then to the right, to give them a chance to "track" it.

Supporting the baby's head and back, have the baby do sit-ups on your lap.

Look at your baby and move your face back and forth in front of them. They'll love to track your movement and anticipate what you're going to do next.

When your baby makes a sound, react with delight, repeat it back to them, then pause and give them a chance to respond. They'll love this kind of turn taking and anticipating what's coming next.

While bathing or dressing your baby, name body parts so that she begins to associate a word with their nose, her leg, her belly, and so on.

Show your baby how things work around the house: Flick a light switch on and off, or open and close a drawer, and describe what's happening.

To reinforce your baby's budding interest in language, keep up a running dialogue with them while you're going about the ordinary activities of your day.

Talk to the baby about what you're doing throughout the day, while you're diapering them, bathing them, or tidying up their room. Take them on a walk around the house and tell them about different objects. Babies prefer simple, clear language that's expressed in a higher-pitched tone (this usually comes naturally to adults when they talk to babies).

While you're sitting, place your baby on your lap so that they are facing you and hold them under their arms for support. Lift and lower your heels so that your knees go up and down and he gets a gentle, jiggly ride. Sing a song or recite a rhyme while doing this—it'll be even more fun!

Sing a song or recite a rhyme and clap your baby's hands together with the rhythm. See the included list of rhythms to use or make up your own.

Let your baby touch different types of textures—smooth, shiny fabrics, corduroy, velvet, wool, aluminum foil, and so on. This helps them learn about their sense of touch and about how objects can be different. Tell the baby how soft, smooth, rough, etc.

Make different faces at baby: happy, sad, surprised, excited, angry, and tired.

Hold one of their favorite toys or some other interesting object slightly out of reach so that she can practice her grabbing skills.

Talk to the baby about what happened during the day: where you went, whom you saw, etc.

While your baby is lying on his back or sitting in an infant seat, place some gentle pressure against the soles of his feet: he will love pushing against that pressure and exercising his newly developed strength.

When you're changing your baby or just hanging out with them, bring your face toward theirs and let them pat your cheeks.

Place your baby tummy down on top of a big beach ball and slowly roll it back and forth and from side to side. This will help them develop balance and gain a new sense of space as they get different views on their ride.

Show baby colors. Then take the baby on a tour of the house finding all the yellow things one day, and other colors on each of the following days.

Help baby rollover from back to front and from front to back.

Blow raspberries with your baby. Or click your tongue at your baby and they'll probably try to imitate you.

Hold your baby in your arms or seat them on your lap and ask, "How big is [your baby's name]?" Then raise one of their hands over their head and answer, "So big!" Eventually they'll learn to raise their hand themselves while you do this.

Take your baby on a walk outside and let them touch a leaf, a brick, a feather, and some grass. Discovering these natural textures will delight them.

Let baby listen to sounds: vacuum cleaner, washing machine, running water, timer, and doorbell. Watch baby's reaction, as they may not like some sounds.

While dressing your baby or changing her diaper, tickle her or play "This Little Piggy" with her toes.

Hold baby's hand against a cool surface (a glass with an icy drink in it, a window on a cold day, etc.). Tell baby it's cold. Do the same for warm surfaces (a sunny window, baby's bottle, etc.). Tell the baby it is warm.

Place your baby on the surface of their tummy and put a non-breakable mirror just in front of them so that they can discover their own reflection.

Put baby in a child swing. Sing songs like ABC's to them in time to the motion.

With baby looking at your mouth say, "Mama" or "dada" and ask baby to repeat it.

Do little exercises with a baby like bicycle their legs gently or stretch their arm out to the side then in or over the head then back down.

Take baby for walks in a stroller. Let the baby look at people and tell baby about the scenery.

Show the baby how to work all the activity center gadgets. Then let them do it on their own.

Dance with your baby.

Lie on your back on the floor and hold your baby overhead. As you slowly lower them toward your face, smile and make a happy sound before raising them in the air again.

Play a tape for baby of children's songs. Sing along with it, as the baby loves to hear your voice.

Throw a cloth over your baby's favorite stuffed animal and say, "Where's Teddy?" Then whip it off and say, "There he is!" At this age the element of surprise will amuse your baby, even if you do it over and over.

Watch Sesame Street with baby and Mr. Rogers. Tell the baby what things, animals, etc. on the screen are. Say, "Oh, look what he's doing!"

Play in front of a mirror. Both of you look into the mirror and touch the "other" baby. Move away from the mirror and then back again so "baby" looks like they are moving. Say, "Who's that baby? Is that you?"

Discover what makes your baby laugh—whether it's shrugging your shoulders or frantically waving your arms—and do it as long as the giggles keep coming.

Sit baby on your lap. Letting them hold onto your fingers help baby stand up, then down to a sitting position saying, "Up we go, down we go". You will soon feel your baby doing the work itself.

Sing "Pop Goes the Weasel", bouncing baby when you sing "pop".

Sing "Pat-a-Cake", clapping baby's hands gently.

Sing "Row, Row, Row Your Boat". Lie baby on your lap facing you, hold their hands and rock up and down first the baby sitting with you lying down then you are sitting and them lying down.

Count your baby's fingers and toes, holding each one as you say the number.

Sing "Itsy, Bitsy Spider" and have your hand "crawl" up baby.

Blow raspberries on baby's stomach and chest.

Do "This Little Piggy" wiggling baby's toes and ending with a tickle.

Sing the ABC's touching a different spot on baby's face (nose, cheek, mouth, etc.) as you sing each letter.

As you sing the ABC's point to the letter of the alphabet on a chart so your baby can see the letter and begin to recognize them.

Play alphabet blocks with baby. Show the baby a letter and let them associate it with something he knows or something fun. For example, "K" is for kiss and give the baby one. "J" is for jumping and doing it – the more active the better, they'll pay attention and want to play.

Ask baby to point to a certain letter. First use a board to help recognize the order that they go in.

Read baby books or magazines and tell them what the large letters in the titles are.
Give baby a tour of the house telling baby, "This is the bedroom, this is the kitchen", etc.

When baby is ready to say the letters, start with the vowels. Have the baby watch your mouth while you over-emphasize the letter. Then encourage the baby to try it.

Let baby turn the light switch on and off, saying "on" or "off" at the appropriate times.

Let the baby ring the doorbell and listen to the sound.

Six to Nine Months

Play peek-a-boo covering your eyes with your hands and pulling them away to exclaim, "Peek-a-boo".

Holding a pillow or cloth in front of you, leave the pillow where it is and you pop out over the top, bottom or one of the sides exclaiming "Boo".

Play peek-a-boo with the toys by hiding them under a baby blanket.

It's true that play is baby's work. Playtime is every day, all day, everywhere, and anywhere! Your baby is ready, full of energy, and acquiring new skills all the time. Play helps them learn about the world and make sense of what's going on around them. At the same time, your baby is developing his motor and language skills.

Your baby can now play on his own with you close by. Place a few toys he enjoys within easy reach and watch them go! Your presence and encouragement will go a long way!

Your baby also needs you to play with them to show them how things work, to describe what is happening, and to deepen his involvement with the activity. When you play together with your baby, he will get more involved and play longer. So join in the fun!

Your baby's eagerness to play can be a part of your everyday care of them. Be playful with them. Your repertoire of songs, nursery rhymes, finger plays, silly faces and noises, as well as a few toys in your diaper bag come in handy when he is upset and in need of distraction.

Your baby is fascinated that objects disappear and reappear. After all, he is trying to figure out where you are when you are not with him and whether you will be back! This is prime time for peek-a-boo games of all sorts. Use your hands, a scarf, and a stuffed toy. Cover your face. Cover your baby's face if he's comfortable. You'll have a great time playing peek-a-boo wherever you are!

Your baby needs toys that he can hold on his own, toys that demonstrate cause and effect, and toys that he can begin to stack and manipulate. Soft cuddly toys are wonderful to hold and play with as well.

A few toys at one time are all your baby needs. If he seems to lose interest in a toy, put it in the closet, and let some time go by. When you bring it out again, your baby may find it exciting to explore with his new skills.

Look around you for wonderful everyday items for your baby to play with. Pots, pans, plastic containers, wooden spoons, or an old pocketbook make great playthings. Also check for rough or sharp edges. Show them how to put things in the purse or bang on pots and he is on his way!

Keep a few different-sized, colorful balls in your toy collection. Roll one to your baby and encourage them to "catch" it. At first, this might be simply touching the ball. Eventually his hands will find it. Before long he will even roll it back! Encourage your crawling baby by rolling the ball slightly beyond them. He'll be on the move to get it!

A large inflatable beach ball offers lots of fun. Roll it to your baby, and he will reach out to its bright colors and appealing shape and size. Use it as a drum to tap on. Toss it up and watch them crawl to get it! Place your baby, tummy down, on the ball and roll them gently back and forth. Be sure he enjoys this activity before you continue.

Your baby loves imitating you. Give them lots of opportunities when you play together. Clap your hands. Shake your head. Stamp your feet. Bang two small blocks together. Stack two blocks on top of each other. Take all the blocks out of a plastic container one by one. Show them how and, eventually he will imitate your actions.

Older babies might enjoy crawling through a hula-hoop or large carton. Try creating a baby-sized "obstacle course" by adding a large cushion to crawl over or around.

Bubbles are great fun for babies! They reach out to grab them and crawl over to chase them. Keep a bottle of bubbles in your diaper bag--they are wonderful to have when you need a little something special to do.

Grab a few lightweight, bright scarves from your drawer. Toss them in the air. Your baby will love watching them float to the floor. He'll quickly crawl over to touch one!

Play with a variety of stuffed toys and soft dolls. Explore the textures of the soft toys. Add a baby blanket, a play bottle and a baby brush to expand play.

Play with an assortment of squeak toys and rattles or anything that makes noise. Help Baby choose toys with different colors, shapes, sizes, and textures. Help Baby to hold, mouth, pat, bang, shake, wave, press buttons, and squeak the toys.

Play with blocks that are different sizes. Blocks can be made of plastic, wood, or fabric. Use a verity of blocks in your play. Bang the blocks together. Experiment with different combinations (i.e. wood and plastic) to see what kinds of sounds you can get from them.

Provide cups or other containers to encourage the development of in and out play. Pick up small objects and drop them into cups. Move the objects from hand to hand. Hide the small objects in and under the cups.

Play with cause-and-effect toys i.e. toys that have buttons or levers to push or pull that make noise. Encourage Baby to make something happen. Help Baby learn that he or she can influence the world.

Share board books with Baby. Choose books with a wide variety of simple photographs or pictures. Show Baby how to turn the pages. Point to pictures and name them. Encourage Baby to pat the pictures. Read to Baby with feeling in your voice. Some books have different textures or smells in them. Help the baby recognize some of these different things.

Get out photo albums of family members and look through them with baby. Point to the people and tell them who they are and something about them.

As the baby gets older ask them to point to a person or object on a page (i.e. grandma or flower.)

Smile and talk to Baby. Pause and wait for Baby to respond by vocalizing or moving. "Answer" Baby back. Use gestures along with words. Make a variety of sounds including "raspberries" and popping sounds. Encourage Baby to imitate you. Imitate Baby's sounds.

Talk to baby about what you are doing. Use words to describe what Baby is doing. Name all the family members as they play with Baby. Name all the toys and objects that you are playing with for your baby as your baby plays with them.

Sing songs to Baby. Recite nursery rhymes. Hum familiar tunes or make up a song. Hold Baby and move to the music. See the included list of action rhymes that you can do with your baby.

Make music using rattles or household items such as wooden spoons and pots or pans.

Take the baby where they can see lots of people. Watch them stare and smile at them.

Dangle a small towel over baby. Let baby get a good grip on it, then whisk it away saying, "no you don't" then let the baby hold it again.

Lightly cover the baby's head with a small blanket and then pull it away exclaiming, "Boo".

Cover your own head with a blanket and let the baby pull it away exclaiming, "Boo" when they do.

Stand up holding baby. Bend over so the baby is upside down and say, "upside down" then straighten and repeat.

Help baby into a standing position in front of couch or coffee table. Holding the baby let them grab for a favorite toy.

Do the crab with your hand drumming the surface with your fingers as you advance toward baby ending with a tickle.

Let the baby hold onto your fingers and walk them around the house.

Let baby "play" piano or another keyboard, holding them on your lap. Guide one finger on each hand to play baby to play chopsticks.

Play tapes in different languages: i.e. opera or language tapes. (Get them from a library.)

Let baby slap surface. Highchair trays allow toys to bounce up and down. Babies love to watch the objects "dance".

Read books to baby.

Point to objects in books or magazines and tell the baby what the name of it is and tell the baby something about it (i.e. "this is a fish, and it swims in water.)

Put baby into a small pool or bathtub making sure to keep a firm hold on them. Let baby play with toys.

Hold a container of water above baby. Pour it slowly in front of them letting them touch it.

Make bubbles in the water.

Get baby to crawl by placing toys just out of his reach – they will stretch for them. As they get better, put them a little further away. Remember to let your baby achieve each goal you set, as this will build self-confidence and reward them for trying.

Hide one of your baby's favorite toys under a baby blanket and let them find it.

While your baby is watching, place a small toy in one of your hands, and then close both hands into a fist. Ask them to choose the hand with the toy in it. If they pick the correct one, tell them how brilliant they are!

Let your baby play with some plain white paper (spare them the dyes from newspapers and magazines). They'll enjoy crinkling it up, reaching for it, throwing it, and unfolding it.

Place a pot or a plastic container on the floor and tap on it with a wooden spoon. Then let your baby take a turn.

Play a drop and retrieve game, baby drops toy, parent retrieves it.

Show the baby a toy. Cover it with a cloth. Ask the baby "where did it go?" And then say, "there it is." When you whisk the cloth off the toy.

Hide toy in container with loosely fitting lid.

Play tag with your baby, crawling after her and encouraging them to crawl away. Or tell them to catch you and then crawl away.

Hide a small (but not small enough to choke on) object, such as a pen or your keys, in a shirt pocket and let your baby take it out.

Sit on the floor a few feet away and roll a ball to your baby. Then try to get them to roll it back. Babies love rolling balls, in part because they go across the floor just as your baby wants to.

As your baby begins to master their crawling technique, create an obstacle course for them by stacking pillows on the floor so that they must crawl over them. Once your baby starts crawling or rolling across the floor, get on the floor and do it with them. They'll get a kick out of this, and it'll encourage them to work on these skills even more. Plus, you'll be able to see just how hard they are working.

Once your baby is mobile, let them see you hide around a corner, then come and find you.

Tell baby what each room is for, (i.e. this is where we cook food.)

Have the baby shake a bottle or jar of small objects, sing while the baby is doing this but stop singing when the baby stops making music.

Count for the baby.

Holding a pillow upright, show your baby a ball on one side of the pillow. Roll it so it appears on the other side. Repeat.

Nine to Twelve Months

Give baby several objects: plastic storage dishes with lids, blocks, etc. Watch how baby knocks one against the other and experiments with several at a time.

While reading a story to your baby, cuddle with one of his favorite stuffed animals or dolls or his blanket. Associating this special object with the comfort of you will help them feel better when you go out.

While you're getting your baby ready for bed, turn on a flashlight or a penlight and let them track the beam as it moves around the room. This can be very soothing.

Place your baby in front of a mirror and let them spend some time flirting with themselves as you watch behind them. At this point they start to understand that it's themselves they are seeing.

Place a handkerchief over your baby's head and pretend you can't find them, saying, "Where's [your baby's name]?" When they whip it off, get excited and say, "Oh, there you are!" This reminds them how much you like being with them, which will make them feel good.

Let your baby entertain you: If you laugh at something silly, they do, they'll repeat it again and again as long as it gets the same response. Not only does this let you share some fun together; it also gives them a sense of confidence.

Look at books together, and while you're turning the pages, show your baby appropriate emotional responses to what you're seeing.

When you say good-bye to other people, make a game out of it: Try to get your baby to wave and say "bye-bye" to you. Or you do part of it—wave or say the words—and try to get them to do the other half.

Make your baby laugh by doing silly things: they'll love to laugh at visual incongruities, so pretend to drink from their bottle. Or mess up your hair while making goofy sounds—something your baby is more likely to do—and try to get them to copy you.

Play name games—ask your baby, "Where's Mama?" or "Where's Dada?" or, "Where's the dog?" and they'll probably point to the right being.

Take turns mimicking each other in the mirror: Wrinkle your nose, then your baby will probably do the same; stick out your tongue, and they'll follow suit; then blow them a kiss and see what they do.

Sit down with your baby in front of a mirror and make faces that illustrate different emotions—happy, sad, scared, and so on—and label each one as you show it.

If your baby seems scared when you're out of the room, talk to them and tell them what you're doing. That way they'll hear your voice and realize that you're still around.

Put a hat on your baby's head, and then put it on your head. Your baby will love this kind of turn taking, and they'll find it funny to see the same hat on both of you.

Show your baby pictures of their favorite people—Mama, Dada, other relatives, and friends—and tell them who they are.

Play pat-a-cake and other clapping, rhyming games with your baby. See the rhyming section included in this book.

Sing "Itsy, Bitsy Spider" to your baby and do the finger movements. As they get to know this routine, they may even try to gesture along with you.

Give your baby an empty shoebox and some small (but not small enough to choke on) objects to put inside and dump out again. This makes them feel powerful and supports their understanding of the concepts of empty and full.

While you're cooking, place a few pots and lids around your baby on the floor and let them try to match them.

To promote her problem-solving skills, give your baby a set of plastic cups to nest inside each other, and then take apart.

Sit on the floor with your baby and place some paper cups in front of the two of you. Fill one with dry cereal and show them how to pour it from one cup to another.

Let your baby play pretend its mealtime—for example, by pretending to drink out of a "big kid" plastic cup.

Tell your baby about her stuffed animals and show them what sounds they make—such as, "This is a lion and he says, 'Roar!'"

Inflate a beach ball and let your baby push against it or hold on to it as they move. For added fun, let them roll over the top of the ball (keeping a hand on them, of course!) and support themselves with her hands on the floor.

Instead of coming to "get" your baby, sit on the floor behind some kind of obstacle—a stack of pillows, a table, a box—and encourage them to come and grab you. When they do, give them a big hug.

Be your baby's personal jungle gym: Sit on the floor with them and let them push themselves up against your legs and crawl or climb up your body.

Stand up and spread your legs wide enough apart for your baby to fit between them. Hold them by the waist and move them back and forth through the space a few times. Then let them try to crawl or walk through on their own.

Read to your baby or tell them a story about your day together. Pause occasionally to let them respond vocally.

Let the baby wipe up spills.

Play open close. Let baby open a drawer, cupboard, or door. Saying open or close when the baby opens or closes the object.

Outside put some toys in a plastic tub with a little water in the bottom. Let the baby sit alongside and play.

Give baby a container and lots of smaller toys/objects to put in it. Let them fill the container then take them out and fill it again.

With two adults facing each other and a small distance between them, encourage baby to walk toward one person. Then turn them around and have them walk to the other person.

Ask baby to point to his feet arms, belly, etc.

Show the baby how to climb stairs and when appropriate how to come down them on their tummy backwards.

Show baby their clothing, naming each piece, like socks - tell the baby where these items go. After a few times ask baby to point to where each item goes.

Get a container and an object to put in it, say "in" when you place the object inside and "out" when you take it out. Let the baby put it in and out.

Show your baby some photos of family members telling them who each is. Ask baby to point to someone in the photos.

Get a ride-on toy and let the baby practice getting on and off it.

Get a push toy. Show your baby how to hold on to it and how to push it around walking behind it. Carpet and grass surfaces work well to start out on.

Recite classic poems for the baby.

Give the baby stackable toys. Help them stack them up then knock them down. Repeat.

Let the baby hold a toy, ask for the toy when the baby gives it to you say "thank you" then give the toy back to them and repeat.

Twelve to Fifteen Months

Go around the house pointing out different shapes. Do different shapes each day i.e. circles, diamonds, squares, etc.

Make silly faces at each other, copying each other's expressions. Imitation is the basis for learning.

Sew a few small bells securely onto two large, elastic hair scrunches or small wristbands. (They should fit comfortably around your child's ankles) Then watch and listen to the fun as your child moves about or jumps up and down. Quadruple the fun by adding jingling bands to your child's wrists or arms. Make a set for yourself, then turn on some upbeat music and jingle, jangle all around!

Stand up and squat down, then rise onto your toes. Twirl like a ballerina. Have your child try to copy you. Copy your child's movements. Your child learns patterns and new ways of moving.

Put your child in the tub with plastic measuring cups. By filling and pouring, your budding scientist is experimenting with the concepts of measurement, size and shape, full and empty. At the bathroom or kitchen sink, tint the water with food coloring to make this game even more fun.

While playing pat a cake, your child begins to memorize words, repeating the singsong lines. This also helps a child to develop a memory of recent events. Sing, "Pat-a-cake, pat-a-cake, baker's man, bake me a cake as fast as you can. Pat it and prick it and mark it with a B and put it in the oven for baby and me!" Include clapping and acting out the words (for example, miming putting a cake in the oven); point to yourself and to baby when you say the words "me" and "baby." See the included list of other rhymes to do with your child.

Hide your feet in the sand (or, for non-beach days, under a blanket). Let your toes pop out. Children love the thrill of "hiding" and "finding" things. A little game like this teaches a child about object permanence (meaning, things that disappear are just somewhere else), a great cognitive lesson.

Get out the shaving cream and put it on a wooden board such as a cutting board. Let your child "finger paint" with this fun-to-mold substance. Experimenting with the molding of shapes helps your child find new and exciting ways to use his hands.

When reading to your child, let his fingers do the walking by asking them to turn the pages for you. A thick board book makes the job easier and encourages the development of fine motor skills.

To help your child work on his balancing ability, get a big round gymnastics ball (it should come up to your child's waist). Hold your child while they sit on it and gently bounce them up and down. Or place your child's tummy down on the ball and roll your child over the ball by holding on to your child's legs. Use gentle, easy movements.

Give your child a little workout and help them perfect their balance by getting a toy-shopping cart to push. Since these little plastic carts are often not heavy enough to help a tentative toddler balance easily, allow the child to fill it with books or cans of juice to weigh it down. Now the cart is steady, and the child feels like a "grown-up" delivering juice from the kitchen to the dining room or wheeling books from the playroom back to the bookshelves.

Set up an environment that encourages your child to practice walking. Move the coffee table away from the couch so that the baby needs to take a couple of steps to get from the stability of the table to the comfort of the couch. If your child isn't yet ready to "let go," place different activities across the top of the coffee table to invite them to cruise around the perimeter. (Be sure, of course, that the table doesn't have any sharp edges.)

Find something that takes your child by surprise—a jack-in-the-box that pops up when you turn the knob, a flashlight that shines when you push the button, or an empty squirt bottle that makes a funny sound when you squeeze it. This age loves life and all its unexpected delights! At the same time, the child is thrilled at being to be able to master the game. They will be the ones who makes it happen!

Your voice is all that's needed to make a book talk. Discuss the characters in the book as you read. "He looks very sad," you might say about the poor little kitten that has lost his mitten, to help your child associate a word with a particular emotion.

Play "Where's your nose?" Have your child touch his own nose with his finger. Ask, "Where are Daddy's ears?" Toddlers love this intimate game of exploration and learning about the name for their own body parts, as well as the important difference between "my eyes" and "your eyes."

Using a sturdy scarf or a towel, sit on the floor for a playful tug-of-war. Be sure to let your child experience the thrill of being "the strong one" sometimes! Tug-of-war is a fun way to help reinforce your child's identity as separate from you, an ongoing process for your little one.

When you sit down to open your mail or pay a few bills, include your little one and make a game of it. Offer her a big envelope to examine or a colorful magazine to peruse. Place a wastebasket next to them on the floor and let them throw papers away. Baby likes to be where you are, doing what you're doing. Imitating you is not only fun for them; it allows you to get a little of your work done. At this stage, don't expect them to play alone with her toys while you're "playing" with your bills.

Letting your toddler help in the kitchen may not be as unthinkable as it first sounds. This is often the social hub of the house, and even 12- to 15-month-olds want to feel they're part of the scene. Give them a bowl and wooden spoon for pretend mixing or an ear of corn to husk. A wet sponge for wiping can be the perfect job for your little helper!

Nursery rhymes (especially those combined with finger play) are great learning activities. Toddlers respond to the sounds and the rhythms, as well as to the one-on-one time with a parent (a crucial component in a child's development). The surprise at the end ("...and this little piggy went wee, wee, wee, wee all the way home") just adds to the silliness and sense of fun. As you sing and play together, your child learns that you can use language to be close to other people.

Learning how to take turns and share is key to social development, but it will take a lot longer than these three months (or even this whole year) for your child to be able to do this. Get them started with some gentle turn-taking games. Give your child a ball and let them hold it as you count to three. Have them pass it to another child (or to you) and count to three again. The lesson here: The fun is in the sharing, not the hogging.

Let the baby help you clean. Talk to the baby while you clean about how you are cleaning and what tools you use.

Tell your baby stories.

Mix flour and water to make dough until baby can use cookie cutters or other object to make shapes in it.

Show baby how to make bubbles with a bubble maker.

Let the baby help you cook. They can stir – well away from the stove.

Fifteen to Eighteen Months

Create an activity book with lift-up flaps, things to touch and feel, or tabs to pull. Make sure the book is sturdy enough to withstand the curious and not terribly gentle hands of a toddler. Check out the book in advance to make sure the manipulatives are age-appropriate for your child, so they won't be frustrating.

Activities with boxes: Children won't think twice about what to do with their box. They'll just do it. They'll find different uses for different sizes and should one use not work out, they'll find another use. There are many advantages when children play with boxes. Boxes are readily available. Children will have fun with an appliance box. Supermarket boxes or smaller boxes such as tissue or food boxes are right in your home. The children can paint them, cut them, glue them, build with them, fill them, or anything else you can think of. Best of all, when your child is done and onto another box project, you can put the old box in for recycling.

Appliance boxes: Houses. They are great for building houses. Let your child determine where windows and doors go and for safety reasons you can do the cutting. They can be placed either horizontally or vertically. Let your child place a child-size chair and a few toys inside. Your child might want to paint "indoors" and "outdoors". Children like to hide inside big boxes. Your child might want to turn it into transportation methods such as: trucks, boats, cars, or airplanes. Your child will enjoy getting in and out of the boxes. They might want a red fire truck, or a trailer. Use construction paper to form props, such as wheels, steering wheel, and mirrors. Take the time to make these props together.

Supermarket boxes: Pull box. Take a supermarket box and cut off the flaps. On two opposite sides of the box make two handles. At 2-3 inches from the rim cut two holes and pass a cord (about 12-15"). Tie the knot inside of the box. Let your child push and pull the box. Toddlers will really enjoy this activity. Easel box. Take a supermarket box and cut off the flaps. On the side, from one corner to the opposite corner, cut diagonally. Do the same on the other side (same corners). Turn the box over, take off the hanging piece and use as an easel, Tape paper onto to box and let your artist draw or paint. Another variation is to cut a door, and this can be a doll tent.

Feelly box. Cut out a hole on the side of the box about 4-5" in diameter. Without your children's present, put various household objects inside the box such as: plastic spoon, small toys, foam, pieces of yarn, sandpaper… Tape the box shut. Have your child put a hand inside the box and feel different objects. Let them describe these objects to you and you must guess what it is they are feeling.

Give your child an empty two-liter soda bottle and some wooden clothespins and show her how to push the clothespins through the top. When shaken, the clothespins make a wonderful sound. Your child begins to understand the concepts of "in" and "out" and "full" and "empty." The delightful rattling sound she creates provides an instant reward while teaching an early lesson in cause and effect.

Give your child a gentle hand or foot massage. Touch is one of the earliest forms of communication. It uses the physical senses to underscore the warm bond between parent and child. At bedtime it can relax a tired little body.

Send a feather or two along a breeze or blow bubbles. Your child will love the thrill of the chase and capture!

Smaller boxes (tissue, cereal, cookie, or food boxes): Box City. Let your child paint each box. Once dry, glue many of them onto a piece of cardboard and make them part of a city. Make roads, use little cars and others props you may have on hand. Bean bag box. Using six to eight different boxes and cut off the tops. Have your child throw bean bags inside the boxes. Use this activity to reinforce words like inside, outside, and beside. They'll be practicing their throwing skills as well. Babushka boxes. This activity might take a little more preparation but find ten boxes. One small box that fits into another and those (2) go into another and those (3) go into another and so on. Your child will enjoy fitting the smaller boxes into the bigger boxes. This will develop counting skills, counting from one to ten, and as you hide a box inside another, how many boxes can you see? Sand box. Fill the box 3/4 full of sand. Inside the sand place tiny objects such as: paper clips, ring, and keys. Using a crochet hook lets your child poke through the sand and try to hook up as many objects as possible. This activity will be good for children over three years of age, as younger children will put the objects in their mouths. Dice box. Use a square shaped box. Cut out circles from construction paper and glue them onto the side of the box to make a big die. Once dry, play games with your child using this die. For example: Roll the dice and that's the number of songs you must sing or hugs you must give each other or minutes before bedtime.

Mom's purse is always one of the most intriguing items in the house. Your toddler loves to empty and fill things and to imitate you. Give them a purse or book bag made for a toddler. It should be easy to open and close. Fill it with real-life items such as an old wallet, plastic keys, a piece of paper, a crayon, and a hairbrush. Pretend you're going out. What do you need in your purse? Say, "Don't forget your keys! Don't forget your purse!" Then "come home," empty it out, and start all over again.

Help your child connect two things by singing a cleanup song while putting toys away. You can make up your own words to the tune of a familiar song like "Row, Row, Row, Your Boat." Soon, once you begin to sing, the child will be immediately aware that it's time to clean up. Routines give your child a sense of security and teach them that there are ways to predict what will happen next in his life. This is also helpful for other routines in a baby's life like brushing his teeth or putting on a bib.

Put pudding in a large plastic bag with a zipper-lock top. Let your toddler "write" or "draw" on the outside of the bag with his finger. No mess, but a lot of fun!

Put on the music you love and hop, jump, and dance along with your child. Movement to music helps your child to learn how to balance and shift his weight. It can help give a child the confidence he needs to move from a waddle to more mature walking.

Put on some music and dance with your child in front of a mirror. Your child will observe where his own body begins and ends. He will also experience a sense of control as he sees what he can do with his body.

Kids love to make noise! Encourage your child to make a joyful sound by turning a pot upside down and adding two wooden spoons. Make a tambourine for her by putting a bunch of small, crunchy cereal between two paper plates and stapling them together. (Tape over the staples so there are no sharp edges.) Making music allows your child to express herself creatively.

Give your child a big cookie that you can break into pieces, a pile of small "O"-shaped cereal bits, or a box of blocks. Ask, "Can I have one?" It's fun to play "some for me and some for you." Your child gets to oversee deciding how much each of you gets.

Turn a sock into a puppet. Slip it on your hand and make it talk. Or make a puppet out of a small paper bag. Pretend the puppet is going on a trip or having lunch. Talk about how the puppet feels (happy, scared, and hungry) and make it "talk." Let your child slip the puppet on his hand and try it themselves. (He's not ready to make the puppet talk back yet, but that's okay. He'll still enjoy the game.)

Eighteen to Twenty-One Months

Ask your child to imagine what would happen if something silly occurred. "What would happen if I put on my glasses upside down?" Or "What if candy bars grew on trees?" Or "What if people walked on their hands, instead of their feet?" Let your child make up some silly questions for you, too. Have fun guessing and acting out these silly questions. You might be pleased and surprised with your child's imagination.

Children at this age love to pretend and dress up. Make masks with paper plates by cutting out eyes, nose and mouth. (You can make just an eye mask using half the plate) Color around eyes, add hair, or clown colors. Then staple or tape a piece of string that's been measured snug around the child's head, onto each side of the plate.

Ramps and chutes can be made from large cartons or several shoeboxes. Cut off the ends of the shoeboxes and tape the boxes together into a long chute. Place it on a slant, and the children will enjoy sliding various objects down it. The boxes may also be used to make the cars of a train. Connect them with string or rope, decorate them, and paint or glue on some wheels and watch how much fun this train can be for the children.

Children love to punch holes with a whole puncher. Colored paper and hole punchers will keep children busy for quite a while. Save the dots in an envelope or bag for art projects or confetti for a party. Have the children punch holes from wax paper and put the dots in a jar filled with water. Screw on the lid, shake it, and watch the children's very own snowstorm.

Make or buy some beanbags and have the children toss them to each other or throw or drop them into a box or bucket.

Strike up the band. Help your child make other instruments that she can play along with her guitar. Use household items such as cans, small screws, and juice cartons to make a shaker and a drum. Or use your imagination to make up your own instruments! Your child can decorate them to create a colorful band.

Making musical instruments with your child can be easy and fun! You can use a variety of household objects to get your hands clapping and your toes tapping in a creative activity that will enhance your child's motor skills, coordination, and expressive language. Parts List for a Great Guitar: shoe box, four large rubber bands, paper-towel tube, tape, scissors, construction paper, glue, markers or crayons. Ask your child if he or she knows what a guitar is. Then discuss the parts of a guitar and how it's used. Put out the shoebox, rubber bands, and paper-towel tube and let your child experiment with them. Together, talk about how you might make a guitar using these materials. Help your child tape the cover onto the shoebox. Then cut a five-inch hole in the center of the top and a two-inch hole on one end of the box. Ask your child to push the tube through the two-inch hole to make the guitar neck (to use as a handle). Then help her to carefully stretch the rubber bands around the box, from one end to the other (two on each side of the tube). Make sure they are stretched directly over the hole in the top. Put out construction paper, glue, markers, and crayons, and invite your child to decorate her guitar. Now she's ready to strum away!

Fold a piece of paper or cardboard in half. Draw a picture of a bowl of water with an object on top of the water on one side, and a bowl of water with an object on the bottom of the bowl on the other side of the paper.

Write your own songs. Ask your child what she would like to sing about. If she needs help, suggest subjects such as her favorite foods or toys. Then together make up lyrics for the song. Use your set of instruments to add the melody. Record a tape. Use a tape recorder to make the fun last! You'll be able to listen to the music you've made together anytime you like!

Write out a list of about five items (rock, leaf, grass, dirt, etc.). You carry the list and let the child carry a small paper bag. Go for a walk and see if you can find the items. Encourage the child to find each item by asking, "Can you find a rock?" Look for one thing at a time. When all the items are found, sit down together and talk about the items. Smell, touch, and look at them. Talk about color, shape, texture, and weight.

Provide a small bowl of water and various objects from around the house that will float or sink. Sitting down with the child, place an object in the water and talk about whether it is on top of the water or at the bottom. Does it float or sink? If the child does not grasp the concept, do not pressure them. Let them place things in the water and talk about "on top" or "on the bottom."

On a piece of poster board or cardboard, trace around four or five small objects you have in the house such as a cookie cutter, clothespin, battery, or scotch tape dispenser. Use a wide, dark colored magic marker. Put the items in a box where they can be kept permanently. The child can take objects out of the box and match them with the outline on the cardboard, feel the objects, and talk about them.

Miscellaneous items: Let children make a collage out of beans and macaroni and scraps of material. Make it on newspaper, paper grocery bags, or paper plates. Use flour paste as glue.

A child can glue squares of cloth on paper and make colorful scenes. To teach children to notice similarities and differences, cut two squares of each scrap of material and mix them up in a box. The children can match them or sort them by color, texture, or design.

Cover a piece of heavy cardboard with felt or flannel. Cut out various shapes and colors from felt, flannel, non-woven interfacing, wool, or other fabrics. Make up stories together, holding the flannel board on your lap and using the shapes you have cut out to illustrate the stories. Magazine pictures backed with flannel will also work well. Children can also name shapes, colors, or objects while you work together. They love putting things on the board and taking them off. A felt person cut into parts to be put together will help teach body parts. A cardboard pencil box is a good place to store your shapes, glue a piece of flannel to the inside of the lid, this now becomes your background. Then place various shapes in the box. It is now ready to be played with. This makes an excellent quiet or travel toy.

Use a tape recorder to record familiar sounds (washer, vacuum, or car) so the child can identify these as a game. Record short stories and then play them back when the child wants you and you are busy. He can hold a book and listen. Talk and sing together on the tape and then play back the recording and let the child listen to his own voice.

Take a walk in the house and feel a variety of items (wallpaper, bedspreads, rugs, curtains, wood).

When setting the table, talk about the shapes on the table—round plates, squares, or rectangles. What shape is the table?

Sort the knives, forks, and spoons and let the child put them away. Let the child help dry and put things away.

Go on a shape hunt in your house. Look for circles, squares, rectangles, and triangles.

Count! Count the chairs in the kitchen, books, buttons, steps, windows, beans, plates, or anything else you can think of.

Make up guessing games. "I live on a farm. I'm little and black, I like milk and say meow, meow. What am I?"

Take a button and tap it on the table two times, then say, "Now you do it." Have the child repeat a rhythm you clap. Or say several words and have them say them back to you.

Children love to put puzzles of them together. Have a photo of a child's face enlarged to eight-by-ten inches. Mount the photo on heavy cardboard with rubber cement. Cut it into three or four pieces. Store it in a box.

Different kinds of dough or clay are favorites of many children. See the craft recipe list for some easy recipes.

Let the children try using watercolors.

If you use tempera paints (powder paints mixed with water), add some dishwater soap to the paint so it will wash out of clothes.

Let the children try painting on rocks.

If paints aren't available or practical, give the child a can of water and a brush and let them paint the house!

Draw on paper with chalk. Put butcher paper on the wall and have the child draw a mural on it. Try wetting paper with a sponge and then drawing on it with chalk. Chalkboards are a good addition to a child's toy supply.

Cut out pictures from magazines and show the child how to paste them on paper, boxes, paper cups, or plates. Talk about the pictures. Tissue scraps, material scraps, colored paper shapes can also be cut and pasted.

Make pinwheels, hanging mobiles, paper-bag or paper-plate puppets (attach popsicle stick to paper plate and make a face on it). Make a chain out of construction paper. Hook one link inside another and talk about colors.

Put some powdered paint in an old saltshaker. Take the child for a walk in the snow and let them shake paint on the snow to color it. Take a picture on the snow.

Have the child lie down on a piece of butcher paper. Trace around the outline of his body. Talk about what you are doing. "Now I'm drawing around your fingers." Color the picture together. Talk about body parts and where they belong. Hang it up.

Take a head-to-toe picture of the child. Have it enlarged so that it measures ten to twelve inches high. Mount the picture on 1/8-inch hardboard (or heavy cardboard). Use white glue or rubber cement to mount the photo. Hang the picture on the wall or set it on a stand. (A short piece of one-inch diameter half round molding with a slot makes a good stand.)

Cans are easily made into a variety of toys. Poke holes in cans and run a string through the holes. Toddlers will enjoy pulling this toy behind them. Cans, as well as cartons, also make interesting blocks to stack and build with. Let children play with them in the kitchen area, putting them on the shelves with food for the family, or using them to play with store. (If cans have sharp metal edges, cover with tape or avoid using them.)

Buy a little bottle of soap bubbles or pour some dish soap, diluted with a little water, into a paper cup. A piece of bent wire or a plastic ring will do as a blower.

Even a two-year-old can help load silverware into a dishwasher or sit on a stool and help mother wash some dishes. Before mealtime, when a little one is underfoot and impatient for meals, try this: Give them an apron, a stool, some sudsy water and the cooking utensils you've finished using. For additional fun, add a few drops of food coloring to the water.

Going shopping? Take along labels from empty fruit and vegetable cans or cereal and cracker box fronts and let your child help shop for the groceries by matching labels.

Let the child choose which vegetable, fruit, or dessert the family will have for supper. Let them select the pan to cook it in.

Sit in a familiar room with your child. Look around the room and pick out something you can talk about in two ways: 1. What it looks like, 2. What it does. Say both and ask your child to guess what you are thinking of. For example: "I can see something that is red, and rolls along the floor," or "I can see something that is white, and you drink from it," or "I see something that is tall, and you sit on it." Then ask: "What is it?" Let your child have a turn asking you to guess, too.

Tease your child with "I'm going to get you!" and she'll run away! She'll squeal with delight and look forward to being "caught" and wrapped up in a big hug. Toddlers delight in the silliness of such playacting.

Face your child and copy whatever he does—stretching up high, then bending down to touch the floor. Now it's your turn to move and your child copies you. This give and take is the basis for many social behaviors. By making you do whatever he does, your 1-year-old gets to experience a sense of power.

Your toddler will be delighted when Dad "disappears" behind the sofa. Finding Dad gives your toddler quite a sense of accomplishment. Hide and seek is also a great social game because it involves turn taking.

Let your child look through your photo albums, or better yet, make one especially for your toddler. Point out the pictures. Say, "Here's Mommy," or "Look! There's your big sister, Ellen." Show pictures of your child as a baby: "Look how small you were when you were a baby! You're so big now!" This helps a child label and reinforces familial relationships—mother, father, sister, and brother.

Line up the chairs in the kitchen and board the Snack Time Express. This is super for exercising "pretend" skills and learning about how the world works, as well as a great game to play with more than one child. Kids can take turns being the conductor. Everyone can toot and chug. As kids slip off the chair, they can pretend they've arrived in a whole new place!

A few months ago, your child could be found talking on the toy phone or trying to use your lipstick. By 21 months she is ready for more representational plays. In other words, a banana can be "answered" like a telephone. A pickle can be tooted like a horn. A plastic disk can be "eaten" as a make-believe cookie. Broaden your child's understanding with this silly, imaginative play.

As you go about your day with your toddler, give names to different things in your house and around your town—truck, dog, piano, and the like. Or ask them to tell you the names of objects he's familiar with—point to them and say, "What's that?" (Your child will eventually return the favor with a barrage of "what's that?" questions for you!) You're helping your child build his memory and make sense of the things in his world.

Take the cushions off the couch and make a tunnel your toddler can crawl through. Drape two chairs with a sheet to make another crawl space to explore.

For fine motor skills, offer your toddler colorful wooden blocks for building. Help make a long line of blocks (point out how this is like a fence) or a tower of blocks (like a building). Once the building is "up," allow your toddler to knock it back down. It's almost as much fun for her to have the power to tumble the blocks down as it is to be able to stack them up.

Let your child work on his fine motor skills by "drawing" on the sidewalk with easily gripped fat sidewalk chalks. Show them how to make a big circle and then "decorate" inside it.

Sing this simple command to your child (you make up the tune) while you model the appropriate action: "Spinning, spinning, spinning, everybody's spinning; spinning, spinning, spinning, and now it's time to stop!" Continue with clapping, hopping, and other motions your child enjoys. You are practicing fun physical skills, helping your child put names to the motions, and reinforcing the notions of starting and stopping.

Create a pull toy by stringing together some empty orange juice cans. Or buy an animal pull toy. Not only do children love this activity, but they also learn to walk forward while checking over their shoulder periodically for the object behind them.

Play "Ring Around the Rosie." This one little nursery rhyme offers multiple fun—the child gets to move themselves around in a circle and practice falling and getting back up again. It's an activity that supports the child's new physical sense of themselves. It's also a delightful social activity, a great way to support language skills and cognitive exercise (learning to follow commands). "Hop (or jump) around the Rosie" makes a nice change of pace.

Your child will love to squish, and shape play dough. Serve up the fun with some plastic knives, plastic cups, and cookie cutters for some great fine motor play. Have these ingredients on hand to make play dough: 3 cups of flour, 1 1/2 cups salt, 6 teaspoons cream of tartar, 3 cups water, 1/3 cup vegetable oil, and food coloring (optional). Mix dry ingredients in a saucepan or bowl. Mix liquid ingredients separately in a bowl. Add food coloring if desired. Slowly add the liquid mixture to the dry mixture. Mix well. Cook on low heat until mixture is rubbery. Let cool. After use, return to a plastic bag or sealed container to keep it fresh.

Do a beginning somersault along with your child. Both of you can bend over, look between your legs, and giggle about how funny the world looks this way. Then you can help her to gently tumble over for a fun introduction to the gymnastics toddlers love.

Toddlers can act out some of their new skills, as well as their empathetic responses, by doctoring their baby dolls or stuffed animals. Let them put a Band-Aid on a baby doll's leg or wrap her up and put her to bed.

Take out the cups and saucers. Let your child pour the imaginary tea into your cup.

Pretend you don't know whether your baby's shoes go on her hands or her feet. Or point at her nose and ask, "Is this your ear?" Besides giving your child a lot of laughs, this silly game gives your baby a sense of power and competence when she appears to "know" more than you do.

Simple songs involving finger play help your child to understand more about his own body. This song also involves repeating a cordial greeting and encourages interaction. Sing (to the tune of "Are You Sleeping, Brother John?"): "Where is Thumbkin? Where is Thumbkin? Here I am"—show your thumb—" here I am." Show the other. "How are you today, sir? Very well, I thank you." Have thumbs talk to one another. "Run away, run away." Hide thumbs behind your back. Do the same with the pinky and "pointer" fingers.

With your child holding one favorite doll or stuffed animal and you holding another, suggest acting out a little scene with them that's familiar from daily life, like going to the park or having a snack. Let her take the lead and observe how she makes one toy interact with the other. You'll probably see her imitate many of your own actions and words!

Let your child fall into your arms. It's even more fun if she gets a running start. She loves the sheer physical pleasure of it. Even better, she feels deliciously secure: She may fall, but your protective arms will be there.

Get a big cardboard box and cut a door and window in it. Keep it safe by reinforcing boxes (put one inside another) and use plenty of tape. (Remove any staples that could hurt a child.) Children love to go in and out and to answer the door. Let your child decorate the house with crayons. When he gets a bit older, he'll be able to amuse themselves with this or playact with another child, but for now you (or another caregiver) make his best playmate.

Twenty-One to Twenty-Four Months

Children this age love to find hidden objects. They also love to dig. Bury some small toys in his sandbox and let them dig them up.

Play follows the leader through a maze of big pillows, using words to reinforce the concepts of "around," "through," and "on top." Let your child play at being the leader to give them a rare opportunity to have power over you (which he loves!).

Cover the top of a low, child-size table with paper and tape it down. Offer your child jumbo crayons and let her sit at the table, scribbling to her heart's content.

Make reading interactive by stopping to ask your child questions as you go along: "I wonder what will happen next?" or "What do you think the fireman will do?" This gets her thinking about sequence: what happens before and after. It also encourages the give and take of conversation.

Use a natural line in your home, such as a floorboard or even a long strip of masking tape on a rug, to practice walking a straight line. Try not to fall off!

Nothing beats banging with a toy rubber hammer. The noise! The power! Let your child use the hammer to force a peg through a hole in a toy tool bench or an old plastic jug.

Let your child hold a small bouquet, carry it home, and arrange the flowers in a vase. What a lovely (and fragrant) way to exercise those fine motor skills!

Get out the big cardboard boxes. Take the pillows off the living room couch. Climbing season has begun. Children this age want to challenge themselves and show you how powerful they are.

For a good "feeling" experience for your toddler, as well as some practice with fine motor skills, put uncooked rice in a basin along with measuring spoons, plastic cups, and sieves. He'll love to mix and measure! (If done outdoors, the birds can eat the spills!) You can dye the rice with drops of food coloring if you like.

Give your child a plastic jar with a screw-on lid. Help them figure out how to unscrew it, to build fine motor skills. This is a challenging activity that may take your child some time to learn.

Assuming your child is in an infant or "bucket" swing, you can add a challenge. Give your child a beanbag to throw to you as he gently sways back and forth.

Give your child one small thing to carry home from the supermarket—a package of spaghetti or a small box of tissues, for example. This and other common household activities, such as wiping off a counter, encourage playacting and appropriate development of autonomy in a safe environment. The point is not that your child learns how to do a chore, but that she feels important doing the things she sees you do.

Put on some music and let your child dance. When you turn off the music, see if he can "freeze" in place.

Challenge your little athlete to a race. Toddlers really enjoy the idea of "winning" and thinking "I can go faster than you!" Children this age love to challenge themselves and show how powerful they are.

Use scarves or long strips of cloth for dress-up fun. Your child can wrap it around herself, drag it behind her, or watch it flow and flutter. Hats, old Halloween costumes, and other accessories can be added to the dress-up wardrobe. Let the drama flow!

Pretend to be an animal. Get down on all fours and bark or moo. Your child may simply enjoy watching you pretend to be an animal (and guessing which one), or he may try to join in. Pretend play is one of the most fun forms of social interaction a toddler can have!

Collect three or four balls of various sizes. Sit on the floor with your baby and roll the balls back and forth. Ball playing is great for eye-hand coordination, of course, but it also has a very social element. The message is: I get something, and I give it back to you.

Line up a couple of friends or siblings and let them march to the tune of a drumbeat or kazoo. Marching together teaches kids how to get along with their peers and become more confident in-group situations. Have them take turns being the leader.

Toys, Games, and Activities that Cost Almost Nothing Over 400 Fun Activities for You to do with Your Child

Art

Sticker Star Art – Supply the children with star shaped stickers to place on another piece of paper. This activity is great for fine motor skills!

Outdoor Water Painting – On a hot summer day give your children outdoor paint brushes and buckets of water. Let them paint the sidewalk, walls, etc. Watch how the water evaporates in the warm sun. Painting on rocks, trees, the sidewalk, anything!

Blueberry Paining – Give children blueberries to look at, touch, smell, and taste. (Good for the young). After the children have observed the blueberries add a little water to them and cook them in the microwave for one minute. Have children mush them up. Use the blueberry juice to paint a beautiful blue blueberry picture.

Salt Art – Saturate hot water with salt. Let the water cool, and have the child use the salt water to paint on black paper. Then after it dries, have the child look at the crystals of salt on the paper.

Rubbings – Cut shapes from paper doilies or sandpaper. Tape these shapes to the table. Have the children place a piece of thin white paper over the shapes and lightly rub a crayon over the shape. Find other things to make rubbings of. Some examples of other things you can use is textured wall, basketball or football, leaves, hard cover books will sometimes have a texture to them or an embossed emblem, etc. Cut out all your rubbings and make a collage.

Natural Dyes – You can get color by collecting items from nature, such as grasses, leaves, and berries! Cut a 7" x 14" piece of muslin. Place the items on one half of the fabric, then fold the other half over. Have the children pound the items through the muslin with a small hammer or mallet. This will make a wonderful hanging.

Bubble Gum Art – Give each participant a piece of bubble gum to chew, a toothpick and an index card. Allow them 10 minutes to chew the gum, place their gum on index card and then design something on the index card using only the toothpick as a tool (No Hands).

You Are a Star – Cut stars out of construction paper, one for each child. Have the children draw pictures of themselves on the stars. Variation: Glue a photograph of each child on a star cut out of foil. Then pin the stars on a bulletin board.

Musical Fingers – Select a variety of music to play. Give the children large pieces of paper with spoonful of finger-paint placed in the centers. Play the music and let the children finger-paint it. Encourage them to move their fingers and hands to the rhythms and tempos of the different kinds of music. This is very fun to do when the tempo (how fast or slow the music is going) changes frequently. This can be found in some classical music.

Feather Painting – Provide each child with a feather, paint and paper. Ask the children to paint a picture using the feather as a paintbrush. Have use the different parts of the feather and see how it changes the look and feel of the painting.

Star Art – Cut out star shapes for the children and have them decorate the shapes with markers, crayons, pens, paint, glitter, torn paper or create your own ideas with materials you have. Hang the stars in their room. You can then use different shapes and have the children decorate them as well.

Cereal Flowers – Use a Paper Plate, Green Construction Paper, Glue, and Green Pipe Cleaners. Paste colorful cereals on paper plates in the shape of flowers. Add pipe cleaner stem and leaves cut out of construction paper.

Kool-Aid Painting – Sprinkle unsweetened Kool-Aid on a piece of paper. Have the children move a piece of ice over the Kool-Aid. Watch as the Kool-Aid turns to liquid and makes a yummy smelling picture.

Stamping Patterns – Use rubber stamps to create a simple pattern on the top half of a piece of paper. Ask your child to help you recreate the pattern on the bottom half of the paper. Tip: Start with one stamp and have your child pick which stamp you used. Start slowly and work your way up to more complicated patterns.

Spray Paint Art – Obtain a few clean spray bottles. Add water and a little bit of liquid or powdered tempera. Then, place a large piece of shaped paper on an easel over a regular piece, (you can use tape to hold the shaped piece in place) and have the children spray the colored water onto the shaped paper. Spray mostly the edges of the shaped paper. Lift the shaped paper up and repeat the process using different shapes or colors of paint until you have the design you want.

Stencil Art – Provide the children with stencils to trace. They may use markers, glitter, paint, crayons, etc. to decorate the shapes. Cookie cutters are also good shapes for them to trace and then decorate.

Contact Paper Art – Tear tissue paper into 1–2-inch pieces, and then cut a circular shape from contact paper. Leave the backing on until ready to stick the tissue paper on top. Remove the backing, leave the sticky side up, place the tissue paper all over the paper, and use different shades of colors. Leave a little space uncovered around the edges. Make a top, remove the backing and lay over the first circle. Trim it a little to make the edges even. Hint: tell the children to just lay the tissue paper on gently so their fingers don't stick. They usually get the idea after their finger sticks the first time!

Sock Splash Painting – Materials: box, Paper, dried beans, old socks, paint. Make "bean bags" out of the socks and dried beans. Put the paper in the bottom of the box; dip your sock in the paint and hold above the box...then drop! Splat!!! :-) The Thinner paint will make a bigger splash The box acts as a splash guard... no mess!

Bubble Prints – In a small margarine tub, mix one part liquid tempera paint with two parts liquid dishwashing detergent and stir in a small amount of water. (If you wish to use several colors, make a separate solution for each one.) Let the child put a straw into the paint mixture and blow through it until the bubbles rise above the rim of the tub. Then lay a piece of white paper on top of the bubbles and let the child rub across it gently. As the bubbles break, they will leave delicate prints on the paper. Try various kinds of paper for different results.

Printing with Balloons – Pour three or four different colors of tempera paint into separate aluminum pie tins. Partially blow up a small balloon. Then have the children dip the balloons into the paints and press them on sheets of white construction paper to create balloon prints.

Apple or Potato Printing – Cut an apple or potato in half. Put some paint in a shallow container, (a pie tin works well) and show your child how to dip the apple or potato into the paint and press onto a piece of paper creating a print. You can also cut shapes into the apple or potato to make more designs. Variation: Use a cookie cutter that will fit the potato half. Press the cookie cutter into the flat side of the potato. Then, using a knife, cut the potato around the outside of the cookie cutter, leaving a shaped potato stamp. Give the child the potato stamps, different colored paints, and paper. Have the child dip the potatoes in the paint and press them firmly onto the paper. Note: If the potatoes are not cut evenly the shapes will not appear clearly.

Rice Rainbows – Ahead of time you will need to dye the rice in the seven rainbow colors. See the recipe section for how to color your rice. Have the children draw rainbow shapes on paper. Show them how to use a brush to spread a thin layer of glue over one band of the rainbow and then sprinkle a thin layer of rice over the glued area. Now let the children glue-and-sprinkle to make their own rice rainbows. Make other designs to suit the season or what you are working on like Easter eggs, pumpkins or Christmas trees.

Draw With Chalk – Put butcher paper on the wall and have the child draw a mural on it. Try wetting paper with a sponge and then drawing on it with chalk. Chalkboards are a good addition to a toy supply.

Marble Art – You need a container with a top (the larger the better). Cut out pieces of paper to fit inside the top of the container. Place a piece of paper in the top of the container, a small amount of water or paint will help it stick to the lid. Place a small amount of paint in the bottom of the container. Use a few different colors. Add four or so marbles. Place the lid on the bottom. Flip the container upside down. Have your child shake the container. When they are finished, open the container and take out the paper.

Nighttime Surprises – Use a white crayon to draw stars on a piece of white construction paper. (Press down hard with the crayon while drawing.) Set out the paper along with brushes and black tempera thinned with water to make a wash. Then let the children brush the tempera wash over their papers to discover the star surprises that will show through. This can also be done with other things as well for example drawing a bunch of leaves on the paper then using green, red, yellow.

Seed Painting – Cut a piece of manila or finger-paint paper to the height of a Pringles can. Put a small spoon of paint inside the can, pour in a few seeds, and then slide in the paper. Put lid on can and shake well. The seeds have a cool design, similar to splatter painting but less messy!

Torn Paper Stars – Draw a star shape on a piece of paper. Provide the children with paper to tear and glue inside the star shape. Or do other shapes.

Paint with Jell-O – Paint or finger-paint with Jell-O. Use several different flavors. Or use unflavored gelatin and add food coloring to it.

Spool Print Flowers – Have at least three spools. Put a small amount of green tempera paint in a small shallow container. (A metal juice lid works well) Put a small amount of two other colors in two more containers. Each color should have a separate spool. Have your child dip a spool in one of the colors of paint (not the green), then press it gently onto a piece of paper. This will be the center of your flower. Then dip a different spool into the other paint, and have them press the spool onto the paper, around the center of your flower. Then dip a different spool into the green paint and press the spool onto the paper on either side of the flower for leaves.

Koosh Ball Painting – Hang a long piece of bulletin board paper on your outside fence. Place pans of paint and Koosh balls on the ground. Encourage the children to throw the Koosh balls at the paper. This makes a great design and is a lot of fun. If possible, have the children do this activity in the bathing suits so you can hose them off when they are done. Other things you can use are fly swatters, spray bottle, water gun, and so much more.

Pictures – Cut out shapes from white paper, and add some finger-paint, and let your child paint. See the recipe section of this book for different fingerpaint recipes.

Piece of Beach – Materials: Sandbox Sand, White Glue, Small Shell, etc. Mix sand and glue until sand is syrupy. Pour the mixture into a bowl, plate, cup, etc. Push shells into the mixture to form a sculpture. Leave this to dry undisturbed; it may take a couple of days. When dry--the glue converts the sand to a plaster.

Apple Art – Give a child a paper plate and one of the following colors... red, yellow or green. Have them paint the paper plate. Attach a paper stem to create an apple. You can also make balloons, flowers and other objects this way. This one is great for younger children.

Blob – Draw a shape on a piece of paper, this is your blob pattern. Cut out the shape. Place the pattern on top of another piece of paper, you can tape it down so it will not move. Use a sponge to dab paint along the edges where the pattern and piece of paper meet. Remove the pattern. Use crayons to draw a face on your Blob any way you like it.

Shaving Cream – Put a small mound of shaving cream on a tabletop and allow your child to finger-paint with it. To add some more fun, add a little food coloring, for some pastel colors. Supervision is required so the child does not get shaving cream in their eyes, (Have the child be very careful and use smocks because the food coloring will stain their clothing and hands.) Have the child paint the shaving cream on a white piece of paper. Easily cleaned with a damp towel.

Worm Art – Set out a piece of yarn for each color of paint you intend to use. Have the child dip the yarn in one color of paint and run it across the paper. Use a new piece of string for a different color. For the brave, dip real worms in paint, and let them crawl across the paper. Be sure to wash them off and return them to their environment. (They usually survive.)

Pine Painting – Supply the children with a pine branch, with pine needles on it, instead of a paintbrush. Other things to use to paint with are cotton balls, Q-Tip's, yellow dandelions, carrot tops, celery leaves, etc.

Bubble Art – Supply the children with a bowl with bubble mix in it and a straw with a hole near the top to prevent children from sucking the soap up. Have the children blow into the straw while it is in the bowl creating bubbles. Then, have the child place a drop of red or blue food coloring on the top of the bubbles and quickly press a piece of paper on the top of the bubbles to create bubble prints.

Golf Ball Painting – Cut out a large piece of paper and put it in the bottom of a very small plastic pool. Place golf balls dipped in different paint colors on the paper. Together the children can hold the edges of the pool and roll the golf balls around. This makes a great design when you are done.

Finger Paint – You can finger paint with instant pudding. Shaving cream or whip cream is also fun to finger paint with. Add color with food coloring.

Popcorn Flowers – Popped Popcorn, Powder Tempera Paint, Green Construction Paper, Glue, Cardboard. Pop the popcorn. Put handfuls of popcorn in plastic bag and add powdered tempera paint to each one. Shake well to distribute paint all over the popcorn. Cut stems and leaves out of green construction paper and glue them to cardboard or construction paper. Glue on the colored popcorn to make spring flowers. For younger children, use dry food coloring instead of paint. This will make it edible in case they decide to have a snack while making these colorful flowers.

Sand Pictures – Spread newspaper over your working areas. Draw a design on construction paper or tag board. Apply glue along the outlines of the design. Pour sand on to the glue and allow it to dry. Gently shake the picture over the newspaper or a wastebasket to remove the excess sand. See the recipe section for how to color the sand.

Crayon Melting – Cover an old heating or warming tray with aluminum foil and heat up. Let older children lay their papers on the tray and draw with crayons. The wax melts and soaks into the paper. Let the wax dry. For younger children color pictures on paper, then when finished put them in oven at 200 degrees until the crayon markings melt. These are fun to hang in windows for a stained-glass effect.

Sidewalk Paint – You will need equal portions of water and corn starch. Mix well. Add a drop of your favorite food coloring color! Paint this wonderful concoction on the sidewalk. Give it a few minutes to dry and you'll have a wonderful work of ART!

Fingerprint – Supply each child with a piece of white paper and non-toxic stamp pads. Show the child how to make fingerprints on the paper, using only one finger at a time. When finished, add leaves for apples, legs for bugs, strings for balloons, or faces, with a black pen.

Kool-Aid Art – Sprinkle a little dry Kool aid mix onto a shaped piece of paper. Have your child spray water from a spray bottle onto the paper. For added adventure, you may choose to take your children out into the rain with a piece of paper that has Kool-Aid on it.

Backyard Mural – Take painting outdoors and transform an old white sheet into a wonderful work of art. You need: An old solid color bed sheet, Tempera paints, Paint brushes, Squirt bottles, Sponges. Start by soaking an old sheet in water and then hanging it on a clothesline or draping it over a fence. Get out various tempera paints and applicators -- sponges, paintbrushes, squirt bottles -- and create pictures or colorful designs. You can also mute and mix colors with a water-filled spray bottle. Whenever you don't like what you see, just hose down the canvas and start over. For art on a smaller scale, try the same techniques with a pillowcase or an old T-shirt. You can also use newsprint instead of a sheet.

Print with Fruits and Vegetables – Try corn, strawberries, pears, cucumbers, radishes, oranges, carrots, beans, lemon, cauliflower, peppers, avocado, mushroom, apples, shapes carved in a potato. Cut the fruits and vegetables in half and dip them into paint and print. Note you can use the edible paint recipe and then you can still eat the yummy food.

Dessert Toppings Finger Paint – Dessert topping in a can, finger paint paper, food coloring. Spray dessert topping directly onto paper. Tint topping with a few drops of food coloring. Use mixture like finger paint.

Rock Paining – Using tempera paint, paint designs on medium sized rocks. If paints aren't available or practical, give the child a can of water and a brush and let him paint the house!

Sand Art – Give each child a piece of construction paper and have them draw a picture or write words with the glue. Make sure that they do not put gobs of glue in any one spot. Before the glue dries, with the hand, pour/put sand onto the glue. Let it sit for a few minutes and then shake off the excess sand. It should dry flat for about a half an hour depending on how much glue was used.

Easy Rainbows – Tape three or four different colored crayons in a straight line. Now draw a rainbow with one stroke.

Shining Stars – Have the children dip star-shaped cookie cutters (or potatoes cut into star shapes) into paint and press them on paper to make prints. Let them sprinkle glitter on the wet paint to make shining stars.

Squeeze Bottle Paining – Use paint made of equal parts of flour, salt, and water. Food coloring can be added to paint mix, just a couple of drops. Mix till it squirts out of the bottle. Squirt it out onto a paper plate or paper. Let sit for a few days and then let the children add decorations if they want.

Sandbox Painting – a Sandbox or large dishpans filled halfway with sand (fill a few pans to share) Spray bottles filled with water Food coloring small sand shovels Add 20 or more drops of food coloring to spray bottles to make colored water. At the sand area give children several bottles of colored water. As they spray, the sand will change color, creating a wonderful painting. If the kids want to 'paint' a new picture, direct them to mix under the top layer with their shovels. Be sure to protect clothing from the food color!

Shades of Colors – Supply the children with any color of paint and white paint. Allow the children to mix a small amount of the paints together. What happens? For younger children, you child add paint to a zip lock bag to minimize the mess.

Cookie Cutter Art – Get some cookie cutters. Have the children dip the cookie cutter in a shallow container of paint, then press onto a piece of paper to make prints.

Pudding Finger Paint – Mix instant pudding according to the directions and paint on wax paper. Add food coloring for a verity of colors. Great for children who like to eat their art or for toddlers who don't know not to eat it.

Marble Painting – Get some tempera paint, paper, marbles, a container and a muffin tin. Place different color drops of paint into the muffin tins. Drop a few marbles in each color. Lay the paper into the bottom of box or roll it up for round container. Place marbles from one color into the container and roll around by moving the box from side to side etc. Remove that color and continue with the other colors.

Saltshaker Art – Put some powdered paint in an old saltshaker. Take the child for a walk in the snow and let him shake paint on the snow to color it. Take a picture on the snow.

Chalk Colors – Add a small amount of acrylic craft paint for color to the basic chalk recipe. Use a toilet paper tube or a 5-oz. Dixie cup for your mold. Another tip is to line your molds or tubes with wax paper to allow the chalk to slip easily out of the molds.

Flowers – Glue paper cupcake liners on paper. Add stems. Spray some flowery perfume on the flowers.

Squiggle Sand – Give each child a piece of wax paper. Have them make squiggles and different designs with glue. Then sprinkle the glue with colored sand. After the glue has dried (overnight) peel the design off the waxed paper. Hang the creations around the room.

Nature Arts, Crafts, and Activities

What is Sand – Talk about sand with the children. What is sand? Where does it come from? How is it made? Set out sand, rocks, shells and magnifying glasses. Explain to the children that powerful waves smash rocks and shells into tiny pieces, which we call "sand". Then let the children use the magnifying glasses to explore the similarities and differences between the sand, the rocks, and the shells.

Nature Collage – Collect a variety of nature items: Seashells, dried wheat, grasses, flowers, sand, rocks, pebbles, bark, twigs, seeds, and small branches. Put these out with glue and sanitized foam trays for the children to create!

Cloud Watching – Lie on your back and point out different shapes in the clouds.

Flower Walk – Pay special attention to the flowers you see. Name the ones you can for your child. This is especially fun in the springtime when the flowers are blooming. You can also do this at other times of the year looking for specific things in nature. For example, a fall walk can be looking for different colored leaves.

What does a plant need to grow – You can ask the children; do a few experiments to see what plants need to grow. Sunlight, water, air…

Leaf Art – Collect leaves and draw around them. Color in the details with crayons or paints. The leaves could then be stuck on to paper collage style or dipped into paint and then pressed firmly on to paper for a lovely leaf print. You can also press them into play dough and dry them to make leafed objects. Experiment with other toys or objects and see what you can produce.

Nature Exploring – Head out to a nearby park, woods, or nature trail and discover the great outdoors. You can simply walk and observe or make your trek into a scavenger hunt by preparing a list of animals, plants, and other objects to spot. A nature guidebook might also come in handy to identify flora and fauna that you don't recognize.

Watch the Ants – But be careful not to touch them if they are fire ants.

Sponge Flowers – Supply your child with different flower shaped sponges, paint and a piece of paper, with lines drawn vertically on the paper. You can take your kitchen sponge and cut it up into petals, centerpieces, or the entire flower. Ask your child to add the flowers with the sponges, as if the lines were stems.

Evaporation – Obtain two clear plastic glasses of the same size. Measure one cup of water and place it in each cup. Mark the water level of each cup with a permanent marker. Place one in a sunny window and the other somewhere else in the room. Observe the glasses of water over the next couple of days. Ask the children where the water is going. Which is evaporating more quickly? Evaporation occurs when the particles of water become warm enough that they turn into vapors and leave the cup and escape into the air. Why did the water in the sun evaporate faster?

Bug Hunt – Go on a bug hunt outside. Provide a box or plastic jar to collect them, and magnifying glasses to allow the children a better view. Return the bugs to their homes so they do not die.

Weathervane – Show the children how a weathervane works.

Sorting – Sort pictures of animals or plants on a basis of observable physical characteristics.

Nature Walk – Take a plastic bag with you on your next nature walk. Encourage your child to collect leaves, small sticks, and acorns, and put them in the bag. (You can go on a nature walk in your back yard too.) Ask your child about each item that they chose to put in the bag.

Sun Prints Fall Leaf – Materials: Colored construction paper, leaves gathered from yard, glue stick, masking tape, picture frames. Dab a bit of glue onto the back of a leaf and attach it to a piece of construction paper. Tape the paper to a sunny window, with the leaf facing out. Leave up for THREE TO FOUR days, or UNTIL YOU NOTICE that the paper's color has faded. Remove from window and gently peel leaf off to reveal the print. Frame and hang.

Measuring Rainfall – On a rainy day, set out a container to measure the rainfall. Measure how much rain fell that day. Continue to measure the rain each day, and record for a few weeks. Ask your child to predict how much water will be collected. Ask at the beginning of the day and ask when it is raining. Did their answer change? Chart your child's progress and see how well they guess.

Caterpillar to Butterfly – Watch a caterpillar turn into a butterfly.

Paint Like a Bird – Supply the children with paper and paint and have the children paint like a bird might paint (this is a version of finger painting). You may want to have them put a pair of clean socks on their hands to help them imagine not having fingers to use.

Dirt – Examine dirt with a microscope or magnifying lens.

Binoculars – Take two empty toilet paper rolls and staple together to look like binoculars. The child can decorate them with crayons or paints or stickers and you can even add a string around them. They can then go out and "bird watch", look at the mountains, etc.

Which Seed is It – Place many kinds of seeds on a paper plate. One of each kind. Talk about the seeds with your child. Then tell your child that you are going to describe a seed, and you want them to guess which one it is. Take turns trying to guess which seed the other is describing. Do other things also like birds, shapes, fruit, vegetables, letters, numbers, colors, etc.

Pinecones – Collect pines cones. Tie a ribbon around the top of the pinecone. Have the children apply glitter glue to them. Use them on a tree for decoration.

Flower Bottles – Clean out and empty plastic water bottles. Place different parts of flowers into the bottle, potpourri works well. Fill about halfway with potpourri, and then fill about 4/5 with baby oil. This will preserve the flowers. You may add glitter if you choose or a little food coloring. Seal the top of the bottle with a little hot glue and allow it to dry.

Dinosaurs – Talk about dinosaurs; discuss that they are extinct and ancient. Explain the term fossil.

Rain Catcher – Obtain a flat-bottomed jar with straight sides. Tape a ruler to the side, so that the number 1 is 1 inch from the bottom. Set out the jar on a rainy day and later that day see how much rain was collected. Obtain a newspaper to check the forecast to see whether they match your results.

Dandelion Hunt – See if you can find yellow dandelions, ones that have seeded. Ones which are closed, big, and small.

Florist – Give your child flowers, and a vase. Have your child pretend to be a florist and have them arrange the flowers. You can pretend to go the flower shop and buy the flowers. Or they can pretend to deliver them to you.

Leaves – Crunch dry and green leaves. Which are easier to crunch?

Seed Collage – Glue all kinds of seeds on a paper plate or paper. You can do a bird theme and use only birdseed, or other themes.

Tadpoles – Have tadpoles in your house and watch them turn into frogs.

Rust – Cut an apple in half and watch it rust.

Dandelion Seeds – Have your child paint glue onto a piece of paper, and then blow the seeds from a dandelion onto the paper.

Parts of a Flower – Show your child a flower. Ask them about the parts of a flower. Ask them if they know where the stem is, or the pedals. Explain that there are roots too. You can even go outside and show your child the roots of a weed, when you pull it out of your garden.

Bird Walk – Next time you go for a walk pay special attention to the birds that you see. Name the ones you can for your child. Check to see if you have a nature park near your city.

Gardener Play – Supply your child with plastic gardening tools, hats, gloves, seeds, flowerpots, flower packets and watering cans to pretend to be a gardener.

Examine Feathers – If you can obtain some feathers, allow your child to examine the feathers with a magnifying glass. Do feathers float in water?

Counting Flower Petals – Draw four or five flowers with different numbers of petals, and different colors. Make a match for each one. Now you can play two games with these. First you can have your child count the petals on each flower. And the second game, you could have your child find each flowers match.

The Sun is Hot – Have your children stand in the sun on a hot day for a few minutes. Then have them stand under a tree or in the shade of a building. Ask your child which is warmer, in the sun or in the shade? Ask your child "What warms the earth?" Place a thermometer in the sun and one in the shade to compare the differences of temperature.

Watch the Rain – Talk about the sounds that you hear during a rainstorm. What are the signs that a storm is coming? Talk about storm safety!

Water – Talk about bodies of water. Lake, river, ocean etc.

Dandelion – Blow a dandelion and watch the wind carry away all the seeds.

Observing Shells – Obtain many kinds of shells and rocks. Allow the children to feel them and look at them with a magnifying glass. Bury the shells in some sand then have the children dig them out.

Plant a Garden – Let your child help you plant your flowers in the spring. Or let your child plant a seed indoors. Make sure the plant receives the proper care so it will grow.

Trees – Discuss and point out the different kinds of trees on your next walk.

Vinegar and Eggs – Place a hard-boiled egg in a cup of vinegar and see what happens. After one day, take out the egg, wipe it off with a paper towel and feel the egg. Ask your child questions about what you see and feel.

Nature Walk – Go for a Nature Walk. Point out trees, grass, bugs, rocks, etc.

Count the Seeds – Before you cut an apple, have your child try to guess how many seeds will be inside. Cut open the apple and count them. How close were they. Write down your child's guess, and how many seeds were in the apple. The next day, repeat the process. Compare your results. Were there more, less, or the same number of seeds in the two apples.

Rocks – Examine different types of rocks. Try looking at them through a magnifying glass and comparing the differences between different types of rocks.

Adopt a Tree – Pick a tree outside. At Various times of the year, spring, fall winter, and summer, take a picture of you and the children outside by the tree. Talk with your children about the differences in the trees, and the clothing that we wear in the different times of the year.

Predict the Weather – Have your child go outside in the morning; ask them what they think the weather will be like. Will it rain, snow, or be sunny? What will the temperature be like? Record your child's answers and compare them to the weather.

Flower Scent – Go to a floral shop or a greenhouse, have your child smell the different kinds of flowers.

Grass Textures – Have kids paint green designs on white construction paper. While the paint is still wet, sprinkle them on grass clippings.

Snowflakes – Try to Catch Snowflakes on your Tongue.

Crafts

Toothpick Sculptures – Make a design on a piece of waxed paper using toothpicks. Then glue the ends of toothpicks together. When they are dry, they will come off the paper easily. Then you can stand them up for display on a piece of clay.

Hand Pictures – Mix tempera paint to consistency of cream and spread it on a sheet of plastic. Let the children place their hands in the paint and then decorate pieces of construction paper with handprints. Variation: An upside-down handprint makes a nice "Christmas Tree", and two overlapped handprints make a pretty "heart", or make a turkey, or any other object that you can think of.

Fun Frames – You will need six popsicle sticks, glue, decorations, two small magnets, construction paper and a picture of the child. Then you make a frame with four popsicle sticks. Lay two sticks parallel to one another (stick 1 and 2) then complete the form with sticks 3 and 4. Then to make the picture stay in you will need to add sticks 5 and 6 on the top and bottom of the frame. Connect these sticks with glue. When dry, then have the children decorate these sticks with paint, glue and glitter, macaroni, string, lace, puzzle pieces etc. Let them dry. Cut a piece of paper to fit the back of the frame. Glue that on. Cut the picture to fit in the frame and insert the picture. Then glue the magnets at the top and bottom of the back of the frame.

Bead Necklaces – Have the children make necklaces out of colored macaroni noodles and yarn. See the recipe section for how to color the pasta.

Torn Paper Apples – Draw an apple on a piece of white paper or use a white paper plate. Tear red paper into dime sized bits (enough to cover your apple drawing.) Cut out one or two leaves for the apple from green paper. (Or if possible, use real apple leaves.) Have your child glue the torn pieces of paper onto your drawing of an apple. Then have your child glue on the apple leaves.

Cotton Ball Clouds – Have children take a large blue piece of construction paper and draw, color, paint a landscape or summer scene. Glue on clumps of white fluffy cotton balls to create cotton clouds in any shape desired. Add a bright shining sun in the sky!

Paper Hand Puppets – Get two paper plates for each hand. Place the child's hand in the center of the plate, fingers together, and trace around the hand, leaving about an inch of space around the hand. (Leave part of the fluted edge at the top for a crown effect and staple along the inside edge of the fluted edge). Make two tracings for each hand. Cut out the tracings, then have the child draw or paint a face or character on one for each hand. Tape or staple one of the characters (with picture facing out) and a back together along the top edge and sides. (If stapling, keep the staples close to the edge to assure enough space for child to slip hand in through the bottom).

Clothespin Butterflies – Open spring-type clothespins then insert a rectangular-shaped piece of tissue paper. Add a pipe cleaner to make antennae.

Froot Loop Sand – Need a Box of Froot Loops Cereal. Have children sort the colors. Put the different colors into baggies and crush them till powdery. Put individual layers in a baby food jar, or clear plastic or glass bottles... as you would color sand. This is good for younger children without the hazard of sand.

Collage – Cut out pictures from magazines and show the child how to paste them on paper, boxes, paper cups, or plates. Talk about the pictures. Tissue scraps, material scraps, colored paper shapes can also be cut and pasted.

Fishing Game – Tie 3 feet of string to a wooden spoon. Attach a magnet to the end of the string. Cut and laminate many different colored, and sized shapes from construction paper (not too big though). Attach a paper clip to each shape. Spread the shapes on the floor and let your child try to catch the shapes. Have them try to catch the red shape, or the biggest shape. For a twist, label the shapes with letters or numbers. Ask the children to catch a specific shape or ask them which shape they caught. This is lots of fun when you have a group of children. They can fish for a numbered shape and the number corresponds to a number on a list of songs they are then picking out songs to sing while they are fishing.

Spring Flowers – Construction Paper, Scissors, Glue. Trace around 1 hand on yellow paper, and trace around 1 hand on red paper. Cut them out; these will be the flowers. Cut out a long & short stem out of green paper. Cut out four leaves out of green paper. Glue the cut-out hands on the stems on the brown paper, add leaves.

What is This – Gather four or more different objects with different scents and tastes. Blindfold the child, then place the object close to the child's nose, and ask the child to smell it and try to identify what it is. Then have the child taste it and see if it is easier to tell by scent or taste.

Homemade Crayons – This is a wonderful way to recycle all the small broken pieces of crayons. Melt the crayons in small glass jars in the microwave then pour (or spoon) into plastic candy or sucker molds. These can be found in the craft section of most stores. This will create some interesting, shaped crayons that your children will love. Another way to melt the crayons would be to foil muffin tins. Melt the crayons in the oven at 200 degrees until they are all melted.

Let them cool completely. Take them out of the tins and remove the foil. You can make them one color or put more than one color in the mold. Kids will love to draw with these multicolored crayons. Note because when the melted crayons come out of the microwave if doing this activity with small children make the crayons first and then give them to the child to color with. Always remember safety first. Also note that some crayon residue will always remain in the jar or on the spoon I would recommend that you use disposable jars and plastic spoons. The molds will be fine as the crayons will pop out when finished cooling.

Place Mat – Have the children cut out pictures from magazines. Have the children glue the pictures onto a piece of paper. Laminate the paper and use it as a place mat.

Flowered Plate Hat – Use sturdy Styrofoam plates. Cut a circle in the middle big enough for your child to wear as a hat. Provide many kinds of either dried flowers, artificial flowers, or make construction paper flowers, for your child to glue onto their hat. Provide ribbons and lace as well. Have a hat parade where the child can walk around the neighborhood showing their hat.

Paint Tray - Take a margarine container lid. Then, about 5 or 6 plastic pop bottle caps. You hot glue the caps to the inside of the lid, fill each one with a different color. The kids can use small paintbrushes, or even their fingers. They get a variety of different colors, but don't use up too much paint!

Lilacs – Show your child what lilacs look like. Precut 2-inch squares of purple or white tissue paper. Twist the tissue around a pencil to create a lilac blossom. Put a little glue on the end of a popsicle stick and show your child how to glue the tissue onto the stick. Repeat until the upper half of the stick is full of blossoms. To display, put them in a small vase.

Monster Madness – Get a paper bag (large enough to fit over a child's head) Cut an oval shape around where their eyes are let the children create and decorate their own monsters.

Puppet Projects – Gather an empty cereal box, scissors, construction paper, glue, yarn. To make the puppet, find the middle of the box and cut across the width and down each side (only one side of the box will remain uncut). Next, bend the box over the uncut side. You now have the puppet created - place your hands in the open ends of the cereal box. To decorate your puppet, use construction paper, scissors and glue. First glue construction paper over the outside of the cereal box (you may need to cut the construction paper to make it fit). Next cut out eyes and any other features you want the puppet to have. Glue them onto the puppet. If you have yarn, macaroni, old, shredded cleaning rags etc. you can use them for hair, simply cut and glue.

Wands – Each child will need an unsharpened pencil or dowel and a few pieces of streamers and tape. Have the child tape the streamers onto the pencil; they may also add star stickers on the pencil for decoration.

Sun Prints Indoor – Cut shapes from paper, and spread re-stickable glue on the back, then stick them to the construction paper. Tape the paper to a sunny window, facing out, and leave for at least a week (longer for higher contrast), then peel off cutouts. You can also lay three-dimensional objects (try rickrack, toothpicks, or buttons) flat on a piece of construction paper in a sunny place where they will not be disturbed.

Ultimate Paperweight – Supply each child with some modeling clay. Let them shape it however they wish. Let them add marbles, buttons, glitter, sand, pebbles, string, or whatever you can think of. After it dries it's a paperweight.

Colored Water Fence Paining – Hang a long piece of bulletin board paper on your outside fence. Give the children bottles of colored water and have them squirt the paper. For young children, this is a lot of fun and a great way to see how secondary colors are made. Example: Spraying blue and yellow water on paper makes a beautiful green design.

Apple Tree – Cut out an apple tree from brown and green paper. Glue the pieces together. Supply your child with red tempera paint, and a pencil with a new eraser. Have the child make prints on the tree with the eraser to make apples. After the picture has dried ask your child how many apples are on their tree. Variation. Have the child dip a cork in paint to make the apple prints.

Dandy Dogs – To make a dog, the child will need a paper plate, brown and black construction paper and two paper brads. Have your child cut ears and eyes from the construction paper. Glue the eyes on the paper-plate head and connect the ears to the head with paper brads. Add additional features with paper scraps. Yarn or string could be added so that it could be used as a mask.

Exploring Hands – Have the children examine their hands. Then let them experiment with different ways of moving their hands, fingers, and wrists. Have them stand still and see how far out and how far up and down they can stretch their hands. How would they use their hands to pick up something heavy? Could they lift it high over their heads? How would they pick up something slimy, something sticky or something round? Can they make their hands look like gentle hands, mean hands, strong hands, weak hands, working hands, or playful hands?

Collages – Have the children cut out pictures of things that interest them from magazines, and glue them onto a piece of paper for a collage.

Popsicle Flowers – Have your child draw pedal and leaves for a flower. They may color them or glitter them if they would like, and then cut them out. Have your child glue the flower parts onto a popsicle stick. For younger children, have the child color the pedals and leaves that you have drawn.

Paper Plate Streamers – You will need crayons or markers, two paper plates, streamers, and tape. Cut out the center of both paper plates. Have the children decorate the top of one paper plate and the bottom of the other with crayons or markers. Then on the side of one plate that undecorated have them tape on many streamers. Place the other plate on top of the first so that the two decorated sides are on the outside and the streamers are on the inside. Tape closed. Put on some dance music and dance with the streamer plates.

Ocean Bottle – Clean out a clear plastic pop bottle. Add water, blue food coloring, glitter, and maybe a few pebbles. Seal the bottle closed using a little glue to allow it too completely dry before the children can play with it. Tip the bottle back and forth. Roll the bottle on the floor.

Tissue Butterflies – Place a butterfly pattern on a flat surface and cover with a piece of wax paper or plastic wrap. Use colored tissue paper to cut into two or three-inch squares. Paint them onto the wax paper with liquid starch or watered down glue. Follow the outline of the butterfly and fill it in completely. Make two to three layers of tissue; dry overnight. Carefully peel away the wax paper. Thread a length of string through the top of the butterfly and hang from the ceiling. Or tape the butterflies to a window for a stained-glass effect.

Collages – Cut sandpaper background for the beach; glue to tag board. Draw waves with markers or pencils, or glue on some rickrack. Cut out shoreline creatures and figures from fabric scraps or use pictures from magazines. Glue to background. Add shells, buttons, etc.

Flower Mask – Cut out the middle of a paper plate. Have the child cut out petals from a variety of different colored construction paper. The child should paint the plate and add the petals after the paint is dry. Finally glue a popsicle stick to the bottom of the plate for a handle. They can now pretend to be a flower growing big and tall. You can also do the same thing for different animals and plants they will have hours of fun pretending to be these different things.

Wagon Fun – Get something heavy in your home that is not bulky, a large brick works well. Ask the children if they can move it. Then place it in a wagon and have them pull it, which way is it easier to move?

Balloon Bugs – Blow up a large balloon for your child. Cover them with newspaper strips dipped in wallpaper paste. Put on three or four layers of sticky paper. Let the balloons dry for two or three days. Then let the children paint their own giant bugs. They may glue construction paper features on them. You can also make faces, globes or anything else you can think of.

Head Bands – Have the children cut paper strips to make a headband out of. They may glue, staple or tape the head band together. Provide the children with feathers, glitter, sequins or other materials for them to decorate the headband with.

Sun Prints Outdoor – Have children place colored construction paper out in the sun----Then have them put various shaped objects on the paper, such as, silverware, flowers, keys, a toothbrush, a box, etc. Leave everything out in the sun until the colored paper fades. When the objects are removed, you should find prints of colored shapes on the paper. Take the paper inside, so it won't fade any more. Try this with different translucent (you can see through them) objects such as glass, plastic or others and see what kind of mark they leave on the paper.

Cotton Balls – Let your child glue different colored cotton balls onto a piece of egg-shaped paper. Cut out a lamb shape and have the child glue on the wool or a bunny shape and have them glue on the tail.

Hand Shaped Flowers – Have each child trace their hand onto a piece of paper. Then have the child cut it out. Obtain a picture of the child to place in the middle with glue. Have the child paint a popsicle stick green. When the stick is dry, glue or tape the hand shape on the stick to make hand shaped flowers. Variation: Supply each child with a cup to decorate. Place a little bit of play dough in the bottom of the cup and stick the flower in the cup.

Pillow Art – On a white pillowcase draw a picture using crayons. Once the picture is complete place it between two pieces of paper and iron it with the iron on low setting (just enough to melt the crayon). Then using tie dye fabric dye, dye the pillowcase or fabric the desired color or colors.

Puppets – To make paper mâché puppets, props or other fun stuff, mix up one of the pastes below. Mold your prop out of non-hardening clay and cover it with petroleum jelly. Tear newspaper into strips about the size of a 12" ruler. For smaller projects use smaller strips. Soak the strips in the paste. Apply to the mold. Cover with one or two layers and let dry for 24 hours. Do a few more layers and let dry again. Cut the whole thing in half. Take molding clay out. Tape paper mâché forms back together. Put three or four or even five layers of paste-soaked newspaper strips over the tape. Make sure it covers the split well. Let dry. Paint.

Pom-Pom Ball Caterpillar – Glue pastel-colored pom-pom balls onto a tongue depressor. Add facial features with markers, then glue on pipe cleaners for antennae.

Yarn Balls – Blow up a round balloon. Dip yarn into a mixture of one part glue and one part water. Wrap yarn around the balloon until completely covered. Let dry, then pop balloon. Decorate as desired.

Star Scopes – Give each child an empty toilet tissue tube with a black paper circle taped over the end. Let the children gently punch holes in the paper-covered ends of their tubes with toothpicks to complete their star scopes. To use, have the children hold their scopes up to the light and look through the uncovered ends. The light will shine through the holes, creating miniature planetariums.

Make an Instrument – Use a pot or pan and a spoon, an empty coffee tin with lid, or two pot tops for cymbals.

Sponge Print – You can find already shaped sponges at craft stores, or you can make your own. The children can dip the sponges into paint and press on a piece of paper. They can also go outside on a sunny day and do this with water on the sidewalk the water will dry so they can start over again creating more fun pictures. Have fun talking to the children about what kinds of interesting shapes are found within the sponge (the holes) and how they add to the artwork to make it more interesting. If you create your own shaped sponges some stores will sell flat sponges that only need a little moister to expand. These are great to create the shapes and then cut them out then expand. Also, you do not need to be good at art or make intricate shapes. Tracing cookie cutter shapes will work very well for this activity. You will simply need to trace the cookie cutter on the sponge using a Sharpe marker then cut out the shape and have fun.

Flower Picture Collage – Obtain a catalog for flowers, an advertisement, or a gardening magazine. You can either cut out the pictures of the flowers or have your child cut them out. Tell your child the name of each flower in the pictures. (Optional) Ask your child to sort the pictures according to color. (Optional) Then, ask your child which is their favorite. Have your child glue the pictures on a piece of paper for a flower collage. Make collages from other themed catalogues.

What is It – See if children can guess an object by the shadow it makes.

Show and Tell – Show pictures of objects and ask, "Is it alive?" Show pictures of plants and animals and ask, "Am I a plant or an animal?" Do this for other things like fruits and vegetables, big and small, or any combinations you can think of.

Miniature Gardens – The foil trays that pies and prepared foods arrive in or meat trays make lovely containers for miniature gardens. The children can enjoy hunting around the park or garden for twigs to make trees, moss for a lawn, stones to arrange as a waterfall. Keep twigs or stones where you want them with a little glue. Add toy people or animals and maybe a little water if the container is watertight. A variation is to use play sand to make a beach scene, maybe adding shells, stones and a blue paper sea.

Necklaces – Cut out shapes from different colors of paper. Older children can do the cutting for themselves. Then depending on the ages, either punch holes in the shapes or allow the children to punch the holes. Then supply the children with yarn that is about 18 inches long with one end that is wrapped with a little piece of masking tape. Have the children lace the shapes onto the yarn then tie it to make a necklace.

Feather Headbands – Measure your child's head and cut a piece of construction paper long enough to create a headband. Glue the paper together so the headband fits snugly on your child's head but is loose enough to take off easily. Glue the feathers to the headband.

Hand Wreath – Trace your child's hands several times onto a piece of green paper. Cut out these hand shapes. Give them a paper plate and show them how to cut out the center of the plate. Have the children glue their green hand shapes onto the plate to make a wreath. You could also have them use a paper hole punch on red paper and glue the holes on for holly.

Flag Design – Have an older child design their own flag.

Painted Pots – Obtain small clay pots. Have the children decorate them with non-toxic paint. When dry add dirt and flowers.

Puzzle Box – A small gift box can become the base for an endless variety of puzzles. Begin by gluing a piece of felt onto the lid of the box. You and your child can then select a variety of pictures and cut them to make a puzzle. Then glue strips of flannel onto the backs of the pieces. Puzzle pieces backed with flannel stick to the felt covered box and can be stored inside the box. You can create another type of flannel box puzzle by filling the box with felt pieces cut into basic geometric shapes in a variety of sizes and colors. These shapes can be used to create a picture on the box lid.

Picture Matching – Find stickers that will interest your child, or you can draw shapes. Place 2 identical stickers or shapes on the left and right sides of an index card. Cut the index card in half, cut in a jig-jag form. Use a highlighter to highlight the edges. Do this with many different stickers or shapes. Have the child match the stickers or shapes, and line up the two halves of the index card.

Heart Fish – Give your child one very large heart shape for the fish's body, one large heart shape for the tail, two or three heart shapes for the fins, and one tiny heart shape for the mouth. Have the children glue the extra-large and large heart together by the points, and then add the fins to the body, then the tiny heart is the mouth.

Egg Carton Caterpillar – Cut the bottom of a cardboard egg carton in half. The long, six-cup section will be the body of the caterpillar. To make the legs, cut a small section from both sides of each cup. Paint the outside with green paint and let it dry. Glue the body to a piece of black paper. After it has dried in place, trim around the edge of the caterpillar with scissors. Cut the head from green paper and draw on features with a marker. Add wiggly eyes. Make the antennae from black paper and glue to the head.

Pussy Willow – Make pussy willows with cotton balls and Popsicle sticks.

Q-Tips – Make structures out of Q-tips and play dough or clay. This is a variation of using craft sticks or toothpicks.

Play Time

Blocks – Build towers with blocks then knock the towers down.

Paper Airplane – Make a paper airplane. Try to fly your airplane. Use different designs and see which ones work better.

Is it Full – Experiment with filling up a container with large rocks, small rocks, sand and water. Which one can you put more into the container? Can you put them all into the container at one time? Experiment with how you could do this (hint – go from largest to smallest.)

Ramp It – Provide the children with an inclined plane. This can be made with a propped-up board. Have your child pick an item around the house. Show the children a few basic items, like a car with wheels, a marble and a book. Ask the children if the item will roll down or slide down the ramp, or if it will not move. Then try it with each item. Have each child guess what the item that they picked out will do.

Telephone – Poke a hole in the bottom of two Styrofoam cups. Place a piece of string in the bottom of one cup and tie a knot at the end of the string to prevent the string from coming completely out of the bottom of the cup. Then thread the string through the bottom of the other cup and tie another knot. Have one child talk in one cup while another listens with the other cup. How long can the string be before the phone won't work?

Bean Bag Toss – Obtain a large piece of cardboard. A large, unfolded box works well. Cut one or two shapes out of the cardboard. Paint the cardboard. When dry let the children throw beanbags through the holes.

Balloon Puppets – For each child, blow up a balloon until it is about the size of a large cantaloupe. Tie several strands of curled ribbon around the knot and attach a loop of ribbon large enough to slip over the child's hand. Then let the children make faces on their balloons by sticking them on gummed reinforcement circles. When they have finished, let them wear their balloon puppets on their wrists.

String – Can be tied to chair legs to make a jump, dipped into paint and twirled on to paper, plaited, knitted with, or made into a parachute or mobile, used as a measuring aid or for learning how to tie shoelaces and bows.

Glass and Water Music – Fill a couple of identical glass cups, at least four, with varying amounts of water. Tap the side of each glass with a metal spoon. Which is the highest sound and the lowest? How could we change the sound?

Beach Ball Bat – Hang a beach ball from the ceiling just within the child's reach. Allow the children to bat at the ball.

Evaporation – Set out three cups, half filled with water. Add food coloring to the water. Have your child use an eye dropper to drop the colored water onto a paper towel. Notice how the water evaporates, leaving the color behind.

I Spy – Show the children a variety of different objects or images. Then give clues, like "I spy something with a green rectangle." Keep giving clues until the children can tell you which object or picture you have chosen.

Balls in the Basket – You need some small balls and a small laundry or bushel basket. Ask your child to place the balls in the basket. Count with your child as they place the balls in the basket. How many balls will fit in the basket? Have your child guess how many will fit, and then see how many it takes to fill the basket. You can also tape numbers onto the bottom of the baskets, and have your child place the appropriate number of balls into each basket.

Sand Dough – Add sand to the play dough for a different kind of texture experience. Encourage the children to describe how the play dough feels as they work with it. See the recipe section for how to make your own play dough.

Popping Balloons – Let the children help you pretend to blow up balloons and fill the room with them. Then have them pretend to tape sharp pins on their knees and elbows so that they can "pop" the balloons. Encourage them to reach their knees and elbows way up high and way down low until all the balloons have popped.

Will it Dissolve – Fill five clear jars with water. Take five different substances, like sugar, cereal, salt, paper, things that will dissolve, and some that won't. Ask your child which will dissolve, and which will not. Test each item in the water.

Directions – Talk about directions, north, south, east and west. Post these labels on the walls in your home and play "Simon Says" using the directions, (i.e. "Simon Says face North")

Sensory Fun – Supply the child with many different items to feel, smell and touch. Like pine tree branches, leaves, dirt, rice, etc.

Musical Instruments – Make your own musical instruments, clap your hands, and tap your belly. Use a coffee can with lid for a drum. Make maracas with two paper plates and beans.

Flexibility – Supply the children with different items that range in flexibility. Rubber band, pencil, string, a stick. Which is the most flexible? Which is the least flexible?

Floating Bubbles – Let the children pretend to be bubbles. Play soft music and have them "float" like bubbles around the room.

Indian Play – Provide the children with Indian clothing, cradle boards, beaded necklaces, set up teepees and allow the children to pretend to be Indian.

Shades of Green – Supply the children with three clear cups of water, one with a drop of blue food coloring, one with a drop of yellow food coloring, and one empty cup. Supply the children with plastic eyedroppers and let them mix the colors in the empty cup. (Add more coloring as desired). Try mixing other colors as well.

Faster and Slower – Talk about faster and slower. Roll a ball on the floor slowly, then faster. Ask the children how to get the ball to roll faster.

Shaving Fun – Spray shaving cream on your pumpkin. Shave the pumpkin with safety razors that have the blades removed.

Black Play Dough – Make play dough then use Wilton's Black Cake Paste to color it. Use a lot of the paste to get a deep rich black.

Feelie Box or Bag – Place items in a box or bag and see if the children can guess what they are.

Paper Puppets – A picture of anything carefully cut out and mounted onto card stock, then glued onto a Popsicle stick. This becomes a very easily made puppet. Magazine pictures can be stuck on to folded card to make theatre set background and wings.

Noisy Cause and Effect – Toddlers will love to play games where they can see the cause and effect. A simple light switch can be a source of entertainment, (as well as the not so desirable toilet flushing); toys that resound by touch, like music books, and pop-up toys, jack in the boxes and activity centers are great toys for this age.

Balloon Fish – Partially blow up ten small balloons. Place them in a dishpan full of water. Set the pan on the floor and let the children take turns fishing for balloon fish with a wire food strainer. Help each child count his or her catch before putting the fish back in the pan.

Cafes – Use a picnic set or microwave cookware for this game. Giving the waiter/waitress a little notebook and pencil to take orders and making a tall white hat from a cylinder of paper for the chef will add realism. Sit dolls and teddies around as well as willing Aunts and Grannies for extra customers.

Silly Putty – Play with silly putty. Or other gooey substances. See the recipe section for some ideas.

Treasure Hunt #1 – Draw a simple map of your house. Hide a "treasure" somewhere in your house, something like a snack, or maybe a treasured toy. Explain the map to your child. Tell them where each room is. Next say there is a hidden treasure in the house, and the map is going to help them find it. Draw an X on the map where you have hidden the treasure. Help your child look for the treasure.

Treasure Hunt #2 – Make a list of items you would like your child to find on a walk. Like a stick, leaf, fire hydrant, or blue car. Explain to your child that you are going on a treasure hunt and go over the list with your child. First the items should be very easy to find. And later can increase in difficulty. Go on the walk with the paper and mark of the items as your child finds them. For older children try: Find an item that is: taller than you, can fit in your hand, is too heavy to lift, if your arm, is three different colors. Etc.

Pinwheel Fun – Play with a pinwheel. Try blowing on it, putting it out on a windy day, have a fan blow on it etc. What angle does the wind need to come at it. What makes it go faster or slower etc.

Balloon Jump – Blow up balloons and tie them with long strings. Then hang the balloons from the ceiling at a height that will tempt the children to stretch, jump and bat the balloons around.

Star Experiment – Ask the children why they think they can see stars only at night. Then ask them to help you do this experiment. Turn on all the lights in your room. Have two or three children stand away from the group and give them each a flashlight that has been turned on. Ask the group if they can see the light from the flashlights. Gradually darken the room. What happens to the light coming from the flashlights? Does it become easier or harder to see? Help the children to understand that just as they can't see the light from the flashlights when the room lights are on, they can't see the light from the stars when the sun is shining.

Rainbow in a Jar – Take a large glass jar, fill it 3/4 with water. Drop a single drop of food coloring into the jar from about a foot above the jar, so the coloring makes its way almost to the bottom. Try different colors.

Octopus Color Changes – Discuss with your child how an octopus will change colors to blend with its surroundings. Cut four or five different colored octopus from construction paper. Set out four or five matching sheets of construction paper. Ask your child to match the octopus with its background.

Magnifying Fun – Use a magnifying glass. Observe lots of different types of objects. Notice what you can see with a magnifying glass that you can't see with only your eyes.

Bowling for Boxes – Stack gift boxes of varying sizes. (Be sure to stack them up high). Roll a softball at the stack. Count the ones that are knocked over and the ones that a still standing. The object is to knock over as many as you can.

Stages of Growth – Explain the stages of growth of a bean. If you can draw, or find pictures of the stages, laminate them, and ask your child to arrange the picture from first to last. This can also be done with other things like a butterfly or whatever interests the child. Laminate the cards for longer life. See the next activity for another idea to use with these cards.

Races – Have the children run as fast as they can a measured distance outside. Record the time. Have them run the distance every day at least a few times. Then at the end of the week, have them run again and time them. Compare the time with their first time.

Inclined Plane – Roll the ball down an inclined plane that is very steep vs. almost parallel to the floor. Which ball rolls faster? Try different angles.

Teepees – You can show the children how to make teepees from paper by making the paper into a cone shape and taping it. Then have the children decorate.

Dance – Play some music and dance with your child.

Paper Bag Face – Stuff small lunch bag with crumpled paper. Twist the top closed then paint the top, this becomes your hair. Then paint the bottom and make into a face.

Nesting Hen – Place some plastic eggs under a pillow. Have the child sit on the pillow and guess how many eggs are under the pillow. Count the eggs with the child.

Match the Shapes – Cut out two shapes from 4 or 5 different colors of construction paper. You may laminate them to make them last longer. Have the children pick a shape and then find its mate. Variation: Use the same color for the shapes and draw on different designs.

What Is Missing – You will need a tray and various objects like jar tops, a spoon, a spool of thread, and crayon. Place the tray with the objects on it on the table or floor. Start the game by asking the child to look closely and try to remember everything that is on the tray. Allow the child time to look at each object; he may want to touch and ask questions about each object. Then ask them to close their eyes. While his eyes are closed, take one thing off the tray, and hide it. Then ask the child to open his eyes and try to tell which object is missing. You can make the game harder by adding more objects.

Play with a Kaleidoscope – Talk to the children about what they see, how it works and if they see any shapes, etc.

Hide and Seek – Play hide and seek with a group of children.

Weighing – Supply the children with a balance and some small objects to experiment with and plenty of various items. This can usually be tied in with your theme. If you are doing winter, let them weigh snow vs. water. Which weighs more? If you are doing Valentines Day have them weigh heart shaped beads or find different objects from around the house to weigh.

Texture – Supply the children with different textured items to feel. Is the item rough, smooth, or bumpy?

Hardness – Supply the children with different items that range in hardness. Which is the hardest? The softest?

Sand and Water Play – A dish tub filled with sand or water can provide entertainment as well as a great learning experience. Ideas to add to water play: a drop of food coloring, funnels, cups, dish soap, boats, plastic toys, brushes and sponges, ice, cold or warm water, baby dolls or play dishes to wash, toddler safe balls, items that will sink or float.

Popcorn Pop – Have the children pretend to be popcorn. Use some upbeat music or a recording of popping corn to stimulate the children to jump more.

Dump and Fill – Toddlers like to dump and fill just about anything. Coffee cans, large formula cans, any of your kitchen containers, and boxes make great items to be filled. You can have the children fill with toys, tops from baby food jars, and other toddler safe items.

Summer or Winter Cloths – Gather an assortment of clothes for summer and winter seasons. Show your child each piece of clothes and ask your child if the clothing is winter or summer clothing. This can also be done with images cut out of magazines or catalogs.

Square Balloons – Fill a balloon half full with water. Place the balloon in a square container, and then place in the freezer. When frozen take out of the freezer. Show the children what you have done. Ask them what will happen when the ice melts. Find out.

Find that Shape – Show the children a variety of different flags. What shapes do you see in the flag?

Sand Writing – Place a tray of sand in front of the children. With your finger, write an alphabet letter in the sand. Ask the children to identify the letter. When they have done so, smooth out the sand and write another letter. Follow the same procedure for reviewing numbers and shapes. Then let the children take turns writing letters, numbers and shapes in the sand themselves. Use dry and wet sand to see what is easier to use.

Flag Match Game – Obtain pictures of the flags of the world. Make two color copies of each (they need to be about the same size) then glue each flag to an index card and play memory.

Light – Play with color filters or "gels" on the end of a flashlight, to change the color of light. Try different color combinations to see how it affects the light. What colors make white light? (Red, Green, and Blue.)

Find that Color – Show the children a variety of different images. What colors do you see in the images?

Pass the Object 1 – Played like hot potato, Have the children sit in a circle and pass an object around the circle while music is playing, when the music stops the child holding the object sits in the middle until the music stops again and the next child replaces the first. You may also chant "hot ___, hot ___, 1, 2, 3, 4, 5, 6, 7, 8, 9, and 10" and the child who has the object on 10 is in the middle.

Pass the Object 2 – For older children. Have one child hold an object such as an apple or orange, under their chin and try to pass the object to a friend. You could do this in a circle, or you can do a relay race where the children must run with the object under their chin.

Body Trace – Have the children lay down on a long piece of construction paper and trace their bodies. After this is finished, let the kid's color and draw on the paper what they think they look like.

Look at a Mirror – Help the children identify different body parts in the mirror.

Cookie Monster – Pretend to eat like Cookie Monster. The toddlers seem to really like this a lot. I ask them for a cookie or ice cream, and they pretend to give one to me and I make a lot of noise while pretending to eat it.

Which Color is Missing – Draw several different rainbows on small pieces of paper for each one; exclude a color that should be in the rainbow. So, the first exclude red, second orange... etc. Then make a rainbow that has all the colors. Show the children the rainbow with all the colors on it. Ask what colors they see. Then show each card to the children and ask them if they can guess what color is missing. Variation: Put the colors in the wrong order. See if the children can see which color is not in the right place.

Posters and Photographs – Large, colorful posters can be cut into delightful puzzles. It is possible to buy inexpensive reproductions of famous works of art as well as other types of posters. Glue the posters onto tag board (strong cardboard) before you cut them into puzzle shapes. Family photographs can become very personal puzzles. A photograph that has been enlarged will probably be more satisfying since the image is clearer.

Color Stars – Make a matching game for the children by cutting a star out of cardboard and coloring each of its five points a different color. Then color the ends of five clothespins to match the colors on the star points. To play the game, have the children clip the clothespins on the matching-colored star points.

Growing Flowers – Have your child pretend that they are a seed. Turn the lights off. Ask your child to "grow" just a little when it rains. You can either make rain noises or use a tape recording of the rain. After your child grows a little, turn the lights on, tell your child that they have just grown above the ground a little and they can see the sun (light). Tell them to grow a little faster, until they can grow no more.

Sing – Sing the ABCs with the children or any other song that you know. You can use the rhyme section to come up with some ideas.

Where is My Home – Cut out bird and nest shapes from many different colors of construction paper. Have the children match the bird to the correct nest. Do other types of animals such as dogs and doghouses.

Singing Balloons – Blow up a balloon and demonstrate how its "sings" by stretching the opening as you let out the air. Ask the children to tell you whether the air is coming out quickly or slowly. Experiment with different rates of escaping air. Let the children feel the air escaping by placing their hands over the balloon opening.

Sensory Fish – Use Blue Hair Gel, Ziploc Bag small, Plastic fish, Glitter. Place the fish, glitter and gel into the baggie. Seal the bag, and then tape it shut. Let the children feel and play with the bag. Watch the child closely so the bag is not punctured.

Make a Playhouse – Drape a blanket over a table for a fun place to play. This is also fun if you use an appliance box to make the house.

Flag Talk – Show the child pictures of many flags. Name a few of the countries the flags belong to. Ask the children which is their favorite. Why do they like it?

Prism Fun – Show your child the prism, and how to see all the colors of a rainbow in the prism.

Rainbow Bubbles – Have the children blow bubbles and look at them closely. When the reflection from the sun hits the bubbles, a rainbow of colors can be seen. Ask the children to look for the different colors and name the ones that they see.

Grow a Bean - Place a wet paper towel in a small zip lock back along with one bean seed. Place the bag in a sunny place and watch the bean sprout. You can do this activity with other seeds and watch other things grow. Try placing different types of seeds in the same back and guess which one will sprout first.

Rubber Band Music – Place a rubber band on your index finger and thumb and pluck it to make a twang sound. Can the sound change? How can you change it? How does it change?

Winter Activities – Ask your child what activities can be done in the summer, but not the winter. And vice versa.

Balloon Power – Blow up 20 to 30 small balloons and put in a large garbage bag. Fully inflate a small balloon. Ask your child what will happen if he/she sits on it. Let your child try it. If it doesn't pop have your child jump on the balloon to pop it. Inflate enough of the small balloons to fill the garbage bag. Seal the bag and have your child sit or even jump on the bag.

Riddles – Gather some everyday objects from around the house, such as a spoon, scissors, crayon, or thread. First place the items in front of the child. Say something like; "I am going to make up a riddle about one of these things. Look at the things and listen to see if you can guess which one I am talking about." Then give clues, one at a time, until the child guesses correctly: "You see me on a table. You cannot eat me. But you use me to eat your soup. What am I?" "Yes, I am a spoon." See if the child can make up the riddles for the other two items. Remind the child not to say the name of the object. Give help, if necessary, by whispering suggestions to the child. Expand this activity by describing something in the room that both of you can see. Have the child tell you its name from what you tell about it. Then let the child describe something for other family members to guess.

Pretend to be Asleep – Let the children wake you up, pretend to be surprised. Snoring adds a lot more fun to this game.

Hot and Cold – Hide an object. Then tell the children individually whether they are "hot" or "cold" to the relation of the object. Allow the other children to have a chance to hide the object and tell children whether they are "hot or cold". It may be a good idea to discuss the meaning of hot and cold before you play this game.

Ring Around the Rosie – Play Ring around the Rosie with the children.

Measure It – Place something to be measured in a dish pan, (i.e. beads, rice, water, sand etc.) also provide the child with measuring cups, and containers of various sizes. Experiment with how many of one will fit in the larger containers.

Compare and Contrast – Find two things in the room. Ask the children how they are the same. Ask the children how they are different.

Bean Game – Take a certain amount of large beans, or small items to hold in your hands. Decide on a number to work on like 8. Have your player count out 8 beans. Place the beans in your hand and hide them behind your back. While they're behind your back put some beans in each hand. Like 3 in one hand and 5 in the other. Show the player the beans in one hand. They must tell you how many you have in the other hand. Play this again using another combination. This helps your child learn all the combinations of a number sum.

Star Folders – Draw eight stars on the insides of a file folder and number them from 1 to 8. Draw matching stars on construction paper or index cards and cut them out. Use dots to number the stars from 1 to 8. Give the children the file folder and cutout stars. Let them take turns matching the numbers by placing the cutouts on the corresponding pictures on the file folder.

Name that Flag – Have the children guess which flag belongs to which country.

Bubbles – Blowing bubbles provides endless fun.

Hand Coupons – Have the children each make handprints on four or five sheets of paper. Staple the papers together and let the children give them to family members or friends as gift coupon books. Recipients can tear out the pages and present them to the children when they need helping hands.

Playdough Apples – Let your child use red or green play dough to make apples.

Will it Absorb Water – Supply the children with pieces of material to test like pieces of cotton, plastic, wool, tin foil, etc. Supply the children with eyedroppers and a cup of water. Which materials absorb water, and which do not?

Creating Ice – Place water in a plastic ice tray and place it in the freezer. Every half-hour takes it out to inspect the ice. Ask the children why it is changing? Then after it is frozen, set it in a cup and allow it to melt again.

Capes – Kings, queens, Batman, Superman - they all need capes or cloaks. Make one by attaching ribbon ties to an oblong piece of fabric or towel in the color of your child's favorite character.

Sand Fun – Build with dry sand, and then build with wet sand. What is the difference? Is it easier to build with dry sand or wet sand?

Post Office – Get a Cardboard mailbox, stamped envelopes, wagon, bag, stickers for stamps, used mail, file boxes, pens, pencils, paper, and junk mail. Let the children use the material to pretend they work for a post office. The children can write letters, address the envelope, buy stamps, put the letters in the mail, deliver the mail and receive mail.

Obstacle Course – An obstacle course can turn a rainy day into an adventure. Use whatever you have available. A bench to walk the plank, cushion steppingstones across shark infested seas, through a cardboard box tunnel, up a chair mountain or through a duvet cave. The wilder your imagination the more your children will love it.

Scarf – Dance with a scarf to music and have the child see how the air holds it up.

Books and Reading – It's never too early to start reading to children. Kids love the ritual of cuddling on a parent's lap and hearing their mom or dad's voice as they read to them. As children get older, ask them to turn the pages for you. Look at the illustrations and point out all the different elements. Ask your child questions about the story you are reading to increase their comprehension skills.

Sidewalk Chalk – Use sidewalk chalk to draw different pictures.

Gravity – Watch a feather fall to the ground, and then watch a ball. Use all kinds of objects to see which ones fall faster than others.

Magic Balloons – Blow up several balloons. Let the children rub the balloons on their clothes or their hair and place them on a wall. Have the children try guessing what causes the balloons to stay up (static electricity).

Buried Treasure – Fill a box with sand and hide five small objects in it, such as a shell, a pebble, a crayon, a bead, and a button. Let the children search for the "buried treasure." When they have found as many of the treasures as they can, ask them to count the objects or to match them to cards with pictures of the hidden objects drawn on them. Provide a sifter for the children to use when searching for the treasure, if desired. Variation: Hide plastic letters in the sand. Each time the children find one, have them name words that begin with that letter.

What Will Happen If – Record the children's answers then try it and see. Some examples: What will happen if I flip this light switch? What will happen if I put oil in water? What will happen if I drop this ball?

What's in my Sock – Find a very colorful sock. Place something in the sock, like a block, or a toy. Let the child feel the object and try to guess what it is.

Ramp and Roll – Create a ramp with a large block or book. Then gather toys and show how the toys roll or slide down the ramp.

Bean Bag Toss – Obtain a laundry basket, bushel basket, large formula cans, or large coffee cans. Beanbags, or small balls. Use masking tape to tape a line on the floor. Place the basket a couple of feet away from the line. Have the child stand behind the line and try to toss the balls or bags into the basket. If you are using a ball have the children toss it gently so it does not bounce back out at them.

Shadow Tracing – On a sunny day take some chalk outside and have the children trace each other's and your shadow. When the outline is complete fill the shadow in with facial features and whatever you are wearing.

Paper Plate Shaker – Take two sturdy paper plates. (The stronger the better). Place some seeds, beans, un-popped popcorn, rice, or other small objects on one of the plates and place the other plate on top of the first so that both eating surface areas are facing each other. Use masking tape or staples seal the plates together. Have your child decorate with markers, glitter, construction paper, or ribbons. When dry, shake. Shake to music or shake it each time you take a step.

Search – Cut out many shapes and hide them around the room. Have the children search for them like an Easter egg hunt.

Apple Chart – Prepare sliced apples for lunch, some green, red and yellow. Ask each child which colored apple they ate. Allow them to mark the column on a graph that corresponds to their answer.

Balloon in the Air – Stand in a group with the children and have a blown-up balloon and tap it up in the air. (Use two or three balloons for a large group.) Have the child closest to where the balloon starts to come down, tap it up again with his or her hand. The object of the game is to see how long the group can keep the balloon in the air.

Sounds – Make a tape of sounds around the house. Water dripping, the door opening, the phone ringing, children drawing with markers, etc. Play the tape back and see if the children can guess what the sounds are.

Counting Bubbles – Let the children take turns blowing all the bubbles they can with one breath. Have the rest of the children count the bubbles.

Cause and Effect – Use a large mailing tube or a shoebox with the ends cut out of it, and a toddler safe ball. The child places a ball or any item that will fit in the tube have them watch it come out the other end.

Egg Carton Fun – Use a white plastic egg carton for this activity. Fill each hole 3/4 full of water. Add red food coloring to one hole, blue to another, and yellow to another. Give your child an eyedropper, show them how to use the eyedropper to move the colored water to clear water, notice how the color changes. Let them experiment. For older children, ask them how to make green, purple, brown, and aqua colors.

What do You See – You will need one large envelope and a cutout picture of familiar objects such as trucks, cars, or animals. Place the cutout pictures in the large envelope. Pull one picture out slowly to show only part of the picture. Start the game by asking, "What do you see in the picture?" (Four wheels, two legs, etc.) "What do you think it might be?" If the child, after several guesses, seems to lose interest, show the picture and name the object. A variation of this game would be to write the letters of the alphabet or numbers on pieces of paper and play the same game.

Prism Fun – Play with a prism. Try different angles and different lighting to see how the prism changes the light.

Measuring Distance – Have children use a ruler to measure different items and distances.

What is a Real Heart – Discuss with your children the purpose of our heart. Our heart is like a pump that pushes our blood to our cells and lungs. Show the children where in their body it is. Show the children how to take their pulse.

Stores – Save all your empty grocery boxes, cartons, bags, cans, etc. You will soon have a store that any kid will love to pretend to go shopping in. The boxes will need to have their flaps glued down and you will want to open the cans with a can opener that does not leave sharp edges if you give the child empty ones. Other things can also be used to create "stock" such as clothing, shoes, toys, office supplies, etc. Also, you can use bags, toy cash registers, and play money to add to the fun.

Paper – Blow paper across a table with your breath. Try it while blowing with a straw. Have a race. Try it folded into different shapes and see how they work.

Condensation – Obtain two jars and their lids. Fill one jar with ice cold water and the other with room temperature water. Observe the results. Condensation occurs when the vapors in the air become cool enough to condense and form water droplets.

Mommy Says – Played like Simon says. Replace mommy with other family members.

Jet Balloons – While blowing up balloons, let a few of them go before tying them closed and watch them fly around the room. Have the children try to guess why this happens. What makes the balloons go? How far will they go before they stop? How can you make them go again?

Who is It – Make a tape of each child saying, "Hello! Can you guess who I am?" See if the children can tell whose voice is whose.

Shadow Tag – This is done the same as regular tag only instead of trying to touch a person you try to touch their shadow.

Hunt for Gold – Get some plastic gold coins, candy coins or just make some from yellow tag board. Hide them around the room and have the children hunt around the room for them.

Phone – Pretend to talk on a play phone. Talk about phone edict.

Jingle Bell in a Bottle – Place a jingle bell in a pop bottle. Seal the top very tight with hot glue. Allow it to dry. Let the children play with the bottle.

Mom's Helper – Get the help of your child to make dinner. Kids love measuring and mixing, and they can also set the table or make something simple, such as a salad, entirely on their own.

Sequence Cards – Make simple sequence cards for your child. Draw the various stages of a chick hatching from an egg, a butterfly's life cycle, or how a plant grows. Draw an egg in its' nest, an egg cracking, a chick partly out of the egg, and a chick that is completely hatched. Or a caterpillar egg, caterpillar, cocoon, then a butterfly. Or a seed, roots, plant stem, flower. Mix the cards up and have the child put them in order. You can also use different sized objects like balls and have the child put them from biggest to smallest. If you do not want to make cards, use actual objects such as different size balls. If you are using objects have the children sort by weight. You can also number the shapes or objects and have the children line them up by number.

Creative Movement Fun – Let the children watch you blow up a balloon and then slowly deflate it. Have them pretend that they are limp balloons, expanding as they breathe air in and whistling as they let air out. Let the children spring and dash around like balloons that have been inflated and released. Or let them pretend to be inflated balloons floating lazily about the room while gently bumping into things.

Bubble Games – When blowing bubbles with the children, reinforce the concept of big, little, few, many, high, and low. Ask questions such as these: "Can you blow big bubbles? Little bubbles? A few bubbles? Many bubbles? Can you blow your bubbles high in the air? Can you blow them down low?"

Stilts – Take two strong tins, coffee, baby formula, or clean paint tins and drill a hole about one inch from the bottom on opposite sides of the tin. Insert a length of rope and knot securely. Check that the handle is at a comfortable length for the child before knotting the other side.

Apple Tree – Supply each child with a tree shape, and a red, green, or yellow non-toxic bingo dabber. Have the children put "apples" on the tree with the dabber.

Lacing Cards – Cut colored poster board into different shapes and punch holes around the edges. Then let your child lace yarn or a shoestring into the cards.

Play With a Puppet – Children like to have a puppet talk and play with them. Have the puppet tell a story. Have the children act out different situations and show how they would react to them. For example, stranger danger, drugs, argument with siblings, etc.

Parachute Fun – Play with a parachute. You can put balls on it and let have them grab around the edge and bounce the balls with it or other fun activities that you can think of.

Balloon Lotto – Make a balloon lotto game by dividing a piece of heavy white paper into six sections and drawing a different colored balloon in each square. Cut matching-colored squares out of construction paper. To play the game, have the children take turns placing the construction paper squares on top of the matching-colored balloons. Use other objects depending on the interest of the children.

Graph It – Show the children how to make a simple graph. Graph anything!

Leg Exercises – Lie on your back, with your knees bent and feet on the floor. Ask a child to sit on your feet or place them on your feet, facing you. Lift your legs slowly so they are parallel to the ground. If the child holds on you can lift them upside down.

Wish Upon a Star – Cut a star out of cardboard and cover it with foil. Tell the children that it is a special wishing star and that whoever holds it gets to make a wish. Then give the star to one child and let him or her make a wish. Pass the star around the group until everyone has had a turn making a wish.

Pretend to be a _____ – Pretend to be a dog, cat, dinosaur, baby, etc.

Make a Puzzle – Stick a favorite picture on to card stock and allow it to dry with a heavy book on top. Cut it into pieces for an almost instant and personal puzzle. How many depends on the age of the child.

Paper Balls – Paper balls are easily scrunched up from torn out magazine pages. When it's time to tidy up, stand the wastepaper basket in the middle of the room and see who can throw the most in. A rolled-up magazine makes a good "bat" too.

Play in a Mirror – Make silly faces into a mirror. For added fun, place a mirror on the floor and let the child walk on it.

Roll Around – Roll around on the floor or down a gentle hill outside.

Foam Play – Use a tear-free bath foam or fragrance-free shaving cream to create a good lather. Let your child have fun styling his or her hair and creating "disguises" with foam or shaving cream. Create a Santa beard, moustache, and mane of hair on your child. Hold up a mirror so your child can see how funny he or she looks.

Play Basketball – Supply the children with a large ball and a laundry basket. Show the children how to put the ball in the basket. Try the same with beanbags or small pillows.

Tubes – Cardboard tubes from paper towel roll, foil, plastic wrap, or wrapping paper. These make instant telescopes for sailors or pirates, or tunnels to roll marbles through. Children love to watch things disappear then reappear out of the bottom.

Bean Bag Fun – Play with beanbags, toss them in a basket, up in the air, balance them on your head or the back of your hand, toss them to a friend.

Paper Plate Fun – Use two or more paper plates. Draw faces of different characters and glue a popsicle stick on the back for holding. Use the plate characters like you would finger puppets. Make up a story or pretend to be the characters. Let the child's name his character and discuss other qualities or aspects of the character.

Story Box – This is a variation of the Puzzle Box. Using a small gift box glue a piece of felt to the lid of the box. Then find pictures that can represent different characters in a favorite book and also objects that are mentioned in the book. Glue strips of flannel on the backs of these pictures and objects then use it during story time to tell the story. As your child gets older, they will be able to pull out the box and tell you the stories. The same box can be used for multiple stories by storing the pictures for each story in small zip lock bags then pulling out that bag when a particular story is wanted. These bags can be stored in the box. Older children will love to tell you stories or they can tell them to younger siblings.

Rhythm Sticks – Supply the children with rhythm sticks to experiment with. Play soft and loud. Can the noise change? What different sounds are made when you hit the table different ways? Try hitting them together and rubbing them together. Try hitting the floor. Rhythm sticks can be easily made from long blocks, chopsticks, or silverware.

Hot or Cold Weather – Cut out many articles from magazines that represent hot or cold weather. Ask your child to tell you which pictures are hot weather, and which are cold weather.

Paper Tear – Provide paper that the child may tear.

Dominos – Play with dominoes or have a domino rally. You can make a set of dominos easily by taking some 3 x 5 cards and drawing a line down the center. Then put dots or shapes on both sides.

Popping Popcorn – Ask the child "What happens when you heat up corn kernels?" Get an air popper and let the children watch the corn kernels pop. Be sure to let the children know that the container is hot. WARNING: Popcorn is a choking hazard, and young children should be supervised while eating popcorn.

Penguin Hop – Play the bunny hop song and have the children pretend to be penguins hopping around.

Indian Vests – Make and decorate vests from paper grocery bags.

Float or Sink – Have several different items on a tray, and a dishpan of water. Ask the children if they think an item will sink or float.

Name It – Point to something and name it for your child. Or say what color it is or describe it. Encourage your child to point out objects for you to name.

Hide and Seek – Have all the children hide their eyes while you "hide" an object in the room. Tell the children to find the object.

Magnets – Supply your children with magnets and various items. Have the children guess which things will stick to the magnet.

Puzzles – Collect old greeting cards. Cut off card fronts and save. Using a black marker, draw several squiggle lines on the backside of the card front (not the picture side). Cut card along these lines. Place all pieces in a plastic bag.

Friendly Monster – Tape a large sheet of bulletin board paper or newsprint on the tabletop. Draw an outline of a monster and provide the children with various collage materials and art equipment. Let them create their own friendly monster. Cut out and display! Great for scaring off the monster under the bed or in the closet.

Masking Tape – Allow the children to play with a small piece of masking tape.

Mimic Me – Repeat your child's vocal sounds. Make simple sounds for your child to mimic.

Mother May I – Have the children stand at one end of the room and you at the other. Have the children ask, "Mother may I take __#__ little steps forward?" have them use a different number each time. Replace mother with other family members.

Wind – Play with a streamer or kite in the wind.

Record Your Voice – Record your child's voice and play it back for them.

Dress Up – Play dress up with your child.

Up and Away – Lie on your back and lift the child above you for an airplane ride.

Cause and Effect – Try different cause and effect experiments, flipping the light switch on and off; jumping up and down, the earth pulls you down etc.

Box – Add a large cardboard box to a toddler's room. The children will have fun climbing in the box and hiding.

Peek a Boo – Place your hands on your face and say "(child's name) where are you?" Encourage the older children to pull your hands away from your face.

They really like to have control over the game. Let them put your hands over your face and pull them away.

Make a Map – Make a map of your classroom, school, home, or neighborhood.

Toys – Play with a windup toy. How does it work?

Box Train – Attach a short piece of yarn to a small box to make a train for your toddler's stuffed animals. For added fun link several boxes with string to be pulled by the child. Add wheels for an added effect.

Where is Your _____ – Ask your child "where is your nose?" eyes, head, etc.

What Sound Dose a _____ Make – Ask your child what sounds a car makes, a cow, a dog, etc.

Food

Fall Trees – Prepare ahead of time two or three pans of Jell-O in thin layers using fall colors (cherry, lime, lemon, etc.). Get pretzel sticks and place one large one for the tree trunk on a paper plate for each child. Let the child use small leaf cookie cutters to cut out the "leaves" of their trees from the Jell-O. Have fun eating your tree after you make it.

Plants We Eat – Show the children some common plants we eat. Name the various parts of the plants, while you show the plants to the children. Help the children sort the plants. By types of fruit, and veggies. Sort again by the part of the plant we eat, like we eat the roots of carrots and potatoes, and we eat the leaves of lettuce, and spinach.

Eating Your Colors – Learn your colors by eating different colored foods, for example if the color is yellow, you can feed them yellow apples, golden potatoes, bananas, lemons, pineapple, cheese, etc. You can also add food coloring to favorite foods, for example green eggs add some green food coloring while cooking some scrambled eggs. Vanilla Pudding is another fun food to add food coloring to.

Pizza Heads – Get some refrigerator biscuits (the larger ones work best), Pizza Sauce, Cheese, Pepperoni, sausage, olives or whatever foods you can think of. Flatten biscuit for each child and help them put sauce on it, and then let them use their own imaginations for designing their person's face.

Different Apples – Next time you go to the store with your child. Point out all the various kinds of apples. Tell your child their names. Buy a few various kinds, and when you get home, let your child try them. Ask your child how each one tastes. Ask your child how each one is different. Do this also with cheese, oranges, and other types of food that there is a variety of.

Hand Cookies – Use a favorite recipe to make cookies and let the children help roll out the cookie dough. Place the children's hands on the dough and trace around them. Then cut out the shapes and use a toothpick to write the children's names on their hand cookies. Bake according to your recipe directions. Variation Let the children roll out the dough and use shaped cookie cutters to cut out cookies. Arrange the cookies on a cookie sheet and let the children sprinkle them with colored sugar crystals before baking.

Shaped Sandwiches – Let the children use cookie cutters to cut shapes out of pieces of bread. Have them spread softened cream cheese or any other topping they want on their shapes before eating.

Tea Party – Pretend to have a Tea Party. Invite a favorite stuffed animal. Serve everyone milk or juice and a cookie.

Animals

Leg Count – Show pictures of a crab, octopus, starfish, frog and other animals. How many legs do each of the animals have?

Paper Bag Bird Masks – Let children use yarn, paints, crayons and paper scraps to create their own bird mask. You may have to cut out the eyes, mouth and shoulders for younger children.

Starfish and Seahorses – Explain to your child that starfish and seahorses have an exoskeleton, (their bones are on the outside.) Let them examine dried, dead seahorses and starfish. You can also go to an aquarium and see some live ones.

Beautiful Beasts – Gather tissue paper, glue, jumbo rickrack, Styrofoam balls and luncheon size paper plates. Scrunch up and glue tissue paper squares to the back of a paper plate. Cover the whole plate. Allow for drying time. Cut a Styrofoam ball in half. Using black permanent marker, color a pupil on each ball half. Then glue the halves to the tissue paper for eyes. Also glue rickrack to the tissue paper for the mouth. You can also add a tissue paper mane or beard, ears, or accessories.

What do ____ Eat – Talk a little about what we eat. What do bears eat? What do lions eat?

Baby Chicks – Give each child one eggcup cut from an egg carton and two large yellow Pom-Pom balls. Have your child glue their Pom-Pom balls in their eggcups, one on top of the other. Then let them add an orange construction paper beak, and black construction paper eyes.

Feathers or Fur – Ask the children if a dog has feathers or fur? What about an owl, bear, etc.

Compare – Animal parts with human parts of the body, i.e. paws with hands and feet, legs to arms and legs.

Paper Plate Masks – Draw some masks on a 9" paper plate, or glue on items to make a mask. Let dry and cutout (making slits for eyes, nose and mouth). Add string, as above, or glue on a popsicle stick for holding.

Bird Memory – Find bird stickers. Place 2 identical stickers on the left and right sides of an index card. Cut the index in half, cut the index card in half. You can use these cards to play memory.

Ducks – Trace a duck shape on a piece of paper and have children glue different colored feathers onto the duck.

Animal Families – Talk about animal families. What do we call a baby chicken, baby dog and so on?

Are You My Mother 1 – Make a game like Memory: only with mommies and babies (cows, goats, chickens, pigs, etc.). Give each child a baby and place the mommies on a table face down. Each time a child guesses which is the mommy to their card they say, "Are you my mother" and if the card is not the mother the child and other children can say "you are not my mother".

Are You My Mother 2 – Play this like doggie, doggie where's your bone! Except you choose one child to be the baby bird in the middle and the child with a block or toy is the mommy. The baby bird points to a child and asks, "Are you, my Mother?" the child answers "Yes" if they have the block or "No I am a ___" fill in the ___ with cat, dog, boat. Etc. On the third guess, if the child guesses incorrectly the child should respond "I am a Snort" and everyone can point to the "Mother".

Fish Watching – Go to an aquarium, pet store, or a fish store. Observe the fish pointing out the various parts of the fish such as body, fins, eyes, gills, tail, etc. Discuss with them how the fish swim, why they have the coloring that they do, etc. You can also do this with other types of animals as well.

Animal Sounds – Buy a tape of animal sounds or make one, can the children name the animals that make the sounds?

Does it Fly – Talk about different kinds of birds and whether they can fly or not.

Zoo – Visit a nature center or zoo. Discuss the things you see there.

What do Ants Like to Eat – Set out a paper plate outside with different items on it. See which ones the ants take away first.

Feed the Ducks – Help your child crumble old bread for the ducks to eat. Then go to a park that has a lot of ducks and feed the ducks and other birds. Be sure to go early so the ducks are hungry.

Animals — Talk about or observe an animal. What unique body parts does this animal have? What are the functions of those parts? (i.e. claws for protection, big ears to hear better.)

Bird Care — Talk about what a bird eats, going to the Vet for shots, grooming, and the things an owner needs to do to keep their Bird healthy.

Fish — Have a fish tank in your home and have your child observe the fish. What do fish need to live? Discuss what a fish needs in the sea, or lake. Where do fish live? What do fish eat? Etc.

Holidays

Note — If you do not celebrate holidays or celebrate different holidays these activities can be modified with just a little imagination. For example many of the Halloween themed activities can easily become fall activities.

Holidays — Different holidays offer children a glimpse of the cultural, racial, and religious diversity they will encounter in the world outside their homes. And because holidays contain so many festive elements, children will be drawn to learning about them. The more visuals you can use in exposing children to this information, the better!

Holiday Cookbook — Take the children aside one by one and ask them, "What is your favorite holiday food?" Then ask them "How do you make that?" Write down word for word their responses. You may find it helpful to videotape the responses so you can get it all down. Then compile all the responses in your recipe book.

Fireworks — For New Years, 4th of July, or Other Holiday that Involves Fireworks

Painted Fireworks — Provide children with red, blue, white, gold, and orange paints; 6-8" pieces of yarn; disposable toothbrushes; and paint smocks. Cover the painting area with newspaper or plastic, and make sure no portion of children's clothing is exposed. Show children how to drag yarn through paint, then over paper to create wavy lines. Next, show children how to use paintbrushes to spatter paint. Finished "painting" will look very much like a picture of a fireworks display.

Fireworks – You will need: watered down non-toxic paint, paper, pipettes (small coffee stirring straws) and straws. Supply each child with a straw and a piece of paper. Allow the children to use the pipette (or medicine dropper NOT GLASS) to place a small amount of paint onto a piece of paper. They may use as many colors as they wish. Then, have them use the straw to blow the paint around their picture.

Milk Fireworks – Pour some milk into a shallow container like a cookie sheet. Drop different colored food coloring all around the pan. At one end of the pan drop one drop of liquid dish soap and watch what happens. You can drop another drop of soap at the other end when the reaction begins to slow down. Repeat as often as you want.

Paint on Wet Paper – Give the child a wet piece of paper and some paint. Then let them paint and watch the paint spread on the paper. The paint will burst like fireworks.

Valentines Day

Heart Shapes – Show your child how to make hearts by folding a piece of paper in half and drawing an ice cream cone along the folded edge and cutting it out. Then let the children try cutting hearts out of paper.

Valentine Mailboxes – Get a small shoebox. Cut a small slit in the top for the Valentines to go in. Then decorate the box.

Spring

Styrofoam Caterpillar – Each child will cut a large leaf shape from a piece of 9 x 12 construction paper. Use a hole punch in the leaves to show where the caterpillar has eaten. Use worm-shaped small Styrofoam or pom-poms for the caterpillars. Attach them to the leaves with a small amount of glue. Dry before handling.

St. Patrick's Day

Shamrock People #1 – Give the children a piece of white paper, and a green shamrock shape. Have the children glue the shamrock onto the paper, and then draw a body as if the shamrock was a head.

Shamrock People #2 – Draw a large shamrock shape from green construction paper. Have the children cut it out with 4 smaller shamrock shapes. Have the children draw a face on the large shamrock shape. Supply the children with 4 strips of paper to fold accordion style for arms and legs. Have the children glue the small shamrocks onto the strips of paper as hands and feet, and then glue the arms and legs onto the body.

Easter

Egg People – Give the children a piece of white paper, and a pastel egg shape. Have the children glue the egg shape onto the paper, and then draw a face on the egg shape and a body underneath.

Eggshell Collages – Save clean eggshells and dye them. See the recipe section for ideas. Crush the dyed eggshells into small pieces. Let the children use glue to apply the eggshells to pastel colored construction paper in various patterns. This is a good way to use your Easter eggshells.

Dyed Easter Eggs – Trace an egg shape onto white construction paper and cut on the outline. Using crayons, draw and color an Easter scene on the cutout. Also add other decorative lines with crayon. Brush on a water-and-food-coloring wash (one cup water to four or five drops food coloring) to cover the entire egg cutout. If desired, use several different colors of wash on the egg.

Shiny Easter Eggs – Mix sweetened condensed milk and food coloring to create several colors of paint. Paint this mixture onto giant eggs cut from 12 x 18 sheets of construction paper. These eggs paints will produce a glistening effect. The more food coloring you put into the milk the darker the paint will be. You can also use tempera paint to make this instead of food coloring, but the child will not be able to eat it. Do this activity for other holidays and themes.

Easter Egg – On a hard-boiled egg draw a picture using a white crayon. Then dye it in easter egg dye and watch as your drawing comes to life.

Eggs in the Nest – Have child place jellybeans in a muffin tin. Tape numbers one through six in the bottom of a muffin tin. Have the children place the appropriate number of eggs in each nest (the muffin holes).

Summer

Celery Dye – Place a stalk of celery in a cup with water and blue food coloring (about 10 drops in 1/4-cup water should do). Wait a day or two and see what happens. This also can be done with carnation flowers.

Summer Collage – Collect different magazines with pictures related to summer. Have the children cut out pictures of what they like about summer. Have them glue their pictures to a bright piece and then tell you what their favorite things about summer are. If they can't write---write what they say under the collage.

Pumpkin or Watermelon Rolling – Have a pumpkin or watermelon rolling contest outside in your yard. Each child takes a turn and rolls the pumpkin or watermelon as hard as they can. Measure the distance and figure out why some pumpkins rolled better/worse than others.

Flower Vase – Use a pumpkin or watermelon as a flower vase by cutting the top off. Scoop it out and arrange colorful flowers in it.

4th of July or Other Patriotic Holiday

Flag Art – Obtain a large piece of white butcher paper. You will also need blue paper, red and white paint and star-shaped sponges. Have the children glue the blue square to the upper left-hand side of the paper. You will then have them use the star shaped sponges in the white paint to make the stars. Then, use the red paint to paint each child's hands and then make the red stripes of the flag with their handprints. Variation I: Use Silver Star stickers instead of sponge painting. Variation II: Use smaller pieces of paper and have each child do their own using their fingerprints to make the red stripes. Variation III: Paint the lines red instead of using handprints. Variation IV: Try doing this with your state flag.

Stars and Stripes – Supply the children with paper, red and blue paints, and sponges in star and stripe shapes (long and thin). Using sponges to create a sponge print picture.

Torn Paper Flags – Supply the children with blue, red and white paper. Have the children make a flag by tearing the paper and gluing it onto another piece of paper. Variation I: Let the children use Silver Star stickers for the stars.

Fall

Worm in My Apple – Cut out one apple shape per child. Have them use a hole punch to punch about 4 holes in the apple. Have them weave a brown piece of yarn in the holes. Then have them glued on a stem.

Bird Feeder – Cut a long piece of yarn or ribbon to hang the bird feeder. Tie the ribbon in a knot around a pinecone near the top or use a cup with a small hole punched in the bottom put your string through that and tie a knot so it will not come loose. Spread peanut butter on the pinecone or cup then roll in birdseed. Hang the bird feeder on the tree.

Halloween

Pumkin Science – This can be done with a fresh pumpkin or a Jack-o-Lantern on November 1st. Cut the pumpkin into several pieces. Put these into Ziploc® bags. The children may decide to add "ingredients" such as salt, water, paint, etc. Label what has been added to the bag and tape these to a window. Each day check these for various types of mold growth or other changes. Keep one piece in the fridge and keep comparing. Variations: Use other types of fruit and vegetables to see how they decompose.

Pumpkin Centerpiece – Purchase a large round pumpkin and make it into a jack-o-lantern. Then stick lollipops all around the top of the pumpkin.

Spiders – Paint a Styrofoam (half ball) completely black. Hot glue eight black chenille stems to the stem. Bend the stems to create joints for the legs. Paint a face or add wiggly eyes.

Pumpkin Bowling – Use small pumpkins for the bowling balls and apples with popsicle sticks stuck in them for the pins.

Squish Pumpkin Art – Fold an 11"x 18" piece of white construction paper in half widthwise (to create 9" x 11" sheet), then reopen. Guide the children by dropping orange and yellow drops of paint, using eyedroppers in a rough semicircle area near the fold on one half of the paper (if it helps, you could lightly mark the area you want covered). Fold the paper in half and rub (SQUISH IT!). When opened it should be a rough circle or oval. Now drop one drop of green paint near the middle top, a drop of black for one eye, a small drop for the nose and a few drops on one side for the mouth. Fold and squish again. Reopen and you have made a jack-of-lantern.

Milk Jug Pumpkin – Take a milk jug and remove label. Pour orange paint into jug, put cap on. Have the child turn the jug upside down and all around. You may need to add more paint. The paint will coat the inside. Remove excess paint. Leave the lid off to dry. Glue green cover on. Have cut out some black triangles, squares, and circles so children can glue them on.

Pumpkin Art – Paint a pumpkin vine (or use die cut) then paint the 'fist' of the child orange between the knuckles. Have the child press down on the paper and it looks like a pumpkin. Add leaves.

Pumpkin – Make a pumpkin shape from felt and then sew on 2 buttons for eyes, 1 for the nose and 1 for the mouth, then cut out different shape eyes, nose and mouths with slits in them for the kids to button on to make a funny face.

Coffee Filter Pumpkins – Have the kid's color on coffee filters with orange and yellow crayons. Then fold into a wedge shape, dip the end in a bowl of water for about 3 seconds, and hold it upside down for a minute or two to let the water soak down through the filter. The colors will bleed together and look cool. Add a stem and leaf to make a pumpkin. They are a fun window display when the light shines through them.

Pumpkin Seed Flowers – Use a piece of poster board or heavy construction paper. Glue pumpkin seeds in a circle with the pointed edge out. Glue another circle of seeds in between, with the pointed edge in. Put gold glitter in the middle and you can paint the seeds any color you like. Or of course you can leave them plain! Draw in stems and leaves.

Ghost Feet – Paint the bottom of your child's feet with white paint and have them step on black paper! Turn the paper so heels are up and make wiggly eyes on them.

Pumpkin Counting Book – Make a counting book out of orange paper in the shape of a pumpkin. One = 1 seed, two = 2 seeds and so on. Optional: glue orange yarn around the seeds to represent the pumpkin "guts". You can create different counting books using different types of seeds.

Pumpkin – Cut a pumpkin in half (vertically) and place it on a table for the child to explore. Provide spoons, scissors, tweezers, cups for collecting seeds, and plastic or rubber gloves.

Haunted House – The night before Halloween, set up cardboard boxes to create a maze in the room. Turn the lights low and play some eerie music in the room. At every turn, place an activity: -feely bags (chicken bones, dried apricots, peeled grapes, etc.) -Guess the smell. Plastic pumpkins (with cotton balls inside) saturated with various smells. (Vinegar, pine, lemon, peppermint, smoke) -Optical illusions. Charts with several optical illusions printed on them. -What's that sound? Cans filled with various objects the kids had to guess. -Taste. At the end of the maze, each child was given the opportunity to taste some "Dirt Dessert" Obviously with worms in it! -Mini golf. Children can golf using plastic eyeballs and trying to get it into the cup.

Pumpkin Snowman – Get (3) pumpkins each a little smaller in size such as a snowman. Paint them with white paint, stack, and decorate for winter.

Thanksgiving

Corn on the Cob – Allow the children to use a cob of corn to paint a picture. You may also use an ear of corn and have the children roll the corn in paint and then on a piece of paper. Another variation includes removing some of the corn from an ear of corn and roll the corn in paint and roll it on a piece of paper.

Paper Bag Turkeys – Give each child a brown paper grocery bag (any size) and several sheets of newspaper. Have the children crumple the sheets of the newspaper and stuff them into their bags until the bags are half full. Twist the bags closed and tie them around the middle with pieces of yarn. To make tails for their paper bag turkeys, have the children make several cuts from the top edges of their bags down to the yarn ties. Let the children paint their turkey tails, using bright autumn colors. Then give each child a precut turkey head shape to decorate. Attach the head shapes to the fronts of the bags to complete the turkeys. You can also do this for jack-o-lanterns, apples, faces, or any other object you can think of.

Turkey – Have the children paint their fingers and palms brown and their thumbs red. Then have them press their hands on a large sheet of butcher paper to make "turkey" prints. After the paint had dried, let the children add eyes, beaks, legs and feet with felt-tip markers.

Turkey Strut – Use pieces of masking tape to make turkey footprints all over the floor. Start playing some music. Let the children pretend to be turkeys and strut around the room. When you stop the music, have the turkeys find footprints to stand on (one turkey to a footprint). When you start the music again, have the turkeys continue strutting around the room. You can also play this like musical chairs.

Pumpkin Pie – Cut a paper plate into fourths. Have the children paint them with brown and orange paint. Glue a cotton ball on the top, and sprinkle with a little cinnamon or nutmeg and they have pumpkin pie.

Paper Collage Turkeys – Cut turkey shapes out of brown construction paper. Give each child a turkey shape and scraps of colorful construction paper. Let the children tear the construction paper into small pieces. Have them glue the torn pieces on their turkey shapes to make colored feathers. Then let them use felt-tip markers to add eyes and other features.

Pin the Feather on the Turkey – Draw a picture of a featherless turkey on a large piece of poster board. Attach the picture to a wall. Put loops of masking tape (sticky sides out) on the backs of real or paper feathers and place the feathers on a table close to the turkey picture. Have the children take turns choosing a feather from the table and then closing their eyes while they try to "pin" the feather on the turkey. (The crazy placement of all the feathers adds to the fun.) This is a variation of pin the tail on the donkey. Other ideas for this game are pin the nose on the clown, the beak on the bird, fingers on the hand, wheels on the car, or any others you can think of.

Turkey Feather Game – Cut five-turkey body shapes out of brown felt and fifteen feather shapes out of red, yellow and orange felt. Number the turkey body shapes from 1 to 5 and put them on a flannel board. Place the feather shapes in a pile. To play the game, have the children take turns selecting a turkey, identifying the number on it and adding that many feathers to it.

Stuff the Turkey – Make a turkey by opening a large grocery bag and rolling down the top edges three or four times. Place the bag on the floor, open end up. Stuff the bottom halves of two small lunch sacks with newspaper fasten the tops with twist ties and mold them into turkey leg shapes. Attach the leg shapes to the sides of the large bag. Give the children 6-inch squares of newspaper. Let them take turns "stuffing the turkey" by crumpling the newspaper squares and tossing them into the large grocery bag turkey.

Winter

Pasta Snowflakes – Give each child a piece of wax paper about 8 x 11, an assortment of pasta shapes and a small tray of glue. Have the children roll pasta shapes into glue and assemble a snowflake design on wax paper. When dry, peel the snowflakes from the paper and spray or paint with white paint. When the paint is dry, spray with adhesive spray and dust with clear glitter. Mount the completed snowflakes on blue poster board.

Hanukkah

Spinning the Dreidel or Spinner – Each player puts one candy, penny, or chocolate in a pot. The first player spins the dreidel. If it lands with nun (1) facing up, it means the player wins nothing. With gimel (2) facing up, and it means the player wins everything in the pot but one object. With hay (3) facing up, and it means the player takes half of what's in the pot and everyone puts in one more piece. With shin (4) facing up, and it means the player must put another object in the pot. The next players take their turns. Everyone plays until there are no objects left in the pot. The player with the most objects wins. Note: you can use a game spinner or dice if you do not have a Dreidel.

Christmas

Paper Plate Santa – Have your child draw a face on a paper plate, and glue it on red triangle for Santa's Hat. Use a cotton ball for his hat and his beard. You can also cut out holes for eyes, and mouth, and punch two holes to make a mask.

Stocking – Draw a stocking shape onto a piece of paper and cut it out. Then have them decorate it with markers, crayons, paint, sequins, glitter, ribbons, bows, lace, and whatever else you can produce.

Christmas Ornaments – Decorate canning lids with string, ribbon, sequins, lace, and odds and ends. Glue a pipe cleaner to the back and hang on your tree.

Stockings – Make a homemade stocking for the fireplace. Take a clean, hole free sock and let your child decorate it with ribbons, bows, lace and whatever else you can think of.

A Real Family Tree – Have the children make a family tree with branches and glue. For this activity try to get branches with Y's and let the children pick the branch to write the names of their family members. This is a great way to decorate a Christmas tree, including photos and other objects that would represent the person.

Christmas Shape Match Up 1 – There are many ways to set this up depending on the skill level or the skill you wish to work on. Use your own Christmas Shapes... wreath, tree, star, bell, ornament, etc. Cut out Christmas Shapes from different colors of paper. Give each child one Christmas Shape. Ask the children to find one person with the same color Christmas Shape. Or cut out Christmas Shapes from different colors of paper. Cut the Christmas Shapes in half using a puzzle type cut, like zigzag or interlocking pieces. Give each child one half of a Christmas Shape and ask them to find the person with the other half. Or give the children two pieces and have the children make a circle, with one child that has one match on one side and the other match on the other side. You may end up with 2 or more circles depending on how the Christmas Shape pieces are distributed

Christmas Shape Match Up 2 – Using Christmas shapes makes puzzle type cut, like zigzag or interlocking pieces. Place matching Christmas stickers on separate index cards. Give each child a card and ask them to find the child with their match. Make a file folder format. Glue one part of the Christmas Shape to the file folder and laminate its match. Some other ideas for a shape match up game are apples, balls, balloons, shamrocks, valentines, other holidays or themes.

Christmas Shape Match Up 3 – Cut the Christmas Shapes from one color of paper. Label one set of Christmas Shapes with numbers, i.e. if you have 20 children; label the Christmas Shapes with the numbers one to ten. The other half, draw one dot on one, two on another, and so on until ten. Give each child one Christmas Shape and have them find the child with their match. Or cut the Christmas Shapes from one color of paper. Place matching stickers on two Christmas Shapes. Give children one Christmas Shape and have them find the child with their match.

Candy Cane Balance – Supply each child with a candy cane. Ask them to balance it on their head. Then have the children walk from point A to point B. (Preset marks) whoever makes it across without dropping their cane wins.

Christmas Tree – Using green tempura paint or rubber stamp ink lightly cover the child's hand with the paint/ink. Have them place their hand upside down on a piece of paper to put the handprint there. Turning the paper right side up you can then use a small square sponge with brown paint or ink on it and put the trunk of the tree at the tip of the middle finger. You can also put a star at the top using a small cut out sponge and yellow paint/ink. Once the tree is dry the children can decorate the tree with their fingers making fingerprint ornaments using a verity of colors. A variation of this is using the child's feet to form the tree. You will need to have them step on the paper with each foot with the heels close together to make an upside-down V. The trunk and the star can then be formed the same way.

Popcorn Garland – Make popcorn. Let it cool. Supply the children with a piece of yarn and a child safe needle (plastic and big) Have the children thread the popcorn onto the yarn to make garland.

What Time is it Santa – This is a fun game to play outside. You can change the name to suit any theme. The children all line up against a wall or fence. And one child, (Santa) or the parent faces away from the children, a good distance away from the children. The children yell, "What time is it "Santa", Santa answers 1 o'clock, and the children all take one step toward Santa. The children yell again, "What time is it "Santa", Santa answers (fill in the blank) o'clock, and the children all take same number of step toward Santa. This continues until all the children are very close to Santa, then Santa will answer it's midnight, and chases the children back to the fence or wall that they started at. The first-person Santa touches will be the new Santa.

Christmas Place Mats – Trace a Christmas shape onto a piece of paper, cut out the shape. Then glue the shape onto another piece of paper. Have the children outline the shape with glue and add gold glitter. Laminate the place mat for longer use.

Christmas Tree Hop – Cut out large Christmas tree shapes from colored paper. Laminate them and cut them out. Place them on the floor and ask the children to hop from one tree to another. Use other shapes for other times of the year. Hearts for Valentines, pumpkins, shamrocks, or other geometric shapes.

Santa Snowball Toss – Cover the bottom and sides of a rectangular cardboard box with wrapping paper. Next, draw a Santa face on a large piece of white paper (making sure to give them a nice, big open mouth), color in, and glue to one side of the box. Cut out Santa's mouth. Now make 6-10 large "snowballs" out of wads of cotton. The object of the game is to toss as many snowballs into Santa's mouth as you can to make his jolly belly as full as can be!

Fingerprint Tree – Cut out a Christmas tree. Then have the child use a stamp pad or paints to put fingerprints (Christmas Ornaments and lights) on the tree.

Santa's Reindeer – Trace each child's hands onto a piece of brown paper. Then cut out these hands. Supply the child with a paper plate and ask them to draw a reindeer face on the paper and use their hands for antlers.

Gifts

Coin Play – Most every home has a collection of loose change in jars, drawers, or piggy banks. At least once a year, collect and sort through the coins. Discuss various charities and what each one does (e.g., homeless shelters, animal human societies, children's hospitals etc.). Then, together with your child, decide on one to receive the money. Talk about how much each coin represents. Point out the faces on the coins and tell your child who each person is. Place coins in wrappers or bags. Take the coins to the bank and exchange them for paper money. Donate the money to a cause you and your child mutually decide on.

Melted Crayon Jars – What you need: Jar, Old Crayons in bright colors, Scissors, Aluminum foil, Ribbon. Choose two or three different crayons into small pieces. If you use a large jar, you will need more crayons than if your jar is small. (Three crayons will cover a baby food jar.) Tear off a square piece of aluminum foil. Place the foil outside in hot direct sunlight. Sprinkle the crayons on the foil. The crayons will melt quickly, so be ready with your jar. Do not wait until the crayons are completely melted or they will blend to make a muddy color. When they have melted, but still have some lumps in them, roll the jar around in the melted crayons to coat it. When you are happy with the design on the jar, take it to a cool place. The crayon will harden and set almost immediately. Tie a bow around the neck of the jar. You can also do this in an oven with the temperature 350 degrees. Watch them really closely.

Flower Jars – Have your child place a small amount of clay into the lid of baby food jars. Provide your child with small, dried flowers to stick into the clay. Have your child screw on the bottle, and tie on a bow to the lid.

Crossed Feet Butterflies – Have the child stand on a piece of black paper with their legs crossed and sides of shoes touching. Then trace around the shoes. After cutting the butterflies out, have the child use brushes to spatter multicolored paint onto the butterflies. These make good cards for grandparents or other family members.

Fingerprint Balloons – Glue five bottle caps (open ends up) in a semicircle on a piece of heavy cardboard and fill each cap with a different color of paint. Have each child in turn dip all five fingers of one hand into the paint in the bottle caps and then press them on a sheet of white construction paper to make prints. When the paint has dried, let the children draw lines down from their fingerprints, turning them into balloons with strings. Try other designs such as making thumbprint bugs, faces, and others. This makes a great card. You can also do other themes depending on the occasion.

Creative Cards – Fold a piece of construction paper in half. Provide children with a variety of materials, wrapping paper, paper, glitter, ribbons, bows, and let them make a card for someone special.

Wrap it Up – Let your child wrap a small box in tissue paper or gift-wrap. Let them pretend to give it to someone.

Tips and Hints

Paint Extender – Mix a thick gravy of cornstarch and water. Cook over low heat until thick, stirring constantly. Add 2 tablespoons of mixture to each jar of paint. This makes the paint thicker, smoother, and more plentiful.

Food coloring is a good substitute for paint for younger children in case they try eating their creations. You can also use Kool-Aid or Jell-O.

Bubble Tips & Tricks – Let your bubble solution sit for a couple days before you use it. Make sure your bubble blower is wet. Don't slosh your bubble maker in the solution. Those little bubbles you make by doing this are big bubble busters. Bubbles do better in the cool shade. Caution: Bubbles are sticky and slick. In short, they make a big mess. It is best to do your bubble magic outdoors. If you do blow bubbles, indoors, be careful of slick floors.

Playdough – For color you can add food coloring, Kool-Aid and fruit flavored gelatin. To add a scent lemon oil, peppermint oil, vanilla extract, ground cinnamon, ground ginger, Kool-Aid. You can also add various essential oils if your children are not likely to eat the playdough. You can add glitter for a sparkle. Try to substitute baby oil for vegetable oil. The dough smells good and will not mold or get a bad odor. It will also remain soft for a long time.

Basic Recipe Tips - Food coloring and Kool-Aid are safe to use especially with younger children, however it can stain hands and clothes. Try wearing gloves and smocks to avoid this issue. Do not put these recipes down the drain. They can destroy your plumbing. Try mixing your recipes in disposable containers using disposable utensils so everything can go into the trash when done. Some individuals are allergic to Borax powder. Wear gloves and safety glasses. Do not use this ingredient with young children who are likely to eat their creations. Alum can generally be found at different drug stores. You may need to shop around.

Straw Blowing – Some of the activities have the children blowing into straws to prevent the children from accidentally sucking up the paint mixture, poking holes near the tops of the straws.

Mixing Colors – Start with the primary colors red, yellow, and blue. Along with white and black to make your tints and tones. The purple is – one part red, one part blue. Green is – one part blue, one part yellow. Orange is – one part yellow, one part red. Brown is – one part red, one part blue, and two parts yellow. Brown is a combination of all the primary colors (red, blue, and yellow) just mix them up; I believe there is more yellow than blue and red. It also depends what shade of brown you want. After you have made your basic colors to your satisfaction add either white or black to make your tints (adding white) or tones (adding black). For example, if you add red you would add white to make pink or black to make burgundy. You can vary the number of colors you add together, this will give you lots of different color combinations. If you are making a large project, make sure you create enough color to complete the project. It is very hard to recreate the exact same shade twice. To make a yellow-green, red-orange or other color like that put two parts of the primary color you want to dominate (yellow for yellow green) and one part of the other primary color. The formula for yellow green would be two parts yellow, and one part blue.

Painting Small Objects – Try using a clothespin to hold small objects that you are trying to paint. This way you won't be painting your fingers.

Drop Cloth – You can use plastic garbage bags to put on the floor to keep any dropped messes contained.

Washable Paint – If you use tempera paints (powder paints mixed with water), add some dishwater soap to the paint so it will wash out of clothes.

Watercolor Paint – When you get new watercolors, put masking tape over the colors you do not want children to use. You will be surprised by how well this keeps your colors usable longer, and most kids will not remove the tape when told not to.

Smock – An old shirt of either mom's or dad's will help protect their clothing for the messier projects.

Messy Fun – Tear off a square of heavy-duty aluminum foil. Fold up the edges to make a tray or get some shallow small aluminum pans. Put a huge blob of shaving foam in the middle of each pan and let the child pick one or two colors of food coloring. Add a couple of drops of the chosen color and let the kids dig in. Make mountains and valleys, faces. Let them dry overnight. The foam will dissolve a lot, but you get a colored froth left.

Paint – Who says Karo syrup is just for cooking? Mix a little tempera paint with it and the children can paint. Just paint and let dry, the artwork will shine.

Borax – Is toxic in large doses. Keep it out of reach of children under 3-years-old; it's also a goodidea to wear safety glasses when working with borax as some have an allergic reaction to it.

Mixing Glue and Borax – When you mix the glue and the borax a chemical change occurs in the polymer in the glue, polyvinyl acetate. Cross-linking bonds are formed, making the glue stick to you less and to itself more. You can experiment with the amount of glue, water, and borax that you use to make the slime more fluid or stiffer. The molecules in the polymer are not fixed in place, so you can stretch the flubber/blubber/slime.

Sand and Salt – When using sand art crafts, snip a very small hole in one of the corners of the baggie and slowly let the salt out for your project.

Bubble Blower – If you don't have bubble blowers around the house, be creative and try using different objects from your utensil drawer, (i.e., apple corner, potato masher, handle of a basting brush, etc. They work.)

Rhyming Fun

Over 50 rhymes, songs, and finger plays

Up and Down the Corn Field

Up and down the cornfield,
Looking for a hare.
Where can we find one?
Right up there!

Walk fingers up and down Baby's leg and tickle Baby's neck.

Five Little Farmers

Five little farmers,
Woke up with the sun.
For it was early morning
And chores must be done.
The first little farmer
Went to milk the cow.
The second little farmer
Thought he'd better plow.
The third little farmer
Fed the hungry hens.
The fourth little farmer
Mended broken pens.
The fifth little farmer
Took his vegetables to town.
Baskets filled with cabbages
And sweet potatoes, brown.

Little Horse

I bought a little horse,
That galloped up and down.
I bridled him, and saddled him,
And sent him out of town.

Bounce Baby to rhyme.

Old MacDonald had a Farm

Old MacDonald had a farm, EE-I-EE-I-O.
And on that farm he had a cow, EE-I-EE-I-O.
With a moo moo here and a moo moo there
Here a moo, there a moo, everywhere a moo moo
Old MacDonald had a farm, EE-I-EE-I-O.

Other Animals
Dog, Cat, Sheep, Horse, Donkey, Chicken, Rooster, Duck, Pig, etc.

Caterpillar Song

The caterpillar said to the bird with a sigh,
"I can only wiggle, but you can fly!"

Bounce and lift Baby to rhyme.

A Kiss When I Wake

A kiss when I give her trouble,
A kiss when I give her joy,
There's nothing like mama's kisses,
To her own little baby boy.

A kiss when I give him trouble,
A kiss when I give him a thrill,
There's nothing like daddy's kisses,

To his own little baby girl.

Clap Baby's hands and kiss to rhyme.

Jelly in the Bowl

Jelly in the bowl,
Jelly in the bowl,
Wibble, wobble, wibble, wobble,
Jelly in the bowl.

Cookies in the tin,
Cookies in the tin,
Shake 'em up, shake 'em up,
Cookies in the tin.

Candles on the cake,
Candles on the cake,
Blow 'em out, blow 'em out,
Candles on the cake.

5 Little Valentines

Five little valentines were having a race,
The first little valentine was frilly with lace.
The second little valentine had a funny face.
The third little valentine said, "I love you".
The fourth little valentine said, "I do too".
The fifth little valentine was sly as a fox.
He ran the fastest to the valentine box.

Hickory Dickory Dock

Hickory dickory dock,
The mouse ran up the clock.
The clock struck one,
The mouse ran down.
Hickory dickory dock.

Walk fingers up and down Baby's body.

Down by the Station

Down by the station, early in the morning,
See the little puffer bellies all in a row,
See the engine driver pull the little handle,
"Chug, chug, toot, toot!" Off we go!

The Lights on the Tree
Tune: The Wheels on the Bus

The lights on the tree go blink, blink, blink,
Blink, blink, blink, blink, blink, blink.
The lights on the tree go blink, blink, blink
All Christmas Day.

The presents at the house go rattle, rattle, rattle,
Rattle, rattle, rattle, rattle, rattle, rattle.
The presents at the house go rattle, rattle, rattle
All Christmas Day.

The mom at the house goes bake, bake, bake...
The dad at the house goes snore, snore, snore...
The grandma at the house goes hug, hug, hug...

Clippery Clop
Tune: Row, Row, Row Your Boat

Clip, clip, clippety clop,
Clippety, clippety, clop.
The old gray horse goes up and down,
Until it's time to stop.

Bounce Baby on knee to rhyme.

The Alphabet Song

a-b-c-d-e-f-g,
h-i-j-k-lmnop,
q-r-s, t-u-v,
w-x-y-and-z,
Now I know my A, B, C's,
next time won't you sing with me ?

Knock at the Door

Knock at the door.
Peek in,
Lift up the latch,
And walk right in.
Go way down in the cellar
And eat up all the apples.
Yum! Yum!

Gesture on Baby's face and then gently tickle Baby's tummy.

The Little Man

There was a little man,
Who had a little crumb,
And over the mountain he did run,
With a belly full of fat,
And a big tall hat,
And a pancake stuck to his
Bum, bum, bum,
And a pancake stuck to his bum!

Run fingers on Baby's body and gesture to rhyme.

Slowly, Slowly

Slowly, slowly, very slowly,

Creeps the garden snail.
Slowly, slowly, very slowly,
Up the wooden rail.
Quickly, quickly, very quickly,
Runs the little mouse.
Quickly, quickly, very quickly,
All around the house.

Walk fingers slowly, then quickly over Baby.

Five Brown Eggs

Five brown eggs in a nest of hay,
One yellow chick popped out to play.
Four brown eggs in a nest of hay,
Another yellow chick cheep-cheeped, "Good day."
Three brown eggs in a nest of hay,
Crack went another one, Hip hooray.
Two brown eggs in a nest of hay,
One more chick pecked his shell away.
One brown egg in a nest of hay,
The last yellow chick popped out to say,
Happy Easter!

Caterpillar

"Who's that tickling my back?"
Said the wall.
"Me," said the caterpillar,
"I'm learning to crawl."

Crawl fingers up Baby's back.

Little Jack Horner

Little Jack Horner
Sat in a corner,

Eating a Christmas pie.
He put in his thumb,
And pulled out a plum,
And said, "What a good boy am I!"

Clap Baby's hands to nursery rhyme.

Kittens Mitten's

My poor little kitten lost her mitten
And started to cry, boo-hoo.
So I helped my kitten to look for her mitten.
Her beautiful mitten of BLUE.

I found a mitten just right for a kitten
Under my mother's bed.
But, alas, the mitten was not the right mitten,
For it was colored RED.

I found a mitten just right for a kitten
Under my father's pillow.
But, alas, the mitten was not the right mitten,
For it was colored YELLOW.

I found a mitten just right for a kitten
On the hand of my brother's toy clown.
But, alas, the mitten was not the right mitten,
For it was colored BROWN.

I found a mitten just right for a kitten
Under the laundry so clean.
But, alas, the mitten was not the right mitten,
For it was colored GREEN.

I found a mitten just right for a kitten
Inside a grocery sack.
But, alas, the mitten was not the right mitten,

For it was colored BLACK.

I found a mitten just right for a kitten
Under my sister's kite.
But, alas, the mitten was not the right mitten,
For it was colored WHITE.

I found a mitten just right for a kitten
Under the kitchen sink.
But, alas, the mitten was not the right mitten,
For it was colored PINK.

I found a mitten just right for a kitten
Inside my favorite shoe.
And this time the mitten was just the right mitten,
For it was colored BLUE.

After a Bath

After my bath, I try, try, try
To wipe myself 'till I'm dry, dry, dry.
Hands to wipe, and fingers and toes,
And two wet legs and a shiny nose.
Just think, how much less time I'd take,
If I were a dog and could shake, shake, shake!

Bath Time Bubbles

Bath time bubbles pop! (clap hands)
Lather up with soap (rub hands together)
Warm water and shampoo (rub head)
Then dry off when you're through! (rub arms)

Little Fishies

Little fishies in a brook,
Daddy caught them on a hook.

Mommy fried them in a pan.
Baby eats them as fast as he can.

Swim hands like fish and clap and gesture to rhyme.

Chubby Little Snowman

A chubby little snowman
Had a carrot nose
Along came a bunny,
And what do you suppose?
That hungry little bunny,
Looking for his lunch,
Ate the snowman's carrot nose,
Nibble, nibble, crunch!

Itsy Bitsy Spider

Itsy Bitsy spider,
Went up the waterspout.
Down came the rain,
And washed the spider out.
Up came the sun,
And dried up all the rain.
And the itsy bitsy spider,
Went up the spout again.

Walk fingers up and down Baby's body.

Right Hand, Left Hand

This is my right hand (This is my right hand)
I raise it up high (I raise it up high)
This is my left hand (This is my left hand)
I'll touch the sky (I'll touch the sky)
Right hand (Right hand)
Left hand (Left hand)

Whirl them around (Whirl them around)
Right hand (Right hand)
Left hand (Left hand)
Pound, pound, pound (Pound, pound, pound)

Tulips

In the garden
Tulips grow
Straight and golden
In a row.

Each one holds its
Empty cup
Drinking rain and
Sunshine up.

Baby at the Kitchen Door

One, two, three, four,
Baby at the kitchen door.
Five, six, seven, eight,
Eating cherries off a plate.

Clap Baby's hands to rhyme

Canty, Canty Custard

Canty, canty Custard,
Ate a pound of mustard.
Hurt his tongue and
Home did run.

Clap Baby's hands to rhyme.

Who's Here Today?
Tune: The Farmer in the Dell

_____'s here today,
_____'s here today,
We're so glad that _____'s here,
Let's all shout, " Hurray!"
"Hurray!"

Name and lift each baby.

This Old Ghost
Tune: This Old Man

This old ghost, he played one,
He played peek-a-boo on the run.
With a boo! boo! boo! and a clap, clap, snap,
This old ghost is a friendly chap.
This old ghost, he played two,
He played peek-a-boo in a shoe.
With a boo! boo! boo! and a clap, clap, snap,
This old ghost is a friendly chap.
This old ghost, he played three,
He played peek-a-boo behind a tree.
With a boo! boo! boo! and a clap, clap, snap,
This old ghost is a friendly chap.
This old ghost, he played four,
He played peek-a-boo behind a door.
With a boo! boo! boo! and a clap, clap, snap,
This old ghost is a friendly chap.

Yankee Doodle

Yankee Doodle went to town,
Riding on a pony.
Stuck a feather in his hat,
And called it macaroni.

Clap Baby's hands to rhyme.

Finger Family

Daddy Finger, Daddy Finger, where are you?
Here I am! Here I am! How do you do? (hold up thumb)
Mommy Finger, Mommy Finger, where are you?
Here I am! Here I am! How do you do? (hold up index finger)
Brother Finger, Brother Finger, where are you?
Here I am! Here I am! How do you do? (hold up middle finger)
Sister Finger, Sister Finger, where are you?
Here I am! Here I am! How do you do? (hold up ring finger)
Baby Finger, Baby Finger, where are you?
Here I am! Here I am! How do you do? (hold up pinky)

Mary Had a Little Lamb

Mary had a little lamb,
Its fleece was white as snow,
And everywhere that Mary went,
The lamb was sure to go.

It followed her to school one day,
Which was against the rule,
It made the children laugh and play,
To see a lamb at school.

And so the teacher turned it out,
But still it lingered near,
And waited patiently about,
Till Mary did appear.

I Love Snow
Tune: Three Blind Mice

I love snow, I love snow.
Soft, white snow. Soft, white snow.
It falls on the ground so soft and white.

Sometimes it falls all through the night.
Did you ever see such a beautiful sight
As soft white snow?

Santa's Spectacles

These are Santa's spectacles (Circle your eyes with your fingers)
And this is Santa's hat (Make a pointed shape on your head)
This is the way he folds his hands (Fold your hands)
And puts them in his lap! (Place folded hands in your lap)

Eeny, Meeny, Miny, Mo

Eeny, meeny, miny, mo,
Catch a baby by the toe.
If he hollers,
Let him go.
Eeny, meeny, miny, mo.

Wiggly Baby's toes to rhyme.

Little Mouse

There was a little mouse,
Who had a little house,
And he lived way, way up there.
Then he'd creep, creep, creep,
Down through his house,
Into a hole down there.

Walk fingers from Baby's head to toe.

Bubble, Bubble, Pop

One little red fish (place a hand on another and enact swimming using your thumb fingers)
Swimming in the water (move your hands around pretending to swim)

Swimming in the water
One little red fish swimming in the water
Bubble, bubble, bubble, bubble… POP! (move both your hands in a circular manner to show bubbles traveling upward and clap to pop)
Continue the same actions for "Two little blue fish," "Three little green fish," "Four little yellow fish," and so on.

Five Little Reindeer

5 little reindeer prancing up and down
5 little reindeer prancing up and down
5 little reindeer prancing up and down
For Christmas Time is near.

4 little Santa elves trimming up a tree
4 little Santa elves trimming up a tree
4 little Santa elves trimming up a tree
For Christmas Time is near.

3 little jingle bells ring, ring, ringing
3 little jingle bells ring, ring, ringing
3 little jingle bells ring, ring, ringing
For Christmas Time is near.

2 little snowflakes twirling in the night
2 little snowflakes twirling in the night
2 little snowflakes twirling in the night
For Christmas Time is near.

1 little sleigh speeding in the snow
1 little sleigh speeding in the snow
1 little sleigh speeding in the snow
For Christmas Time is near.

Head, Sholders

Head, shoulders, knees and toes, knees and toes

Head, shoulders, knees and toes, knees and toes
And eyes and ears and mouth and nose

Point to each body part as you go through the song.

Make New Friends

Make new friends
but keep the old.
One is silver
and the other gold.

The Flower

Here's a green leaf, (show hand)
And here's a green leaf; (show other hand)
That, you see, makes two. (Hold up two fingers)
Here is a bud (Cup hands together)
That makes a flower; Watch it bloom for you! (Open cupped hands slowly)

Roses are Red

Roses are red,
Violets are blue,
Sugar is sweet,
And so are you.

Clap Baby's hands to rhyme.

My Hands

This is my right hand,
I raise it up high.
This is my left hand,
I reach to the sky.
Right hand, left hand,
Roll them round and round.

Right hand, left hand,
Pound, pound, pound.

Move Baby's hands on cue.

Five Little Easter Eggs

Five little Easter eggs lovely colors wore,
Mommy ate the blue one, then there were four.
Four little Easter eggs, two and two you see,
Daddy ate the green one, then there were three.
Three little Easter eggs, before I knew,
My sister ate the yellow one, then there were two.
Two little Easter eggs, oh, what fun!
My brother ate the purple one, then there was one.
One little Easter egg, see me run!
I ate the last one, and then there were none.

Choo Choo Train

Here is the choo-choo train.
Puffing down the track. (children bend their arms at their elbows)
Now it's going forward, (rotate arms forward)
Now it's going back, (rotate arms backward)
Now the bell is ringing, (pull cord "ding, ding")
Now the whistle blows. ("wooo, wooo")
What a lot of noise it makes, everywhere it goes! (children cover their ears with their hands)

Love and Kisses

One, I love,
Two, I love,
Three, I love I say,
Four, I love with all my heart,
Five, I kiss today.

Clap Baby's hands to rhyme.

Round and Round the Garden Like a Teddy Bear

Round and round the garden like a teddy bear, (make circles around your hand with one finger)
One step, (take a step with your fingers up your arm)
Two step, (take another step with your fingers)
Tickle you there! (tickle your shoulder)

Mr. Moon

Mr. Moon, Mr. Moon
You're up too soon,
The Sun's still high in the sky.
Go back to your bed,
And cover up you head,
Until the day goes by.

Clap Baby's hands to rhyme.

Dance Little Baby

Dance little baby,
Dance up high.
Never mind baby,
Mother is by.
Up to the ceiling,
Down to the ground.
Backward and forward,
Round and round.

Move Baby to rhyme.

Twinkle, Twinkle, Little Star

Twinkle, twinkle little star (put your palms up and wiggle the fingers)

How I wonder how you are (move your hand to ask a question)
Up above the world so high (point upwards)
Like a diamond in the sky! (join both index fingers and thumb to each other, forming a diamond)
Twinkle, twinkle little star (put your palms up and wiggle the fingers)
How I wonder how you are (move your hand to ask a question)

Where is Thumbkin

Tune: Frere Jacques (Are You Sleeping)

Where is thumbkin? (wiggle your left thumb)
Where is thumbkin? (wiggle your right thumb)
Here I am! (wiggle left thumb)
Here I am! (wiggle right thumb)
How are you today sir? (shake left thumb at right thumb)
Very well I thank you (shake right thumb at left thumb)
Run away! (hide left thumb behind your back)
Run away! (hide right thumb behind your back)

Repeat the same rhyme for Pointer. You can even draw cute finger faces with markers on your child's fingertips.

Five in the Bed

There were five in the bed (hold up five fingers)
And the little one said,
Roll over, roll over (move your hands around each other in a circular motion)
They all rolled over, and one fell down (fold one finger)
Four!

Continue the same actions for three, two, and one.

Five Little Ghosts

Five little ghosts dressed all in white
Were scaring each other on Halloween night.

"Boo," said the first one, "I'll catch you."
"Boo," said the second, "I don't care if you do."
The third ghost said, "You can't run away from me."
And the forth one said, "I'll scare everyone I see."
Then the last one said, "It's time to disappear."
"See you at Halloween time next year."

Baby's Toys

Here's a ball for Baby,
Big and soft and round.
Here is Baby's hammer.
See how Baby can pound!

Help Baby gesture to rhyme.

Brown Squirrel

Brown squirrel, brown squirrel,
Swish your bushy tail.
Brown squirrel, brown squirrel,
Swish your bushy tail.

Wrinkle up your little nose.
Hold a nut between your toes.
Brown squirrel, brown squirrel,
Swish your bushy tail.

Baby Shark

Baby shark (keep moving your thumb and index finger closer and apart)
Doo doo doo doo doo doo
Baby shark doo doo doo doo doo doo
Baby shark doo doo doo doo doo doo
Baby shark!
Repeat for Mommy shark (join both your palms at the wrist, now open and close them),

Daddy shark (stretch your hands out straight and bring the palms together, now pull them apart),
Grandma shark (repeat the same action as Mommy shark but with fists closed),
and Grandpa shark (same as Daddy shark but with fists closed).
Let's go hunt (join both palms and hold them above your head)
Doo doo doo doo doo doo
Run away (jump in place)
Doo doo doo doo doo doo
Safe at last (wipe brow)
Doo doo doo doo doo doo
Repeat singing and dancing to this poem until the shark hunts down the fish. You can even add some background music to make it more fun.

Sun and Moon
Tune: Loop "D" Loo

Baby go up to the sun,
Baby go up to the moon,
Baby go up to the chimney top,
Every afternoon.

Move and lift Baby to rhyme.

Mix a Pancake

Mix a pancake,
Stir a pancake,
Put in the pan.
Fry the pancake,
Toss the pancake,
Catch it if you can.

Clap Baby's hands and lift to rhyme.

Do You Know It's Halloween
Tune: The Muffin Man

Oh, do you know it's Halloween,
Halloween, Halloween?
Oh, do you know it's Halloween,
This October day?
Ghosts and goblins are at play,
Are at play, are at play.
Ghosts and goblins are at play, This October day.

Little Rabbit

I saw a little rabbit go hop, hop, hop. (Hold up 2 fingers, go hop, hop, hop.)
I saw his long ears go flop, flop, flop. (Hands above head, flop at wrists.)
I saw his little eyes go wink, wink, wink. (Wink or blink.)
I saw his little nose go twink, twink, twink. (Wiggle nose.)
I said, "Little Rabbit, won't you stay?" (Curl finger and beckon.)
But he just looked at me and hopped away. (Use two fingers to hop away.)

Three Blind Mice

Three blind mice, three blind mice,
See how they run. See how they run.
They all ran after the Farmer's wife,
She cut off their tails with a carving knife.
Did you ever see such a sight in your life?
As three blind mice.

Walk fingers on Baby as mice run.

Baby Bumble Bee

I'm bringing home a baby bumblebee,
Won't my mommy be so proud of me (Cup your hands together as if holding bee),
I'm bringing home a baby bumblebee,
Ouch! It stung me! (Shake your hands as if in pain)
I'm squishing up the baby bumblebee,

Won't my mommy be so proud of me, (Pretend to squish the bee between palms of your hands)
I'm squishing up a baby bumblebee,
Ooh! It's yucky! (Open up hands to look at the mess while making a face)
I'm wiping off the baby bumblebee,
Won't my mommy be so proud of me, (Wipe hands off on your dress)
I'm wiping off the baby bumblebee,
Now my mommy won't be mad at me! (Hold your hands up to show they are clean)

Birdie in the Treetop

Birdie in the treetop,
Proud and wise,
Here are his wings,
And here are his eyes.
Down on the ground,
A cat he spies.
Up he jumps, and off he flies!

Gesture and lift Baby to rhyme.

Rain, Rain Go Away

Rain, rain, go away.
Come again another day.
Little Baby wants to play.
Rain, rain, go away.

Clap Baby's hands to rhyme.

Latkes, Latkes

Latkes, latkes, (Make a circle with your fingers)
Sizzling in a pan. (Hold your hands out flat in front of you and move them slightly up and down)
Flip them, (Flip hands over)

Toss them, (Make a tossing motion)
Catch them if you can. (Make a catching motion)

Wheels on the Bus

The wheels on the bus go round and round
Round and round, round and round
The wheels on the bus go round and round
All day long

The doors on the bus go open and shut...
The wipers on the bus go swish, swish, swish...
The engine of the bus goes vroom, vroom, vroom...
The dog on the bus goes bark, bark, bark... (use other animals as well)
The babies on the bus go wah, wah, wah...
The daddies on the bus say shh, shh, shh...
The mommies on the bus say "I love you, I love you, I love you"...
The driver on the bus says "Move on back, move on back, move on back"...
The horn on the bus goes beep, beep, beep...
The money on the bus goes clink, clink, clink...
The people on the bus go up and down...

Do actions that fit what verse you are doing. Make up your own verses.

Bounce Me

Bounce me, bounce me,
On your knee.
Bounce me, bounce me,
Pretty please.
Bounce me, bounce me,
Here and there.
Bounce me, bounce me,
Everywhere!

Bounce Baby on knee to rhyme.

Halloween Is Coming
Tune: I'm A Little Teapot

Halloween is coming,
I like it the most.
I'll be a goblin,
You can be a ghost.
When we get all dressed up, we will say,
"Boo! It's trick or treat day!"

Tiny Turtle

I have a tiny turtle (place one hand over the other and move your thumbs to indicate swimming)
His name is Tiny Tim (bring your thumb and index finger closer together to show tiny)
I put him in the bathtub (make swimming movements using both hands)
To see if he could swim!
He drank up all the water (hold your thumb out and make a drinking gesture)
And ate up all the soap (move your mouth to indicate chomping)
Now he has a bubble (hold your thumb and index finger to form an 'O' shape)
In the middle of his throat! (hold the 'O' shape near the throat)
Bubble, bubble, bubble... POP!! (make a popping sound)

Baby Go Up
Tune: Loop "D" Loo

Up in the air to right,
Up in the air to the left,
Wiggle Baby overhead,
And now give an Eskimo kiss.

Lift Baby to rhyme and then rub noses.

5 Little Monkeys Jumping in the Bed

5 Little Monkeys Jumping in the Bed

One fell off and bumped his head.
Momma called the doctor and the doctor said
No more monkeys jumping on the bed.

4 Little Monkeys Jumping in the Bed...
3 Little Monkeys Jumping in the Bed...
2 Little Monkeys Jumping in the Bed...
1 Little Monkeys Jumping in the Bed...

Five Fat Turkeys

Five Fat Turkeys were sitting on a fence.
The first one said, "I'm so immense."
The second one said. "I can gobble at you."
The third one said, " I can gobble too."
The fourth one said, "I can spread my tail."
The fifth one said, " Don't catch it on a nail."
THEN OUT CAME THE COOK WITH A GREAT BIG PAN
AWAY FLEW THE TURKEYS, THEIR TAILS IN A FAN!

Here, There, and Everywhere

Lift you here, lift you there,
Lift you, lift you everywhere.
Bounce you here, bounce you there,
Bounce you, bounce you everywhere.
Hug you here, hug you there,
Hug you, hug you everywhere.

Lift, bounce, and hug to rhyme.

I Want To Be A Ghost

Tune: Did You Ever See A Lassie?

Oh, I want to be a ghost,
A ghost, a ghost.

Oh, I want to be a ghost,
On Halloween night.

Little Mousie

See the little mousie,
Creeping up the stair.
Looking for a warm nest.
There, oh there, oh there!

Walk fingers up Baby's body and then find a corner, like the elbow, to gently tickle.

Dickery, Dickery Dare

Dickery, dickery, dare,
The pig flew up in the air.
The man in brown,
Soon brought him down.
Dickery, dickery, dare.

Bounce and lift Baby up and down.

5 Little Ducks

5 little ducks went out to play
Over the hills and far away
When mother duck called
With a quack, quack, quack.
4 little ducks can waddling back.

4 little ducks went out to play
Over the hills and far away
When mother duck called
With a quack, quack, quack.
3 little ducks can waddling back.

3 little ducks went out to play
Over the hills and far away
When mother duck called
With a quack, quack, quack.
2 little ducks can waddling back.

2 little ducks went out to play
Over the hills and far away
When mother duck called
With a quack, quack, quack.
1 little ducks can waddling back.

1 little ducks went out to play
Over the hills and far away
When mother duck called
With a quack, quack, quack.
No little ducks can waddling back.

But when father duck called
With a quack, quack, quack.
5 little ducks came running back.

I Hear Thunder

I hear thunder, I hear thunder.
What should we do?
What should we do?
Pitter-patter rain drops.
Pitter-patter rain drops.
I'm all wet.
So are you!

Clap and gesture to rhyme.

I'm Bouncing

I'm bouncing, bouncing everywhere.

I bounce and bounce into the air.
I'm bouncing, bouncing like a ball.
I bounce and bounce, and then I fall.

Bounce baby on beach ball to rhyme.

Little Red Wagon

Bumpin' up and down
In my little red wagon.
Bumpin' up and down
In my little red wagon.
Bumpin' up and down
In my little red wagon.
Won't you by my darling?

Bounce Baby to rhyme.

Pussy Willow

I know a little pussy,
Her coat is silver grey;
She lives down in the meadow,
Not very far away.
Although she's a pussy,
She'll never be a cat.
For she's a pussy willow,
Now what do you think of that?
Meow, meow, meow, meow,
Meow, meow, SCAT!

Five Little Turkeys

Five Little Turkeys were standing by a door;
One saw some corn, and then there were four.
Four little turkeys flew up in a tree;
One fell down and then there were three.

Three little turkeys gobbled as they do;
A dog chased one and then there were two.
Two little turkeys strutting in the sun;
The wind came along and then there was one.
One little turkey saw a farmer with an ax;
Look at that turkey run! run! run!

The Muffin Man

Do you know the muffin man?
The muffin man, the muffin man.
Do you know the muffin man?
Who lives in Drury Lane.
Yes, I know the muffin man.
The muffin man, the muffin man.
Yes, I know the muffin man,
Who lives in Drury Lane

Clap Baby's hands to nursery rhyme.

Make a Pancake

Make a pancake, pat, pat, pat.
Do not make it fat, fat, fat.
You must make it flat, flat, flat.
Make a pancake just like that!

Clap Baby's hands and gesture to rhyme.

A Teepee is My Home

A Teepee is my home Of deer skin it is made.
A place on top where smoke can go It stands in forest shade.
A river runs nearby And there is my canoe.
It paddles up and down the stream Beneath the sky of blue.

Bumblebee
Looking for Baby,

To give him a kiss.
Buzzzzzzzzzzz,
He kisses like this!

Circle finger in air and move in to give Baby a gently buzz tickle.

Five Little Hot Dogs

Five little hot dogs (hold up five fingers)
Frying in a pan (place the fingers on the open palm of the other hand)
The grease got hot
And one went BAM! (clap hands)

Continue the same actions for four, three, two, and one hot dog.

Popcorn, Popcorn

Popcorn, popcorn,
Popcorn is hot.
It flies in the air.
Pop! Pop! Pop!

Bounce and lift Baby to rhyme.

I Use My Brain

I use my brain to think, think, think (touch head)
I use my nose to smell (touch nose)
I use my eyes to blink, blink, blink (touch eyes)
I use my throat to yell (touch throat and yell on word "yell")
I use my mouth to giggle, giggle, giggle (touch mouth)
I use my hips to bump (touch hips)
I use my toes to wiggle, wiggle, wiggle (touch toes)
And I use my legs to jump (jump)

Tickle, Tickle

Tickle, tickle, tickle where?
Tickle, tickle on your hair,

Tickle, tickle on your toes,
Tickle, tickle on your nose,
Tickle, tickle, tickle cute,
Tickle, in your birthday suit.

Gently tickle appropriate body parts.

Father, Mother, and Uncle John

Father, Mother, and Uncle John,
Rode to the doctor one by one,
Father fell off,
Mother fell off,
And Uncle John rode on and on.
And Uncle John rode on.

Slide and bounce Baby to rhyme.

Five Currant Buns

Five currant buns in a baker's shop (hold up five fingers)
Big and round with a cherry on the top (draw a circle in the air)
Along came (child's name) with a penny one day, (point to child)
Bought a currant bun and took it away (tuck one finger down)
Four currant buns in a baker's shop (hold up four fingers)

Repeat until all currant buns are gone

Five Little Squirrels

Five little squirrels with acorns to store.
One went to sleep and then there were four!
Four little squirrels hunting acorns in a tree.
One fell down, and now there are three!
Three little squirrels wondering what to do.
One got lost, and now there are two!
Two little squirrels tossing acorns for fun.

One got tired, and now there is one!
One little squirrel playing in the sun.
He ran away, now there are none.

I'm a Little Dreidel

I'm a little dreidel (Point to self)
With a point and a top. (Make point with hands)
I spin, spin, spin, (Spin around)
Then I drop. (Fall to the ground)

A-Camping We Will Go
Tune: The Farmer in the Dell

A-camping we will go,
A-camping we will go,
Hi-ho and off we go,
A-camping we will go.

First we pitch our tent…
Next we chop some wood…
We light the campfire now…
We cook our dinner now…
We tell fun stories now…
It's time to go to sleep…

Pop Pop Pop

Pop Pop Pop, put the corn in the pot.
Pop Pop Pop, shake it 'til it's hot.
Pop Pop Pop, lift the lid, what have you got?
Pop Pop Pop…. POPCORN!

Lullaby and Goodnight

Lullaby and goodnight,
Sleep is softly around you.

While your dreams fill your eyes,
With a melody of love.
Lay you down now to rest,
May your slumber be blessed.
Lay you down now to rest,
May your slumber be blessed.

Little Bunny Foo Foo

Little bunny Foo Foo (hold up two fingers)
Hopping through the forest (bounce fingers up and down like a bunny)
Scooping up the field mice (make scooping motion)
And boppin' 'em on the head! (tap fist with hand)
Down came the fairyand she said...

"Little bunny Foo Foo, I don't wanna see you (shake head no)
Scooping up the field mice (make scooping motion)
And boppin' 'em on the head!" (tap fist with hand)
"I'm gonna give you three chances, (hold up three fingers)
Then I'll turn you into a goon!"
*Repeat with two chances, one chance, and then no more chances
..." Now I'll turn you into a goon!" (make a silly face)

Wind the Bobbin Up

Wind the bobbin up, wind the bobbin up
Pull pull
Clap clap clap
Wind it back again, wind it back again
Pull pull
Clap clap clap
Point to the ceiling
Point to the floor
Point to the window
Point to the door
Clap your hands together, one, two, three
Put your hands upon your knees

Use your fists to wind the bobbin up and down with circular motions. Pull your fists apart for the "pull-pull" and clap for the "clap..." line. Point to ceiling, floor, or whatever is mentioned in the rhyme and then repeat the first six lines along with the actions.

I'm A Little Pumpkin
Tune: I'm A Little Teapot

I'm a little pumpkin, Orange and round. (Hold arms in circle above head)
When I'm sad, My face wears a frown. (Frown)
But when I am happy, all aglow, Watch my smile just grow and grow! (Smile)

Rig-A-Jig-Jig

Thumbkin, pointer, middleman-big,
Silly man, wee man,
Rig-a-jig-jig.

Point to Baby's fingers one at a time and roll Baby's hands on rig-a-jig-jig.

If Your Happy and You Know It

If you're happy and you know it,
Clap your hands. (Clap, clap)
If you're happy and you know it,
Clap your hands. (Clap, clap)
If you're happy and you know it,
Then your face will surely show it.
If you're happy and you know it,
Clap your hands. (Clap, clap)

If you're happy and you know it, stomp your feet...
If you're happy and you know it, shout "I am!"...
If you're happy and you know it, do all three...

You are My Sunshine

You are my sunshine,
My only sunshine.
You make me happy,
When skies are gray.
You'll never know dear,
How much I love you.
Please don't take,
My sunshine away.

Happy All the Time

I'm inright (point at self)
Outright (point out)
Upright (point up)
Downright (point down)
Happy all the time (clap 3x)

Baby Pie

Baby and I were baked in a pie.
The pie was wonderful hot.
We had nothing to pay,
To the baker that day,
And so we crept out of the pot.

Creep fingers slowly up Baby's body.

Little Robin Red Breast

Little Robin Red Breast sat upon a tree,
Up went Pussy Cat and down went he;
Down came Pussy, and away Robin ran;
Says Little Robin Red Breast, "Catch me if you can."
Little Robin Red Breast jumped upon a wall,
Pussy Cat jumped after him and almost got a fall,

Little Robin chirped and sang, and what did Pussy say?
Pussy Cat said, "Meow!" and Robin jumped away.

The Kissing Rhyme
Up, up, up in the sky like this,
Down, down, down for a great big kiss.
Up like this, down for a kiss,
You're a special Baby!

Lift Baby up and down, then kiss Baby.

Five Little Kittens

Five little kittens
All black and white,
Sleeping soundly
All through the night.
Meow, meow, meow, meow,
It's time to get up now!

Cup Baby's fist and raise each finger to the meows.

Open Shut Them

Open, shut them,
Open, shut them,
Give a little clap, clap, clap.
Open, shut them,
Open, shut them,
Put them in your lap, lap, lap.

Help Baby to open, close, and clap hands to rhyme.

Jack-O-Lantern

I am a pumpkin, big and round. (Make a large circle with arms)
Once upon a time I grew on the ground. (Point to ground)

Now I have a mouth, two eyes, and a nose. (Point to each feature on your face)
What are they for, do you suppose? (Finger at temple - thinking)
When I have a candle inside shining bright, (Hold up forefinger)
I'll be a jack-o-lantern on Halloween night. (Thumbs in armpits - boastful)

Old Mother Hubbard

Old Mother Hubbard
Went to the cupboard
To get her poor dog a bone,
When she came there
The cupboard was bare,
And so the poor dog had none.

Months of the Year

In January I shiver and shake. (shiver)
In February, Valentines we make (draw heart in air)
In March my kite blows in the wind (wave hand)
In April, the raindrop is my friend (wiggle fingers in downward motion)
In May, the flowers grow in the pot (wiggle finger in upward motion)
In June the days start to get real hot (fan self)
July the 4th we celebrate (make pretend fireworks)
In August the swimming is really great (pretend swim)
September welcomes in the Fall (wave hands back and forth like leaves falling)
October the Halloween witches call (make pointy hat with fingers)
November the turkeys are on the go (flap wings)
December ends with a Ho Ho Ho! (rub belly)
Oh the months may come and the months may go, which one's the best?
Well, I don't know!

1-2-3-4-5 Once I Caught a Fish

One, two, three, four five! (count with your fingers)
Once I caught a fish alive; (place palms together to make a swimming fish)
Six, seven, eight, nine, ten. (count with your fingers)
Then I let it go again. (throw hands in the air)

Why did you let it go? (shrug shoulders)
Because it bit my finger so. (one hand bite pinkie finger on right hand)
Which finger did it bite? (shrug shoulders)
This little finger on my right. (wiggle pinkie finger on right hand)

Baking Gingerbread

Stir a bowl of gingerbread,
Smooth and spicy and brown
Roll it with a rolling pin
Up and up and down.
With a cookie cutter,
Make some little men,
Put them in the oven,
Till half past ten.

Pitter Patter

Pitter patter, pitter patter (wiggle fingers to show falling rain)
Listen to the rain
Pitter patter, pitter patter
Falling on my pane (tap fingers lightly on the desk or counter)

Five Little Snowmen

Five little snowmen happy and gay
The first one said, "What a lovely day."
The second one said, "We'll never have tears."
The third one said, "We'll stay for years."
The fourth one said, "But what happens in May?"
The fifth one said, "Look! We're melting away."

Hot Cross Buns

Hot cross buns,
Hot cross buns,
One a penny,

Two a penny,
Hot cross buns.

Clap Baby's hands to nursery rhyme.

Ride a Little Pony

Ride a little pony,
Down to town.
Better be careful,
So you don't fall down.

Bounce Baby on knees and then lower between knees.

Tortillas

Tortillas, tortillas for Mama,
Tortillas, tortillas for Papa,
Tortillas, tortillas,
Who will eat them?
Tortillas, tortillas, for me!

Clap Baby's hands to rhyme.

Leg Over Leg

Leg over leg,
As the dog went to Dover.
He came to a fence,
And Whoops!
He jumped over.

Move Baby's legs back and forth and then lift Baby.

Ten Little Indians

1 little 2 little 3 little Indians

4 little 5 little 6 little Indians
7 little 8 little 9 little Indians
10 little Indians boys.

10 little 9 little 8 little Indians
7 little 6 little 5 little Indians
4 little 3 little 2 little Indians
1 little Indians boy.

Rock-A-Bye Baby

Rock-a-bye Baby,
On the tree top,
When the wind blows,
The cradle will rock.
When the bough breaks,
The cradle will fall.
And down will come Baby,
Cradle and all.

Pat a Cake

Pat a cake, pat a cake, baker's man. Bake me a cake as fast as you can (Hold your baby's hands open and pat them together.)
Pat it and prick it (Touch is open palm with your finger, pat it with your hand.)
And mark it with B (Trace a B on his palm.)
And put it in the oven for baby and me. (Pat his hands together again.)

Five Fat Peas

Five fat peas in a pea pod pressed (hold hand in a fist)
One grew, two grew, so did all the rest (put thumb and fingers up one by one)
They grew and grew (raise hands in the air very slowly)
And did not stop, Until one day
The pod went POP! (clap)

Hands and Fingers

Up and down
Round and round (draw circles in the air)
Put your fingers on the ground
Over (hold hands above lap)
Under (move hands below legs)
In between (you've hidden your hands in between your legs)
Now my fingers can't be seen!
Hands in front
Hands behind
Now my hands I cannot find
Here's my left hand
Here's my right
Hands and fingers back in sight (wriggle fingers)

The Bear Went Over the Mountain

The bear went over the mountain,
The bear went over the mountain,
The bear went over the mountain
To see what he could see,
To see what he could see,
To see what he could see.
The other side of the mountain,
The other side of the mountain,
The other side of the mountain
Was all that he could see.

Peter, Peter, Pumpkin Eater

Peter, Peter, pumpkin eater,
Had a wife and couldn't keep her.
Put her in a pumpkin shell,
And there he kept her very well.
Clap Baby's hands to nursery rhyme.

Pease Porridge Hot

Pease porridge hot,
Peas porridge cold,
Peas porridge in the pot
Nine days old.
Some like it hot,
Some like it cold,
Some like it in the pot
Nine days old!

Clap Baby's hands to nursery rhyme.

Ride Away, Ride Away

Ride away, ride away, Baby shall ride,
And have a wee puppy dog tied to one side.
A wee pussy cat shall be tied to the other,
And Baby shall ride to see her grandmother.

Bounce Baby on knee and lean on cue.

One, Two Buckle My Shoe

One, two, buckle my shoe (hold up one, then two fingers, and pretend to tie your shoelace)
Three, four, shut the door (hold up three and four fingers, now pretend to shut the door)
Five, six, pick up the sticks (hold up five and six fingers, then pretend to pick up something from the ground)
Seven, eight, lay them straight (hold up seven and eight fingers, now pretend to put the sticks straight)
Nine, ten, a big, fat, hen! (hold up nine and ten fingers, impersonate a fat hen)
Now we count all over again.

Mistress Mary

Mistress Mary quite contrary,

How does your garden grow?
With silver bells and cockle shells,
And pretty maids all in a row.

Clap Baby's hands to nursery rhyme.

Hello Spring
Tune: Goodnight Ladies

Hello spring,
Hello spring,
Hello spring,
We hope you're here to stay.

Repeat the song and replace "spring" with other springtime words: blossoms, butterflies, flowers, green grass, rainbows, robins, wooly lambs, etc.

Jack and Jill

Jack and Jill went up the hill,
To fetch a pail of water.
Jack fell down,
And broke his crown,
And Jill came tumbling after.

Slide Baby up and down on knees.

Pitty Patty Polt

Pitty patty polt,
Shoe the wild colt.
Here's a nail,
There's a nail,
Pitty patty polt!
Bounce Baby to rhyme.

Teddy Bear, Teddy Bear

Teddy Bear, Teddy Bear, turn around,
Teddy Bear, Teddy Bear, touch the ground.
Teddy Bear, Teddy Bear, reach up high,
Teddy Bear, Teddy Bear, wink one eye.
Teddy Bear, Teddy Bear, touch your nose,
Teddy Bear, Teddy Bear, touch your toes.
Teddy Bear, Teddy Bear, shut the door,
Teddy Bear, Teddy Bear, count to four.
Teddy Bear, Teddy Bear, climb the stairs,
Teddy Bear, Teddy Bear, say your prayers.
Teddy Bear, Teddy Bear, turn out the light,
Teddy Bear, Teddy Bear, say goodnight.

Counting Valentines
Tune: Ten Little Indians

One red, two red, three red Valentines
Four red, five red, six red Valentines
Seven red, eight red, nine red Valentines
Ten red Valentines.
Ten red, nine red, eight red Valentines
Seven red, six red, five red Valentines
Four red, three red, two red Valentines
One red Valentine.

The Clock

The little clock goes tick, tock,
Tick, tock, tick tock.
The big clock goes ding, dong,
Ding, dong, ding.

Lift and swing Baby side to side.

5 Little Pumpkins

Five little pumpkins sitting on a gate
The 1st one said, "Oh my, it's getting late."
The 2nd one said, "There are witches in the air."
The 3rd one said, "I don't care."
The 4th one said, "Let's run & run & run."
The 5th one said, "It's only Halloween fun!"
WHOOOOO WENT THE WIND AND OUT WENT THE LIGHT
AND THE 5 LITTLE PUMPKINS ROLLED OUT OF SITE

This is the Way the Ladies Ride

This is the way the ladies ride,
Nim, nim, nim.
This is the way the gentlemen ride,
Trim, trim, trim.
This is the way the farmers ride,
Trot, trot, trot.
This is the way the hunters ride,
Gallop, gallop, gallop.

Vary bouncing with rhyme.

It's Raining It's Pouring

It's raining, it's pouring,
The old man is snoring.
He bumped his head,
When he went to bed,
And he couldn't get up
In the morning.

Clap Baby's hands to rhyme.

Where is my Gingerbread Man?

Tune: Oh, where or where has my little dog gone?

Oh where, oh where is my gingerbread man?
Oh where, oh where can he be?
He popped out of the oven and ran out the door.
Oh where, oh where can he be?

Butterfly Wings

Butterfly wings go fluttering by.
Down to the flowers and up to the sky.
Butterfly wings tickle your toes.
Butterfly wings land right on your nose.

Gesture and tickle to rhyme.

The Monkey and the Weasel

All around the cobbler's bench,
The monkey chased the weasel.
The monkey thought 'twas all in fun.
Pop! goes the weasel.

Hold Baby and turn around. Lift Baby on Pop!

I Love Baby

I love Baby over and over.
I love Baby among the clover.
I love Baby and Baby loves me.
That's the lass/laddie I'll go wee.

Clap Baby's hands to rhyme.

Snowflake, Snowflake
Tune: Teddy Bear, Teddy Bear Turn Around

Snowflake, snowflake dance around,
Snowflake, snowflake, touch the ground.

Snowflake, snowflake, soft and white.
Snowflake, snowflake, snowball fight!
Snowflake, snowflake in the air,
Snowflake, snowflake everywhere!

Baby's Face

Two little eyes to look around,
Two little ears to hear each sound,
One little nose to smell what's sweet,
One little mouth that likes to eat.

Touch Baby's body parts.

Here is the Beehive

Here is the beehive (make a fist)
Where are the bees? (ask this question with the other hand)
Hiding inside where nobody sees!
Watch them come creeping out of the hive
One, two, three, four, five (hold up one finger from the fist to show each bee)
Buzzzz! (make a buzzing sound while wiggling the outstretched fingers)

I'm A Nut

I'm a little acorn brown,
sitting on the cold, cold ground.
Someone came and stepped on me,
that is why I'm cracked you see.
I'm a nut (click, click),
I'm a nut (click, click),
I'm a nut, I'm a nut, I'm a nut(click, click).

Easter Everywhere

Rabbits soft and cuddly
Baby chickens, too.

Easter eggs for baskets
White and pink and blue
Easter cards of greeting
Music in the air,
Lilies just to tell us
It's Easter everywhere

Froggie

A Froggie sat on a log,
A-weeping for his daughter,
His eyes were red,
His tears he shed,
And he fell into the water.

Bounce Baby and then gently slide Baby between your knees.

Jelly in the Bowl
Tune: The Farmer in the Dell

Jelly in the bowl,
Jelly in the bowl,
Wibble, wobble,
Wibble, wobble,
Jelly in the bowl.

Gently pat Baby's tummy as you sing.

I'm A Little Spider

Tune: I'm A Little Teapot

I'm a little spider,
Watch me spin.
If you'll be my dinner,
I'll let you come in.
Then I'll spin my web to hold you tight,

And gobble you up in one big bite!

Ride a Crock Horse

Ride a cock horse to Banbury Cross,
To see a fine lady
Upon a white horse.
With rings on her fingers,
And bells on her toes,
She shall have music wherever she goes.

Bounce Baby on knee while shaking jingle bells.

Five Little Scarecrows

Five little scarecrows standing in a row,
The first one said, "Look, here come the crows!"
The second one said, "I am very small."
The third one said, "But, I am very tall."
The fourth one said, "I can bend my head."
The fifth one said, "I can wave my arms, instead."
Five little scarecrows standing in a row,
Count them as they move when the wind blows.

Snowman

Tune: Ten Little Indians

1 little 2 little 3 little Snowmen
4 little 5 little 6 little Snowmen
7 little 8 little 9 little Snowmen
10 little Snowmen
Learning how to read!

10 little 9 little 8 little Snowmen
7 little 6 little 5 little Snowmen
4 little 3 little 2 little Snowmen

1 little Snowmen
Learning how to read!

Sippity Sup

Sippity sup, sippity sup,
Bread and milk from a china cup.
Bread and milk from a silver spoon,
Made from a piece of the silver moon.
Sippity sup, sippity sup,
Sippity, sippity sup.

Clap Baby's hands to rhyme.

Baby, Baby Dumpling

Baby, Baby Dumpling,
Boil him in the pot.
Sugar him and butter him,
And eat him while he's hot.

Clap Baby's hands to rhyme.

A Little Seed

A little seed for me to sow.
A little earth to make it grow.
A little hole.
A little pat.
A little water,
And that is that.
A little sun,
A little shower,
A little while
And then... a flower!

Family Horsie Ride

This is the way the mama rides,
Trot, trot, trot.
This is the way the daddy rides,
Gallop-a trot, gallop-a-trot.
This is the way the baby rides
Hobbledy-hoy, hobbledy-hoy.

Bounce Baby and increase speed.

This Little Toe

This little toe goes
Rub-a-dub, dub.
This little toe goes
Scrub, scrub, scrub.
Rub-a-dub, dub,
Scrub, scrub, scrub.
This little toe goes
SPLASH!!

Rub Baby's toes to rhyme.

Tickle, Tickle, Little Mousie

Tickle, tickle, little mousie,
Right up into Baby's housie.

Walk fingers up Baby, then gently tickle.

This Little Piggy

This little piggy went to market (Squeeze and wriggle your baby's big toe.)
This little piggy stayed at home (Squeeze and wriggle his second toe.)
This little piggy had roast beef (Squeeze and wriggle his middle toe.)
This little piggy had none (Squeeze and wriggle his fourth toe.)

And this little piggy went 'wee, wee, wee' all the way home. (Tickle your baby all over.)

This Old Man

This old man, he played one.
He played knick-knack on my thumb.
With a knick-knack, paddywack,
Give a dog a bone.
This old man came rolling home.

Clap and roll Baby's hands to song. Add verses two-shoe, three-knee, four-door, five-hive, six-sticks, seven-up in heaven, eight-skate, nine-dime, ten-in the den.

A Teepee is My Home

A Teepee is my home
Of deer skin it is made.
A place on top where
smoke can go
It stands in forest shade.
A river runs nearby
And there is my canoe.
It paddles up and down the stream
Beneath the sky of blue.

Little Boy Blue

Little Boy Blue, come blow your horn,
The sheep's in the meadow, the cow's in the corn.
Where is the little boy who looks after the sheep?
He's under the haystack, fast asleep.

Five Speckled Frogs

Five little speckled frogs
Sat on a speckled log

Eating the most delicious bugs
Yum yum!
One jumped into the pool
Where it was nice and cool
Then there were four speckled frogs
Glub glub!

Start with five fingers and fold a finger every time one frog jumps in. Continue until no frogs are left. You can massage your tummy with the line "Yum yum!" Hold your nose and sink on the line "Glub glub!"

Five Little Monkeys Swinging in the Tree

Five little monkeys swinging in the tree
Teasing Mr. Alligator "Can't catch me"!
Along came Mr. Alligator quiet as can be.
Snap!

Four little monkeys swinging in the tree
Teasing Mr. Alligator "Can't catch me"!
Along came Mr. Alligator quiet as can be.
Snap!

Three little monkeys swinging in the tree
Teasing Mr. Alligator "Can't catch me"!
Along came Mr. Alligator quiet as can be.
Snap!

Two little monkeys swinging in the tree
Teasing Mr. Alligator "Can't catch me"!
Along came Mr. Alligator quiet as can be.
Snap!

One little monkeys swinging in the tree
Teasing Mr. Alligator "Can't catch me"!
Along came Mr. Alligator quiet as can be.
Snap!

No more monkeys swinging in the tree.

Mama's Little Baby

Tune: Shortening Bread

Mama's little baby a kiss can blow,
And rub noses just like so.
Two little hands can clap, clap, clap.
Ten little toes can tap, tap, tap.

Follow gestures of rhyme with Baby.

Clap, Clap

Clap, clap, little Baby,
Clap, clap, little Baby,
Clap, clap, little Baby,
While we sing this song.

Clap Baby's hands to song.

Baby Fleas

Giraffes are tall.
Birdies are small.
But little baby fleas,
You can't see at all!

Have your fingers play with the baby gently tickle baby.

Piggy, Piggy

Piggy, piggy, where are you?
Piggy, piggy, where's your shoes?
Piggy, piggy, googly goo
Piggy, piggy, I love you.

Wiggle Baby's toes to rhyme.

FiveLittle Bells

Five little bells hanging in a row; (Fingers hanging down)
The first one said, "Ring me slow." (Wiggle thumb)
The second one said, "Ring me fast." (Wiggle index finger)
The third one said, "Ring me last." (Wiggle second finger)
The fourth one said, "I'm like a chime." (Wiggle third finger)
The fifth one said, "Ring me at Christmas time." (Wiggle fourth finger)

These are Baby's Fingers

These are Baby's fingers,
These are Baby's toes,
This is Baby's belly button,
Round and round it goes.
These are Baby's ears,
This is Baby's nose,
This is Baby's belly button,
Round and round it goes.

Touch Baby's body parts, and then gently blow on Baby's tummy.

Easter Bunny

Easter bunny's ears are floppy. (Hands at sides of head, flop fingers)
Easter bunny's feet are hoppy. (Hop up and down)
His fur is soft. (Stroke arm)
His nose is fluffy. (Wiggle nose)
Tail is short and powder-puffy. (Hands behind back, wiggle)

A Bouncing Mouse

A bouncing mouse is in my house.
It's been here for a week.
It bounced from out of nowhere.

Listen to it squeak.
It bounces in the kitchen.
It bounces in the den.
It bounces through the living room.
Look! There it goes again.

Bounce Baby on knees to rhyme.

Circle Round the Baby
Tune: Ring Around the Rosie

Circle round the baby.
Circle round the baby.
Faster, faster,
Baby gets a kiss.

Make circles on Baby's back or tummy.

Baby Horsie Ride

See the baby on her horsie,
Bouncing every day.
Faster and faster,
She gallops away!

Bounce Baby on knee to rhyme.

Little Bird

Once I saw a little bird,
Go hop, hop, hop.
And I said little bird,
Will you stop, stop, stop?
I was going to the window,
To say how do you do?
But he shook his little tail,
And away he flew.

Bounce and lift Baby to rhyme.

To Market

To market, to market, to buy a fat pig.
Home again, home again, jiggety jig.
To market, to market, to buy a fat hog.
Home again, home again, jiggety jog.
To market, to market to buy a plum bun,
Home again, home again,
Market is done.

Bounce Baby to nursery rhyme.

Humpty Dumpty

Humpty-Dumpty sat on a wall,
Humpty-Dumpty had a great fall.
All the king's horses, and all the king's men
Couldn't put Humpty together again.

You're My Little Baby
Tune: I'm A Little Teapot

You're my little baby.
Soft and sweet.
Here are your hands,
And here are feet.
Let's clap your hands
Just like so,
And tap your feet.
And tickle your toe.

Move Baby to actions.

Baa, Baa, Black Sheep

Baa, baa, black sheep, have you any wool?

Yes sir, yes sir, three bags full!
One for the master, one for the dame,
And one for the little boy who lives down the lane.

Baa, baa, black sheep, have you any wool?
Yes sir, yes sir, three bags full!
One to mend the jerseys, one to mend the socks,
And one for the little girl with holes in her frocks.

Baa, baa, black sheep, have you any wool?
Yes sir, yes sir, three bags full!
One for the sweater, one for the shawl,
And one for the blanket that hangs by the wall.

Baa, baa, black sheep, have you any wool?
Yes sir, yes sir, three bags full!

I Can Make Baby Laugh

I can make a baby laugh,
When I tickle her toes.
I can make baby smile,
When I rub her nose.

Tickle Baby's toes and rub noses.

The Rain

Pitter-patter, raindrops,
Falling from the sky;
Here is my umbrella,
To keep me safe and dry.

When the rain is over,
And the sun begins to glow,
Little flowers start to bud,
And grow and grow and grow!

Round and Round

Round and round the garden like a teddy bear, (Hold your baby's hand open and trace a circle on him palm with you finger.)
One step, (Step your finger up towards his elbow.)
Two steps, (Step your finger up towards the top of his arm.)
Tickle him under there. (Tickle him under the arm.)

Jack Be Nimble

Jack be nimble,
Jack be quick,
Jack jump over
The candlestick.

Bounce and lift Baby to nursery rhyme.

Trot, Trot to Boston Town

Trot, trot to Boston town.
To get a stick of candy.
One for me and one for you,
And one for Dicky Dandy.

Bounce Baby on knee to rhyme.

Fee, Fie, Fo, Fum

Fee, fie, fo, fum,
See my finger,
See my thumb.
Fee, fie, fo, fum,
See my finger
Here it comes!

Gently tickle Baby.

Tic Tac Toe

Tic tac toe,
Round I go,
Where I stop,
I don't know!

Draw X's and O's on Baby's back.

What's For Dinner?
Tune: Frere Jacques

What's for dinner?
What's for dinner?
Irish stew, Irish stew,
Sloppy semolina, sloppy semolina,
No thank-you, no thank-you.

Clap Baby's hands to song.

The Little Flea

The little flea went walking,
To see what he could see.
And all the little flea could see,
Was………
A precious little baby.

Walk finger over Baby's body, stopping and starting and gently tickling.

Criss Cross Applesauce

Criss cross applesauce,
A cool breeze,
A tight squeeze,
And a tickle, tickle, tickle,
As you please.

Draw an X on Baby's tummy. Blow on Baby's neck and tickle and hug gently.

Tickley

Tickley, tickley, where should I tickley?
Tickley, tickley, right on the nose.
Tickley, tickley where should I tickley?
Tickley, tickley, right on the toes.

Sway and gently tickle to actions.

This Little Cow Eats Grass

This little cow eats grass,
This little cow eats hay,
This little cow drinks water,
This little cow runs away.
And this little cow does nothing all day.

Wiggle each finger to rhyme.

Trot, Trot, Trot

Trot, trot to London,
Trot, trot to Dover.
Look out Baby,
Or you might fall over.

Bounce and tip Baby to rhyme.

Baby's Fire

Baby blow the fire,
Puff, puff, puff.
First you blow it gently,
Then you blow it rough!

Blow on Baby gently, then stronger.

Jack in the Box

Jack in the box,
Sits so still.
Won't you come out?
Yes I will!

Hide under blanket with Baby and lift Baby to uncover.

"Daddy," Said the Baby

"Daddy," said the baby,
"Wonderful," said the mom.
"Daddy," said the baby
"Cute," said the son.
"Daddy," said the baby,
The sister looked intrigued.
"Daddy," said the baby.
And Daddy looked pleased.

Clap Baby's hands to rhyme.

You Shall

You shall have an apple,
You shall have a plum,
You shall have a rattle basket,
When the day is done.

Clap Baby's hands to rhyme.

Baby Pie

We had nothing to pay,
To the baker that day,
And so we crept out of the pot.

Creep fingers slowly up Baby's body.

Bouncy, Bouncy

Bouncy, bouncy, we like to bouncy.
Bouncy, bouncy, one, two, three!
Bouncy, bouncy, we like to bouncy,
Bouncy, bouncy, bounce with me!

Bounce Baby on knee while playing.

Craft Recipes

Some of these recipes are edible but others are not also some have high allergy ingredients. Please be careful when working with younger children.

For the edible dough you can give children decorating materials such as: raisins, chocolate chips, raspberry chips, butterscotch chips, shredded coconut, dried fruit, pretzels, smarties etc.

For the inedible dough you can add other decorating materials such as: glitter, rocks, shells, etc.

If clay gets too dry, renew it with a few drops of water.

If clay is too sticky, knead in more flour, cornstarch or baking soda.

Cover extra clay with a damp cloth while working to prevent drying.

To color clay: either knead in food coloring or cake-decorating coloring paste.

Most clays can be colored with acrylic paints when dry.

Bubbles

Long Lasting Bubbles

1/2 cup dishwashing detergent
4 1/2 cup Water
4 Tablespoons glycerin
Container with a tight-fitting lid in which to keep the bubbles
Measuring devices
Spoon

Measure out the water, detergent, and glycerin into container. GENTLY stir the mixture together. If a foam forms, gently skim it off the top. Find something with which to blow bubbles and begin to have fun. The longer you let the mixture set, the larger the bubbles are and the longer they seem to last.

Tears No More Bubbles

1/4 cup Baby shampoo
3/4 cup water
3 Tablespoons corn syrup

Mix then let set for a few hours.

Fancy Bubbles

1 cup dishwashing detergent
12 cup water
3/4 Tablespoons glycerin

Gently stir the ingredients together and leave the solution in an open container overnight. This gives the alcohol in the dishwashing soap a chance to evaporate some. In any case, the solution seems to get better with age.

Super Bubbles

2 parts dishwashing detergent
4 parts glycerin
1 part corn syrup

Mix and store in an airtight container.

Iridescent Bubbles

1 cup of water
2 Tablespoons liquid detergent
1 Tablespoons glycerin
1/2 teaspoon sugar

Mix all ingredients together until sugar dissolves.

Homemade Bubbles

1/2 cup dish soap
1 1/2 cups water
2 teaspoons sugar
Mediumsize mixing bowl or cup
Spoon
Sealed container (jar with lid)

Mix all three ingredients together. Don't stir or shake too much. Store in a sealed container to prolong its effect.

Best Bubble Solution

1 cup water
2 Tablespoons Light Karo syrup OR 2 Tablespoons Glycerin
4 Tablespoons Dishwashing liquid

Mix and have fun!

Bubbles

1 cup water
1/3 cup dish soap
2 Tablespoons light corn syrup

Combine ingredients and enjoy.

Sugar Bubbles

4 cup hot water
10 Tablespoons white sugar
3/4 cup Dawn or Joy

Combine hot water and sugar, gently stir in soap.

Rainbow Bubbles

1 cup granulated soap or soap powder
1 quart warm water
Liquid food coloring
Plastic straws
Small juice cans

Pour water over soap and stir until dissolved. Pour mixture into containers (fill about 1/3). Add food coloring and stir. Put straw in a blow a rainbow bubble. If you blow these bubbles against a white piece of poster board, you can make a beautiful art piece as well. Best for outdoor play.

Desperation Bubbles

1/2 cup Water
1/2 cup Liquid Detergent
1 Tablespoons Cooking Oil

Stir together and use. Although these are not the very best bubbles, they can be made from things found in any kitchen.

Bubble Solution Extender

1/3 cup commercial bubbles
1/3 cup water
1/3 cup liquid soap

Mix and store in an airtight container.

Bubble Blower

1 drinking straw (two if you cut the pop holder into smaller parts)
1 six-pack pop holder (the plasticthat goes around pop cans)
Scotch tape
Bowl or pan

Scissors, optional

Tape the holder to the straw. Pour bubbles into bowl or pan. Dip into bubbles and twirl around. Makes LOTS of BIG bubbles.

Editable - Playdough, Clay, and Molding Dough

Many of these recipes contain peanut butter or another high allergy ingredient.

Spice Dough

2 cup Flour
2 teaspoon Baking Powder
1/3 cup Sugar
1/2 teaspoon Salt
1/2 teaspoon Cinnamon
1/4 teaspoon Nutmeg
1/3 cup Water
4 Tablespoon Salad Oil

Mix dry ingredients. Add water and oil. Knead until dough sticks and form a ball. NOTE: This recipe can be fried in oil until crust forms.

Mashed Potato Clay

Instant mashed potatoes water

Make it just like you were cooking for Thanksgiving dinner. Cover the table with wax paper and play.

Peanut Butter Playdough

1 cup peanut butter
1 cup Karo syrup
1 1/4 cup powdered sugar
1 1/4 cup powdered milk

In a large bowl, mix peanut butter, corn syrup, and powdered sugar together. Add powdered milk and knead until smooth. (Add more powdered milk if you need to.) Although a little on the sweet side, this dough is also very yummy. Mix with your clean hands.

Smooth Peanut Butter Playdough

1 cup peanut butter
1 cup liquid honey
1 cup powdered milk
1 cup rolled oats.

Mix and use. If too sticky add some more powdered milk. When not using MUST be stored in an airtight container.

Candy Clay

10 oz. chocolate, almond bark or candy discs
1/3 C. corn syrup

Slowly melt candy and stir until smooth. Add syrup and blend thoroughly. Pour onto waxed paper and spread with fingers until about 1/2 inch thick. Cover loosely with waxed paper and permit to stiffen for a few hours.

Frosting Playdough

1 can frosting (any flavor)
1 1/2 cup powdered sugar
1 cup creamy peanut butter

Mix until dough reaches desired consistency. Storage: When not using MUST be stored in an airtight container and refrigerated. Next time you want to use it let it come to room temperature for pliable dough.

Yummy Honey Peanut Butter Dough

1 cup peanut butter

1 cup honey
2 cup powdered milk

Stir together peanut butter, instant milk and honey. Knead dough until smooth. If dough is too moist, add more powdered milk. If dough is too dry, add more honey. Store unused dough in the refrigerator. Form the dough into shapes and then eat them for a snack.

Edible Playdough

1 1/2 cups powdered sugar
1 cup creamy peanut butter
Mixing bowl
Spoon
Storage Container
Refrigerator

Gather all ingredients, spoon and mixing bowl. Mix with spoon and hands until it reaches desired consistency. This can be stored in an airtight container and refrigerated. Next time you want to use it, let it come to room temperature.

Cream Cheese Dough

8 oz. package of cream cheese
1/2 cup non-fat dry milk
1 tablespoon honey
Crackers or bread slices

Combine cream cheese, milk and honey in a bowl and mix until well blended. Mold sculptures on wax paper. Unused portions must be stored in an airtight container and kept refrigerated! Because cream cheese is perishable, use the expiration date on the cream cheese package as your guide for how long you can keep this play dough. Note: The shapes can then be placed on crackers or bread slices, decorated with celery or carrot slivers, raisins, dried fruit pieces, nuts, or seeds for a healthy snack...

Edible Candy Playdough

1/3 cup margarine
1/3 cup light corn syrup
1 pound box of powdered sugar
1 teaspoon vanilla extract
Food coloring
1/4 tsp. salt

Mix all ingredients except powdered sugar. When all is combined add powdered sugar. Knead until smooth. Play and eat!

Edible Playdough

1/3 cup Margarine
1/3 cup Light corn syrup
1/2 teaspoon Salt
1 teaspoon Vanilla extract
1 lb. Powdered sugar
Food coloring (optional)

Mix the first 4 ingredients. Add sugar. Knead dough. Divide and add food coloring. Keep refrigerated.

Applesauce and Cinnamon Playdough

1 cup Applesauce
1 cup Cinnamon

Mix the applesauce and the cinnamon until it gets to a nice clay consistency. If it is too sticky, add a bit more cinnamon or even a touch of flour. You can make shapes and designs or use cookie cutters. Put the shapes in a warm, dry spot to dry - this takes a few days! You now have sweet-smelling sculptures to decorate and/or paint.

Chocolate Playdough

8 oz. semisweet chocolate
1/4 cup plus one Tablespoon light corn syrup

Melt the chocolate in a metal bowl set over a pan of simmering water (a double boiler). Stir the chocolate with a spoon until smooth, and then stir in the corn syrup. The chocolate will stiffen almost immediately but stir completely to combine. Transfer the chocolate to a sturdy plastic bag and refrigerate until firm; the consistency will be that of Play Dough.

When firm, the dough can be worked by kneading. If it is too hard cut off small pieces and knead until pliable. If the dough sticks to the counter when rolling, lightly spray counter or breadboard with vegetable spray or lightly grease with vegetable oil.

Hand shape the dough into a rope or braid, making two or three long ropes and twist or braid them together -- can be used as the outside edge on top of a cake or around the base. Make ribbons to cover the cake. To do this, pat your dough into a disk shape and roll dough out to desired thickness using a rolling pin or else use a manual pasta machine. Flowers, too!

Storage: When not using MUST be stored in an airtight container and refrigerate

Potato Dough

4 or 5 potatoes
1 - 1 1/2 cup flour

Bake potatoes, in the skin, until soft inside. Peel, and discard peel. Mash potatoes or flatten and decorate; use a potato ricer to get a nice fine, even texture. Combine 1 - 1 1/2 C. of flour to every 2 C. of mashed potato and form dough. It has no raw egg in it, and leaving it out for a bit, there is nothing in it to spoil. The color will be gray after a while, but if you add food coloring, when you make it, you won't even notice. If you have extra, roll it is balls and press your thumb in one side, and roll it across the backside of a fork. Cook in boiling water for 1 min. and serve either with tomato sauce or butter or even brown gravy. They taste great.

Sweet Smelling Dough

1/3 cup Applesauce
6 Tablespoon Ground cinnamon
2 Tablespoon of each - Cloves, and Nutmeg
Cutting board
Rolling pin
Cookie cutters
Spatula
Tempera paint or fabric puff paints
Yarn or ribbon

Mix warm applesauce and spices together to form a ball. Sprinkle some cinnamon onto a cutting board and roll the dough to about ¼ inch thickness with a rolling pin. Cut out the dough with cookie cutters and make a hole in the top of each figure to use later for hanging. Lift cutouts with a spatula and place them in a cool area to dry. Turn them often. The drying time is usually about 24 hours. Decorate, adding words and names with tempera or fabric paint. Add a hanger made from yam or a ribbon.

Non Toxic - Playdough, Clay, and Molding Dough

While these recipes will not harm children if ingested please be careful with any allergies that they might have and even though some of these are safe they may not taste good.

Jell-O Play Playdough

1 cup flour
1/2 cup salt
1 cup water
1 Tablespoon oil
2 teaspoon Cream of Tarter
1 (3-1/2-oz.) package "unsweetened" Jell-O

Mix all ingredients together and cook over medium heat, stirring constantly until consistency of mashed potatoes. Let cool and knead with floured hands until dry. Storage: This recipe needs to cool completely "before" storing it in an airtight container! Note: The items made from this play dough recipe can be painted when they are dry.

Summer Kool-Aid Playdough

1 cup flour
1 Tablespoon vegetable oil
1 package unsweetened Kool-Aid
1/4 cup salt
2 Tablespoon cream of tartar
1 cup water

Mix dry ingredients together in a large saucepan. Slowly add water mixed with oil and stir over medium heat until mixture thickens to dough. Turn out onto a heatproof bread board or countertop and knead until cool enough for children to handle. Dough will be the color of the Kool-Aid mix and will smell like the Kool-Aid mix. (Can be stored in a tightly covered container for up to six months).

Cooked Playdough

1 cup flour
1/2 cup salt
2 teaspoon cream of tartar
1 cup water
1 Tablespoon oil
1 teaspoon food coloring

In medium saucepan, mix all ingredients. Cook over medium heat, stirring constantly. When dough becomes harder to stir and gathers on spoon (about 5 min.) dump onto waxed paper, cool until able to handle and knead 10-15 times until smooth. Store in sealed container, keeps up to two weeks.

Durable Playdough

Mix in a heavy saucepan:
1 cup of flour
1/2 cup cream of tartar

Add 1 cup of water and 2 Tablespoon cooking oil

Stir while cooking over medium heat until it sticks together in a ball and looks like stiff mashed potatoes, 3-5 min. Dump onto a plate to cool a few minutes and then knead into the clay about 1 or 2 cups of flour. Store in a plastic bag (no need to refrigerate).

Playdough

2 cup flour
4 teaspoon cream of tartar
1 cup salt
1 1/2 - 2 cup boiling water
3 - 4 Tablespoon vegetable oil
Food coloring

Add oil and food coloring to boiling water. Combine the remaining ingredients and mix well. As you kneed it, the dough will get smoother. Store in airtight container. Very pliable and easy to roll or sculpt.

Coffee Playdough

2 cups used coffee grounds
1 1/2 cups cornmeal
1/2 cup salt
water
flour

Mix all ingredients until pliable. Add water, flour as needed to achieve a working consistency.

Pumpkin Playdough

5 1/2 cup Flour
2 cup Salt
8 tsp. Cream of Tartar
3/4 cup Oil
1 Container (1 1/2 oz.) Pumpkin Pie Spice
Orange Food coloring (2 parts yellow, 1 part red)
4 cup Water

Mix all the ingredients together. Cook and stir over medium heat until all lumps disappear. Knead the dough on a floured surface until smooth. This makes plenty for a group.

Oatmeal Playdough

1 part flour
2 parts oatmeal
1 part water

Gradually add water to flour and oatmeal in bowl. Knead until mixed (this dough is sticky, but unique in texture.) Model as with clay. The items made from this play dough recipe can be painted when they are dry. Variations: Add cornmeal in small quantity for texture or add coffee grounds in small quantity for texture.

Rock Playdough (Treasure Rocks)

1 cup flour
1 cup used coffee grounds
1/2 cup salt
1/4 cup sand
3/4 cup water
Treasures – small toys

Mix all dry ingredients together in a medium bowl. Slowly add water and knead until the mixture is the consistency of bread dough. Break off a piece of dough and roll it into the size of a baseball. Make a hole in the center of the ball big enough to hide treasures in. Fill the hole with treasures and seal with some extra dough. Let your treasure stone air dry for 2-3 days or until hard or bake in the oven on a cookie sheet at 150 degrees for 15-20 minutes.

Non-Hardening Playdough

2 cups flour
1 cup salt
Water
Oil, optional (if you do not want it to harden)
Medium sized mixing bowl
Spoon

Mix the flour, salt, and water in a bowl. Add a small amount of oil if you do not want the play dough to harden. Knead the play dough a little and watch the kids have fun.

Coffee Clay

2 cups flour
1/2 cup salt
1/8 cup instant coffee
3/4 cup warm water

Dissolve coffee in warm water. In a separate bowl mix salt and flour. Form an indentation in the dough ball and pour in about half of the coffee. Mix until creamy smooth. Add more coffee water as needed and work until it is a clay-like consistency (not sticky). Design away! Bake finished goods in a 250-degree oven for an hour or until dry. Paint and finish with shellac, varnish or plastic spray finish. Store the remaining dough in a covered jar or plastic bag.

Nature's Own Play Dough

1 cup flour
1/2 cup salt
1 cup water
2 Tablespoon oil

2 Tablespoon cream of tartar
Beet, Carrot and or Spinach juice

Mix dry ingredients. Slowly add oil and water. Cook over low to medium heat stirring constantly. When dough is still take it off the stove. Let cool. Knead dough until it feels like play dough. Knead in Spinach juice for green, Carrot juice for orange and/or Beet juice for pink.

Gluten Free Playdough

1/2 cup rice flour
1/2 cup corn starch
1/2 cup salt
2 tsp cream of tarter
1 cup water
1 teaspoon cooking oil
Food coloring, if desired

Mix ingredients. Cook and stir on low heat for 3 minutes or until mixture forms a ball. Cool completely before storing in a sealable plastic bag.

Chocolate Scented Playdough

1 1/4 cups flour
1/2 cup cocoa powder
1/2 cup salt
1/2 Tablespoon cream of tartar
1 1/2 Tablespoon cooking oil
1 cup boiling water

Mix the dry ingredients. Add the oil and boiling water. Stir quickly, mixing well. When cool, mix with your hands.

Baked Dough

4 cup flour
1 cup salt

1 1/2- 2 cup water
Small pebbles, macaroni, buttons, etc.
Condensed milk
Food coloring

Preheat oven to 250 degrees F. Mix together flour, salt, and enough water to make a stiff dough. Provide macaroni, etc. to children to press into the dough shapes. Bake completed dough models for one hour. For antique effect, brush on condensed milk before baking, or use a mix of condensed milk and food coloring.

Kool-Aid Playdough

1 cup flour
1 cup water
1/2 cup salt
3 teaspoon Cream of Tartar
1 package Kool-Aid Mix (any flavor of unsweetened)
1 Tablespoon cooking oil

Mix dry ingredients together in a large saucepan. Slowly add water mixed with oil and stir over medium heat until mixture thickens to dough. Turn out onto a heatproof bread board or countertop and knead until cool enough for children to handle. Dough will be the color of the Kool-Aid mix and will smell like the Kool-Aid mix. (Can be stored in a tightly covered container for up to six months)

Cloud Dough

1/2 cup water (maybe a little more)
1/2 cup cooking oil
2 cup flour
2 cup salt
Food coloring
Peppermint oil

Mix the cooking oil, flour, and salt. Add a few drops of the food color to the water. Add the water gradually, adding extra if needed to bind the dough. Add a few drops of the peppermint oil. Now, knead the dough until it is smooth and pliable.

Industrial Salt Dough

1 cup flour
1/4 cup salt
2 teaspoon cream of tartar
1 cup warm water
1 teaspoon oil
Food coloring

This is a long-lasting dough that requires cooking. Mix all ingredients in a saucepan and cook over medium heat until smooth. Let the mixture cool slightly and knead. The dough will be very pliable and easy to sculpt.

Place in plastic bag or airtight container to store. Bake in a low oven and paint.

Salt Dough

2-1/4 cup Water
2 cup Salt
3 cup White flour
1 cup Whole wheat flour

Bring the water to a boil in a saucepan. Remove from the heat and stir in the salt. Mix the flours together in a large bowl. Add salt water to the flour and stir. Knead on a flour-covered surface.

Bake finished objects on a cookie sheet at 250 degrees F. for 2 to 3 hours. Check your objects every 20 minutes after the first 2 hours of baking. When cool, decorate with tempera, acrylic or colored marking pens. Spray with a clear acrylic finish to protect and preserve.

Gingerbread Playdough

2 cup flour
1 cup salt
1 Tablespoon ground ginger
1 Tablespoon ground cinnamon
2 Tablespoon vegetable oil
1 cup water

Mix well and knead until smooth. Note: At first it seemed it may be too wet; however, after putting a bit of flour on the hands and kneading---it came together wonderfully.

No Cook Play

1 cup all-purpose Flour
1/2 cup Salt
1/2 cup Very Warm Tap Water
Food Coloring

Mix flour and salt, then pour in water and stir well. Knead for 5 minutes, adding color as desired. Store in sealed container, keeps up to a week. Air dry, or small and thin pieces can be baked at 200 degrees for 2 hours.

Cornstarch Playdough (Uncooked)

1 cup cold water
1 cup salt
2 teaspoon oil
3 cup flour
2 Tablespoon cornstarch
Powdered paint or food coloring

Mix water, salt, oil and enough powdered paint to make a bright color. Gradually add flour and cornstarch and knead until the mixture reaches bread dough.

Rubbery Playdough

2 cup baking soda
1 1/2 cup water
1 cup cornstarch

Mix the ingredients together in a pan. Heat over a low heat until it is thick. Stir constantly. Place mixture on a pastry board or bread board to cool. As soon as it is cool enough to handle, knead well. At this time, you can add tempera paint or food coloring if you choose. Roll out flat. Use cookie cutters or cut shapes freehand. Place unused dough in a plastic bag. It dries fast. Paint your finished projects and brush with shellac or clear nail polish to preserve.

Cookie Clay

2 cup Salt
2/3 cup Water
1 cup Cornstarch
1/2 cup Cold water

Mix salt with water in saucepan. Stir and boil. Add cornstarch and cold water. Keep heating if it does not get thick. Roll out dough on board floured with cornstarch. Dry and decorate ornaments. This recipe is meant to be rolled out, cut with cookie cutters, and left to dry. Great for ornaments!

Uncooked Playdough

3 cup flour
1/4 cup salt
1 cup water
1 Tablespoon oil
Food coloring

Mix flour with salt: add water with the coloring and oil slowly. If too stiff add more water, if sticky add more flour. Keep in airtight container.

Cornstarch Play Clay

1 cup Salt
1/3 cup Water
1/2 cup Cornstarch
1/4 cup Cold Water
Food Coloring

In medium saucepan, mix salt and water over medium heat, stirring occasionally (about 3-4 minutes.) Remove from heat and add cornstarch and cold water. Will resemble mashed potatoes. Stir till thickens, cools, then knead. If it's too sticky, add a little more cornstarch. Store in sealed container with piece of damp sponge up to two weeks.

Salt Dough

1 Large bowl
1 Cookie sheet
1 Rolling pin
1 cup Salt
1 1/4 cup Warm water
1 Mixing spoon or mixer
3 cup Flour
1 plastic bag
1 refrigerator
painting supplies

Pour 1 cup salt into large bowl. Add 1 1/4 cups warm water, mix well. Add 3 cups flour, mix well some more. Knead into ball, seal in plastic bag and refrigerate. Paint, if you wish. You may wish to put on cardboard first.

Bird Seed Playdough

Birdseed
2 cup flour
1 cup salt
Water

Mix flour, salt & birdseed with sufficient water to make play dough texture. When done playing, place outside (with the children) in a sheltered area or tree for the birds!

Craft Clay

1 cup cornstarch
1 1/4 cup salt
2 cup baking soda (1 pound box)
1 Tablespoon oil

Combine the ingredients. Cook until thickened to dough like consistency. Turn mixture out on pastry board and knead. Cover with a damp cloth or keep in a plastic bag. Good for plaques and other models. It can be painted when dry.

Jewelry Clay

3/4 cup flour
1/2 cup salt
1/2 cup cornstarch
Warm water

Mix dry ingredients together. Gradually add warm water until the mixture can be kneaded into shapes. To create the beads: Break dough into little balls, rolling it to the desired shape; pierce the balls with toothpicks. Allow the balls to dry. When dry, paint and string the beads.

1-2-3 Playdough

1 cup cold water
1 cup salt
2 teaspoon vegetable oil
2 Tablespoon cornstarch
3 cup flour

Tempera paint or food coloring (adjust amount for color desired) Mix the water, salt, oil and paint together. Gradually work in the flour and cornstarch until you get the consistency of bread dough.

No Cook Cold Water Playdough

4cup flour
1 cup salt
2 Tablespoon cooking oil
1 to 1 1/2 cup cold water
Food coloring

Mix the salt, water, and vegetable oil in bowl. Add the flour a little at a time and mix until it forms a ball. Knead the ball of dough for about 10 minutes, Store the clay in a sealed container in the refrigerator until ready to use. When it is used—make items and place on a cookie sheet. Allow 48 hours for most items to dry. They can then be painted with a light coat of acrylic paint.

Basic Art Dough

2 cup flour
1/2 cup salt
3/4 cup water

In a bowl, mix 2 cups flour and ½ cup salt. Stir in ¾ cup water. Knead the mixture for 8 to 10 minutes, until it is smooth and pliable. If the dough is too dry, add a few drops of water. If it is too sticky, add a small amount of flour. Have children mold the dough into shapes and press it in decorations when desired. Place the decorated shapes on a baking sheet and bake them at 300 degrees F for about 4 hours, or until hard. If desired, when shapes are cool and dry, in an area away from the youth, spray the painted or unpainted shapes with a clear fixative.

Non-Editable - Playdough, Clay, and Molding Dough

Glue Dough

1 part Glue (try colored glue for different colors)

1 part Flour
1 part Cornstarch

Note: 1/4 C. of each ingredient produces a yield about the size of a tennis ball). Combine in a bowl and knead until well blended. If it's too dry, add a drop or two of glue. If too moist, sprinkle with flour and cornstarch. This dough is very moldable and will dry without baking. You can store it for weeks tightly wrapped in plastic wrap. Air-dry about 24 hours turning several times. You can roll it out on waxed paper and cut it into shapes. Try using cookie cutters, jar lids, bottle caps of free hand. Roll the dough to make ball shapes and press to shape. You can use either a toothpick or plastic drinking straw to make holes for stringing. To cut down on dry time for larger pieces. Use Styrofoam as a base, roll out some dough to about 1/8" to 1/4" and cover the foam. Have fun experimenting.

Non-Hardening No Cook Playdough

3 cup flour
3 Tablespoon alum
1/2 cup salt
2 Tablespoon cooking oil
2 cup boiling water

Add 10 drops food coloring to liquid or 2-3 T. dry tempera to flour. Adjust color intensity as desired. Mix in order given. Can use a dough mixer, Mixmaster, or stir with a spoon. Knead well. Keeps up to 6 mos. in heavy plastic lock bag.

Crunchy Clay Dough

1 Shredded Wheat biscuit
2 Tablespoon White Glue
Food Coloring

Crumble shredded wheat biscuit into bowl. Add glue and several drops of food coloring. Mix until shredded wheat is completely coated. Objects dry hard in 12 hours. This dough does not keep. Use it right away.

Sawdust Dough

1 cup sawdust
1/2 cup wallpaper paste
water

Mix sawdust and paste together, adding enough water to form a soft putty like mixture.

Bread Clay

6 slices white bread
6 Tablespoon white glue
1/2 teaspoon detergent or 2 tsp. glycerin
Food coloring

Remove crusts from bread and knead with glue. Add either detergent or glycerin. Knead until it is no longer sticky. Separate into portions and add food coloring if desired. Shape and brush with equal parts of glue and water for a glossy coat. Allow to dry overnight to harden. Paint with acrylic paint. Seal with clear nail polish.

Microwave Playdough

1 cup flour
3/4 cup water
2 teaspoon cream of tartar
1 pkg. unsweetened Kool-Aid
1/2 cup salt
1 Tablespoon cooking oil
1 teaspoon powdered alum

Combine ingredients. Heat in microwave and stir until mixture forms a soft ball. Stir about every 10 seconds. Put mixture on tray or wax paper and knead until cool. Store in an airtight container.

Toothpaste Putty

1/2 teaspoon toothpaste (cream not gel)
1 teaspoon white glue
2 teaspoon cornstarch
1/2 teaspoon water

Mix toothpaste, glue and cornstarch. Add water until you have a lump of putty. Wash and dry hands. Squeeze and roll putty into a ball, the more it is rolled and pulled the better it gets. It will begin to dry in 20 minutes. Just add a drop of water to soften. Will dry rock hard in 24 hours.

Sand and Cornstarch Modeling Dough

3 cup sand
1 1/2 cup cornstarch
3 teaspoon alum
2 1/4 cup hot water
Food coloring

Mix sand, cornstarch, and alum in saucepan. Add hot water and food coloring. Cook over med. heat until mix thickens. Remove from heat and knead until smooth. Store in airtight container.

Gingerbread Cinnamon Dough

1 cup ground cinnamon
1 teaspoon ginger
1 cup applesauce
1/4 cup white school glue (optional)

Add the cinnamon and ginger to the applesauce. You can also add glue for added thickness. Store unused dough in a bowl and cover it with plastic wrap.

Sawdust Modeling Clay

4 cup sifted sawdust

1 1/2 cup dry wallpaper paste
1/4 cup plaster of Paris

Mix ingredients together and add water to make mixture the consistency of clay. Let projects dry naturally in the sun or a well-ventilated place. To store the mixture, cover with a damp cloth or plastic bag.

Sparkling Snow Dough

2 cup water
2 cup flour
1 cup salt
4 tsp. cream of tartar
4 tsp. oil
Iridescent glitter

Combine ingredients in a heavy saucepan. Cook over medium heat, stirring constantly with wooden spoon- until mixture thickens and pulls away from sides of pan. Form dough into a ball, place on waxed paper and cool.

Bread Sculpting Dough

2 parts bread - approximately 2 pieces or slices
2 parts glue - approximately 1/4 bottle (normal bottle of Elmer's Glue-net4 fl. oz/118ml)
1 part food coloring (optional) - approximately 2 drops

Crumble bread into small chunks. Add glue. Mix immediately. If too dry or sticky add a little water. Add food coloring if desired. This is just like clay, but you need to be careful not to crumble it or hold it in your hand for too long. (It may get sticky and stick to your hand!) When you want colored figures, color the doughbefore working with it. It typically takes one hour to dry, depending on the amount and weight.Leave it in a cool room (for instance, the garage, if clean enough) on a flat cookie sheet, with a nonstick spray, or waxed paper on it. Once dry,spraywith either ceramic spray or hair spray -both do the trick. Also, clear nail polish or high gloss varnish work.Make sure the items have dried before puttingany on them.

Lotion Playdough

1 C. flour
1 Tablespoon vegetable oil
2 Tablespoon hand lotion
1/2 cup salt
2 teaspoon cream of tartar
1 C. water
Food coloring

Mix all ingredients together and create your dough.

Plain Old Playdough

2 cup flour
1 cup salt
2 Tablespoon alum
1 cup water
2 Tablespoon oil
1 Package Unsweetened Kool-Aid or Liquid food coloring

Pour dry ingredients into large pan. Stir together to mix. Stir oil and food coloring into the water. Pour liquid into the dry ingredients while mixing, squeezing and kneading the dough. If too sticky, add more flour. Keeps best in the fridge.

Cinnamon Clay

1 1/2 cup ground cinnamon
1 cup applesauce
1/3 cup white school glue (like Elmer's)
1 medium sized bowl
Flat surface for kneading
Wax paper
Rolling pin
Cookie cutters - various types
Knife
Straw

Non-stick cooling rack
Ribbon
Puffy paints, optional

Mix cinnamon, applesauce, and glue together in a bowl. Remove from the bowl and knead the mixture until it turns into a firm clay. Let sit for about 30 minutes. Clay is best used at room temperature. You may need to dust your rolling pin, hands, or working surface with cinnamon, or use wax paper as a working surface. Roll out clay with a rolling pin to approximately 1/8 of an inch thick. Use cutters to cut out desired shapes (we like gingerbread men). If you are going to hang your shape, use a straw to cut out a hole near the top of the shape. Place shapes on a nonstick cooling rack or wax paper. You will need to keep an eye on them and turn them over occasionally so that they dry evenly and dry flat. Dry shapes for approximatelyfive days. When dry you may put a ribbon through the hole for hanging on the tree or adding to a package. You may add puffy paint to decorate your shapes, if you wish.

This recipe makes a sweet-smelling dough that can be made into ornaments or package decorations. Gift ideas: Make an apple ornament to give to your teacher. Make heart ornaments to give to your mother, grandmother, or aunt for Christmas or Mother's Day.

White Bread Clay

1-2 slices White Bread, crusts removed
1 Tablespoon White Glue

Rip bread into tiny pieces in bowl. Add glue and mix with fork till all crumbs are moistened. Roll into ball. If it is too wet add a little more bread. Knead until smooth. If dough dries out while working, add a few drops of water and knead. Store in sealed contained in refrigerator up to a month. Air-dries in 1 to 3 days. For a semi-gloss finish; brush on equal parts water and white glue. Good for detailed projects-won't crack when drying.

Baby Oil Playdough

2 cup flour

1 cup salt
4 teaspoon cream of tartar
2 cup water plus food coloring
2 Tablespoon baby oil (other oil can work, too)

Mix ingredients and place over low heat and stir often until playdough is consistency of mashed potatoes. Knead when cool.

Sawdust Sculpture Mix

2 cup sawdust
1 cup plaster of Paris
1/2 cup wallpaper paste
2 cup water

Mix thoroughly. Mold with hands.

Mud Playdough

3 cup water
3 Tablespoon vegetable oil
3 cup all-purpose flour
2 Tablespoon cream of tartar
1 1/2 cup salt into a large bowl

Boil water and oil. Then while it is heating mix the dry ingredients in a bowl. Carefully mix the wet and dry together and knead until smooth. Add brown tempera paint (either dry or liquid) and 2 or 3 Tablespoons of coffee grounds.It really looks like dirt!

Bread Dough

4 pieces of bread (remove crusts)
4 Tablespoon white craft glue
A small amount of acrylic paint to color
Zipper type plastic bag

Tear bread into small pieces and place in zip bag, add glue. Mix well until it starts to form a ball. Add paint to the color and mix well. It will form a smooth ball collecting all scraps when ready to use. This takes a while so an adult may want to start before the time for project Keep stored in zip bag in refrigerator until ready to use. Shape as desired and allow to air dry (depending on thickness of shape and humidity can take several days to cure. The project can be made without color and finished shape painted if you prefer.

Cinnamon Ornament Dough

1 C cinnamon
1 Tablespoon ground cloves
1 Tablespoon ground nutmeg
3/4 cup applesauce (drain in a strainer for several hours)
2 Tablespoon white glue

Mix cinnamon, cloves and nutmeg together. Add applesauce and glue. Work mixture with hands until smooth. Roll out to 1/4-inch thickness and cut with cookie cutters. Use a straw to make a hole for ribbon. Place on wire rack and air dry for several days, making sure to turn occasionally.

Bakers Clay

4 cup flour
1 cup salt
1 teaspoon powdered alum
1 1/2 cup water
Food coloring

Mix all ingredients in bowl. If too dry, work in extra water with your hands. Bake on un-greased cookie sheet for 30 minutes in 250-degree oven. Turnover and bake another 1 1/2 hours. Remove and cool. When done, sand lightly if desired and paint.

Rock Hard Sawdust Clay

2 cup fine sawdust

1 cup wallpaper paste
Water

Mix sawdust and wallpaper paste together. Slowly add water. Blend until you have a mixture the consistency of clay. Turn it out on a couple sheets of newspaper and knead until all ingredients are very well blended. Use like any other molding clay. Let it dry for 3 days or bake in an oven at 200 degrees for about 2 hours. Sand to a smooth finish. Paint. Use shellac, spray finish or.

Sweet Smelling Glop

3/4 cup flour
1/4 to 1/3 cup white glue
1/4 cup thick shampoo
Food Coloring

Mix three parts flour, one-part white glue, and one-part thick shampoo. Add food coloring if desired. Makes a sweet-smelling mixture for modeling.

Fragrant Play Dough

2 1/2 cup flour
1 T alum powder
1/2 cup salt
3 Tablespoon oil
2 cup boiling water
a dash or two of food coloring
1 package unsweetened Kool Aid

Mix dry ingredients. Add boiling water and stir quickly. Add cooking oil and mix well. When cool enough, use your hands. Keeps well in airtight container in refrigerator.

Holiday Ornament Dough

1 cup ground cinnamon

4 Tablespoon white glue
3/4 cup water

Mix until the consistency of cookie dough. (Add more water if needed.) Sprinkle cinnamon on the cutting board and knead the dough. Roll out 1/4-inch thick. Cut into ornament shapes using cookie cutters or popsicle sticks. Punch a hole in the top with a straw or pencil before drying (so you can string ribbon through later for hanging). Bake in 350° oven for 30 minutes or until firm. Let them cool, then decorate!

Watermelon Playdough

2 1/2 cup Flour
1 Tablespoon Alum
1/2 cup Salt
3 Tablespoon Vegetable oil
2 cup Boiling Water
1 Package Watermelon Kool-Aid
OR
1 Package Watermelon Jell-O

Combine Flour, Alum, Salt, add Oil, Boiling Water. Stir or knead to mix. Add a package of unsweetened Kool-Aid or Jell-O for color and scent. Recipe can be doubled for LOTS of dough. Store in an airtight container.

Quickie Molding Clay

3/4 cup flour
1/2 cup salt
1 1/2 teaspoon alum powder
1 1/2 teaspoon oil
1/2 cup boiling water

Mix dry ingredients together, add water and oil. Mix well. You can add food coloring or tempera paint if you wish. Mold into anything you wish and leave to dry overnight. Store in jar or plastic bag. It will keep for months.

Traditional Playdough

1 cup flour
1/2 cup salt
1 Tablespoon alum powder
1 cup water
1 Tablespoon oil
2 Tablespoon vanilla
a dash or two of food coloring

In a big bowl combine flour, salt and alum. Gradually add the oil and water. Cook over low to medium heat, stirring constantly. When it reaches the consistency of mashed potatoes, remove from heat. Add vanilla and food coloring. Divide into balls and knead in color.

Crepe Paper Clay

Crepe Paper cut into thin strips (any colors you wish).
1 cup flour
1 cup salt
Large container and water

Place crepe paper into a large container and add enough water to cover the paper. Let that soak for about one hour until most of the water is absorbed into the paper. Pour off the excess water and add small amounts of flour and salt until you have a clay-like mixture. Create sculptures by forming crepe paper clay with your hands. Let dry and apply either varnish or glue and water mixture to seal.

Playdough for Baking

3/4 cup flour
1/4 cup white glue
1/4 cup ivory liquid SHAMPOO
Food coloring

Blend ingredients in a bowl. Knead the mixture together thoroughly, dusting with flour. Roll dough out flat. Make it thin because it expands when baked. Cut the dough with small cookie cutters. If you wish to hang the cutouts, poke a hole through the top. Bake on a cookie sheet for 2 hours at 200 degrees F. When cool, decorate with acrylic or tempera paint. Use for making nearly unbreakable miniature tree ornaments and figures.

Apple Cinnamon Dough

1 cup ground cinnamon
1 cup applesauce
1/4 cup white school glue (optional)

Add the cinnamon to the applesauce until you get a clay-like consistency. You may add glue for added thickness. Once the dough is mixed, create shapes with your hands or roll the dough out and use cookie cutters. Add glitter for fun! Let the dough dry. Store unused dough in a bowl with plastic wrap as a cover.

Modeling Clay

1 cup white school glue
3/4 cup liquid starch

Pour the glue into a plastic container and then add the starch. Stir the ingredients and knead the mixture with your hands. If it sticks to your hands, wipe a little starch on them. If the ingredients don't seem to be mixing well, you may need to heat them in the microwave (heat long enough for them to mix). Allow the mixture to set for a while and store it in a closed container in the refrigerator.

Moon Craters

Liquid Starch
Rock Salt
Glue with food coloring

Mix 1/2 cup of liquid starch with 2 cups of rock salt and 1/2 cup of glue plus food coloring or tempera. This makes a gooey, rocky mixture. Let the children freely pile onto cardboard to create a three-dimensional structure.

Soapy Dough

2cup flour
1/2 cup salt
2 Tablespoon liquid tempera paint
1 Tablespoon liquid soap
1/2 cup water

Mix all the dry ingredients in one bowl and then mix the liquid ingredients in another. Stir the two mixtures together and knead until pliable.

Cotton Ball Puff Dough

1cup flour
1 cup water
1 bag of white, cotton balls

Mix flour and water together to make a paste. Roll cotton balls in the paste and carefully lift them out.
Excess paste will fall off. Have children form the dough into desired shapes on a baking sheet. Bake the shapes for one hour at 325 degrees.

Lint Modeling Clay

3 cup dryer lint
1 cup cold or warm water
2/3 cup flour
3 drops oil of cloves, optional
Old newspapers
Saucepan
Boxes, bottles, balloons or other objects to mold

Stir lint and water in saucepan, add flour and stir to prevent lumps. Add oil of cloves to keep recipe fresh. Cook over low heat and stir until mixture forms peaks pour out and cool on newspapers. Shape over boxes, bottles, balloons or press into a mold or use like Paper Mache. Hints: makes 4 C.; dries in 3 to 5 days; is very hard and durable; dries smoothly if pressed into a mold; dries rougher is shaped over an object.

Salt Dough

2 cup salt
2/3 cup water
1 cup cornstarch
Additional 1/3 cup COLD water
Acrylic paint or food coloring.

Place salt and 2/3 C. water in small saucepan and heat until quite warm. Remove from heat. Mix cornstarch and COLD water together, add to salt mixture stirring constantly. Return pan to heat and keep stirring until mixture forms a smooth mass. Turn it out on a plate and cover with damp cloth until cool. Work in color as desired or leave natural. Place in zip bag & refrigerate. Salt Dough will keep indefinitely. Shape on foil covered cookie sheet and let dry (Several hours in a warm oven or several days at room temperature). You can sand rough edges with an emery board when dry.

Sand Dough

1 cup sand
3/4 cup liquid starch
1/2 cup cornstarch

Mix both starches over low heat. Add sand. Stir for several minutes until thick like oatmeal. Form into ball. Pat into a mold. Let it sit in the sun to dry.

Playdough

4 cup flour
1/4 cup powdered tempera

1/4 cup salt
1 1/2 cup water
1 Tablespoon oil

Mix flour, powdered paint and salt. Mix water and oil, and food coloring if desired. Gradually stir the water and oil mix into the flour mix. Knead the mix as you add the liquid. Add more water if too stiff, more flour if sticky.

Paper Pulp

Put a cup of shredded newspaper into a blender
Add 2 cup water

BLEND WELL. Very well. Strain the mixture so that it is mushy, but still very wet. (Adjust paper and water according to the amount you need.)

Cornmeal Dough

2 cup cornmeal
1 cup salt
Tempera paint for color
Water

Mix cornmeal, salt and paint with enough water to makea playdough texture.

Sand Textured Playdough

1/2cup sand
1/2 cup cornstarch
1/2 cup boiling water

Mix ingredients together and knead.

Chalk

Chalk

1 cup plaster of Paris

1/2 cup cold water
Candy or popsicle molds, toilet paper tubes with tape over one end
Tempera Paint (powdered is best)

Combine Plaster of Paris, water and tempera paint. The amount of tempera you add will determine how dark the colored chalk will be. Pour the mixture into candy or popsicle molds and let dry. Take the chalk out of molds and use for drawing on the sidewalk. This chalk will be most effective right after taking out the molds.

Sidewalk Chalk 1

3/4 cup Warm Water
Toilet Tissue Tubes
1-1/2 cup Plaster of Paris
2-3 Tablespoon Powdered Tempera Paints
Container for Mixing

Cover one end of tissue tube with duct tape. Place a loosely rolled piece of wax paper into the tube to create a liner to keep the plaster from sticking to the tube. Pour water into mixing container then sprinkle plaster; a little at a time, into the water until plaster no longer dissolves (approx.1-1/2 cups). Stir thoroughly. Mix in 2-3 tbsp. tempera paint. Place tubes sealed end down on a flat surface. Pour plaster mix in. Tap the side of tube to release air bubbles. Let dry 1-2 days, pull off mold and have fun drawing! Be sure to rinse containers and spoon outside or in a container of water to avoid clogging indoor sink drains.

Sidewalk Chalk 2

Water
Plaster of Paris
Large Plastic Container for Mixing
Small Plastic Containers for Molding
Water Base Paints (Washable Tempera)

Fill mixing container 1/2 full of plaster of paris and slowly add water. Stir until the plaster resembles pudding. Add paint until you achieve the desired color.

Pour into molds and let set for about a day or until dry. When dry turn containers upside down, hit on hard surface until chalk pops out and have fun drawing.

NOTE: chalk will wash off with the next rain, if you don't want to wait, just rinse off with your garden hose.

Spray Chalk

4 Tablespoon cornstarch
1/2 cup water
Food coloring

Mix until all lumps are out. Pour into spray bottle.

Eggshell Chalk

4-5 eggshells
1 teaspoon flour
1 teaspoon very hot tap water
Food coloring (optional)

Wash & dry eggshells. Put into bowl and grind into a powder. A mortar and pestle work fine for this. Discard any large pieces. Place flour and hot water in another bowl and add 1 T. eggshell powder & mix until a paste forms. Add food coloring if desired. Shape & press mixture firmly into the shape of a chalk stick and roll up tightly in a strip of paper towel. Allow to dry approximately 3 days until hard. Remove the paper towel & you've got chalk! Eggshell chalk is for sidewalks only.

Sidewalk Chalk Paint

1/3 cup quick setting Plaster of Paris
3 teaspoon water
1 Tablespoon paint
Glitter (optional)
Mix all ingredients. Scoop into empty toilet paper tube. Let set for 20 minutes. Peel off cardboard. Let dry for one day.

Paint - Non-Edible

Easel Paint

6-8 Tablespoon extender
1 pound can of powdered paint
3 cup liquid starch
2 Tablespoon soap flakes
Water

Put the extender in a large container, such as a one-quart plastic juice container. Gradually stir in the powdered paint and liquid starch, mixing well. Add soap powder. Add water until mixture reaches desired consistency. This recipe makes a large enough quantity so that it can be stored and poured out into small juice cans each day as needed. The paint will thicken and will need stirring and possibly more water.

Sand Paint

1/2 cup sand
1 Tablespoon Powdered paint

Mix and shake onto surface brushed with watered down glue.

Fluffy Painting Fur

Shaving cream
Glue
Paint (verity of colors)
Squeeze bottles

Use equal parts of shaving cream and glue and fold the glue with the shaving cream in a large bowl. Separate this mixture into separate bowls so you can mix different colors. Add a small amount of them to the shaving cream mixture until you reach your desired color. When finish mixing colors, pour the mixture carefully into bottles. (You will need to use the mixture immediately.) Using the squeeze bottle as your painting tool, paint a picture using several colors of the shaving cream mixture. The colors will blend beautifully. Set aside to dry for at least 24 hours. The shaving cream will retain its fluffy shape and has a beautiful smell.

Gouache Paint

(Opaque paint that dries quickly and can be painted on in layers)

2 cup dextrin (hobby stores have it)
4 Tablespoon DISTILLED water
1/2 cup honey
2 teaspoon glycerin
1/2 teaspoon boric acid solution
Powdered or poster paints

Dissolve the dextrin in the water (will be foamy). Then add the honey, glycerin and boric acid. Stir well or shake in covered jar.

Mix this base with powdered paint or poster paint and store tightly covered. Thin with water if too thick.

Easel Paint

1/3 cup water
1/4 cup liquid starch
1 one pound can powder paint
1 Tablespoon soap powder

Pour liquids into blender. Gradually blend in the powdered paint, using a rubber spatula to scrape the paint down from the sides of the blender jar. Add soap powder, and blend. The paint should be very smooth and thick. Add more liquid if necessary.

Puffy Paint

Flour
Salt

Water
Tempera Paint

Mix equal amounts of flour, salt and water. Add liquid tempera paint for color. Pour mixture into squeeze bottles and paint. The mixture will harden in a puffy shape.

Clown Paint

1/8 cup Baby Lotion
1/4 teaspoon Powdered Tempera paint
1 Squirt liquid Dishwashing Soap

Easily removed by soap and water.

Deluxe Poster Paint

1/4 cup flour
1 cup water
3 Tablespoon powdered tempera paint
2 Tablespoon water
1/2 teaspoon liquid starch or liquid detergent

Measure flour into saucepan. Slowly add water until mixture is smooth. Heat, stirring constantly until mixture thickens. Cool. Add 1/4-cup flour paste into small jar or plastic container. Add tempera paint and water for each color. For an opaque finish add liquid starch. For glossy finish had liquid detergent.

Topography Paint

1 cup powdered tempera paint
1/4 cup wallpaper paste
1/2 cup liquid laundry starch
Thick paint is ideal for creating topographical maps. Mix tempera paint and paste, stirring until smooth. Add liquid starch until mixture is spreadable. Use plastic knives or popsicle sticks to spread on heavy paper.

Body Paint

Baby shampoo
Powdered tempera paints

Add tempera paint to shampoo until desired color is reached. Great for painting designs on bodies, before getting in the pool or lake!

Sparkle Snow Paint

1/2 cup flour
1/2 cup salt
1/2 cup water

Mix and put in a squeeze bottle. Squeeze doughy paint out onto black construction paper. Make anything snowy, snowflakes, snowmen, or snow-covered mountains with the moon and northern lights. Let dry thoroughly and it will sparkle. May also be painted (when dry) and allowed to dry again. This is a great 3-dimensional effect for snow.

Translucent Paint

4 oz. school glue
1/4 cup liquid starch
Food coloring

This is a short-lasting paint that works well for easel painting. Mix all ingredients and store in small glass jars. Make only as much as you will need. The painting will last for almost a week.

Shiny Paint

Sweetened condensed milk
Tempera paint

Mix sweetened condensed milk and tempera paint to create several colors of paint. These paints will produce a glistening effect.

Face Paint

1 Tablespoon cold cream
2 Tablespoon cornstarch
1 Tablespoon water
Food coloring

Mix cream, cornstarch, and water until smooth. Add food coloring, one drop at a time until the desired color is achieved. Store in airtight containers.

Tempera and Starch Paint

2 cup powdered tempera paint
1 cup liquid starch

Mix tempera and starch until it is smooth and creamy. Slowly add water until the mixture has a good, thick consistency.

Frosting Paint (Non-Edible)

1 cup powdered tempera paint
2 Tablespoon wallpaper paste
1/4 to 1/2 cup liquid laundry starch

Mix tempera paint with wallpaper paste. Add starch, mixing until thick enough to spread - like frosting. Place paint on a plastic lid and use popsicle sticks to spread.

Opaque Poster Paint

1/4 cup flour
1 cup water
Pour flour into saucepan. Slowly add 1 cup water, stirring until mixture is smooth. Heat, stirring constantly until mixture thickens. Allow to cool, then measure 1/4 cup of the mixture into each of 4 small jars.

To each jar, add:

3 Tablespoon powdered tempera paint
2 Tablespoon water
1/2 teaspoon liquid starch or liquid detergent

Seal jars tightly when not in use.

Oil Paint

Tempera paint
Liquid dish washing soap.

This paint has a smooth, glossy effect and holds color well. Mix tempera paint and soap. Store in glass jars.

Crystal Paint

1/4 cup hot tap water
3 teaspoon Epsom salts

Sparkle and Shine! Mix hot tap water and Epsom salt. Brush the mixture onto a dark colored paper. When dry the salt will form crystals that shine in the light.

Dazzling Paint

White school glue
Glitter
Food coloring
Small zip type freezer bags.

Pour glue and glitter into small freezer bags. Add food coloring if desired. Mix by squishing around in your hands. Snip off a small corner of the bag and squeeze to paint.

Washable Window Paint

Tempera Paints (powdered or premixed)
Clear Dishwashing Liquid

Mix powdered paint with dish soap until they resemble house paint. Or mix just a little dish soap into premixed paints. Line the window sash with masking tape and be sure to spread newspaper around to protect the area. To erase paint or touch up mistakes just wipe paint away with a dry paper towel.

Watercolor Paints

1 Tablespoon white vinegar
2 teaspoon baking soda
1 Tablespoon cornstarch
1/4 teaspoon glycerin
Food coloring

Do like the famous impressionist painters did and bring your watercolors outside to paint. To make your own watercolors, first mix vinegar and baking soda. Next slowly add cornstarch and glycerin to the mixture. Poor into small paper cups to let dry. Add food coloring. The color is not as intense when it is dry so remember to add a lot of food coloring. When dry peel away the paper cups.

Salt Paint

1/8 cup liquid Starch
1/8 cup Water
1 Tablespoon Tempera Paint

Mix and apply to paper with a brush. Keep stirring mixture. Paint will crystallize as it dries.

Puffy Paint

1/2 cup flour
1/2 cup salt
1/2 cup water
liquid tempera paint

Mix the ingredients well. Pour into all those empty, clean mustard squeeze bottles you have been wondering why you were saving. Mark colors on outside.

Squeeze Bottle Glitter Paint

1 cup flour
1 cup salt
1 cup cold water

Mix well. Pour into plastic squeeze bottles. May add liquid tempera paint before mixing. Effective way to use left over tiny amounts of paint. Squeeze onto heavy construction paper or discarded cardboard. Has a glistening quality and dries with a textural effect.

Powdered Milk Paint

1/2 cup Powdered nonfat milk
1/2 cup Water
Powdered Paint Pigments

Mix milk and water. Stir until milk is dissolved. Combine only as much solution with powdered pigments as you intend to use in one sitting. Makes about 3/4 cup. For a large group, combine any amount of powdered milk with an equal amount of water. This paint dries quickly to a glossy, opaque finish. It does not dust, chip, or come off on your hands the way poster paint does. Mix a small amount of the solution with powdered pigment in a palette pan. Work smooth with a brush. Use water to thin paint and to clean your brushes. Store this medium in a tightly capped jar in the refrigerator.

Soap Paint

Warm water
3 cup Ivory Snow Powder
Paint or food coloring

Add water, a little at a time, to Ivory Snow. Mix to consistency of heavy cream. Color with a small amount of powder paint or food coloring.

Easel Paint

1-part powdered paint

2 parts powdered detergent
2 parts water

Mix powdered paint and powdered detergent together. Slowly mix in two parts water, stirring to eliminate any lumps. This basic recipe can be used to mix either large or small amounts if you keep the proper proportions.

Paint - Edible

Milk Paint

1 can sweetened condensed milk
Food coloring

Add a few drops of food coloring to sweetened condensed milk until desired color is achieved. When this paint dries, it will be very shiny. Give the children paintbrushes and paper or just let them use their fingers. The paint will be a pastel color and when it dries, it will be kind of glossy. Note: This edible paint is perfect for decorating holiday cookies.

Watercolor

2 Tablespoon clear vinegar
2 Tablespoon baking soda
1 Tablespoon cornstarch
1 teaspoon corn syrup
Food coloring

Mix the vinegar and baking soda in a bowl. When the mixture stops fizzing add the cornstarch and corn syrup. Blend - it will be rather thick. Divide between three containers (you can use the lids off liquid laundry detergent like Tide and Cheer - they don't tip easily). Add colors. Liquid food color makes a pastel paint while the paste food colors give a more vibrant result. Only put a bit in the bottom. These can be used immediately or allowed to dry cakes like the purchased watercolors.

*Tip. When using watercolor cakes add a few drops of water to the top of the cake at least a half hour before young artists starts working and the color will come much easier. Another plus to these paints is how quickly they dry, so unless you have a young artist that is totally into the water part, they can hang it on the refrigerator quickly.

Egg Yolk Paint

1 egg yoke
1/2 teaspoon water
Food coloring

Mix egg yolk with water, then add food coloring until intense color is reached. Use a paintbrush to paint on pre-baked cookies. After painting, return cookies to the oven at 200 degrees until egg paint has solidified.

Invisible Paint

4 Tablespoon baking soda
4 Tablespoon Water
Purple grape juice

Mix baking soda and water. Dip paint brush into water mixture and paint a design onto white paper. When the papers are completely dry, paint over the papers with purple grape juice. The designs will change from being invisible to visible. The picture mysteriously appears in blue-green colors. Note: Using a blow dryer will speed up the drying time.

Water Paint

Bucket
Water
Sponges
Brushes

Fill bucket with water and use brushes and sponges or other materials to paint water on sidewalk. "Paint" will disappear as it dries. (This has been known to also create wet children.)

Snow Paint

Food Coloring
Water

Place water and food coloring in an empty spray bottle. Let children spray colors on the snow to make designs.

Finger Paint - Non-Edible

Cooked Homemade Finger Paint

4 cup cold water
6 teaspoon of cornstarch

Mix a small amount of cold water with cornstarch until smooth. Gradually add the remainder of the water. Cook the mixture over low heat until it is clear and the consistency of pudding. Add tempera for color.

Plastic Starch Finger Paint

Liquid plastic starch
Water soluble powder paint in saltshakers
Pour a small amount of liquid starch on dry paper. Shake powder paint on paper and spread with your hands. You might even want to try finger painting with instant pudding. Everyone loves this one! Shaving cream is also fun to finger paint with.

Finger Paint (Uncooked)

1/2 cup liquid starch
1/2 cup soap powder
5/8 cup water

Beat together until the consistency of whipped potatoes.

Snow Paint

1 cup finger-paint mixture
1 Tablespoon white tempera paint or 1 1/2 cup soap powder or flakes
1 cup hot or warm water
1 teaspoon glycerin

Whip with an eggbeater.

Finger Paint 1

2/3 cup dry starch or cornstarch
1 cup cold water
3 cup boiling water
1 Tablespoon glycerin
1 cup ivory soap flakes or 2 T. liquid soap
Calcimine pigment or food coloring.

Dissolve starch in cold water. Smooth lumps and add boiling water. Stir constantly. Thicken until clear but do not boil for more than one minute. Add the rest of ingredients (hot or cold). Use it on glazed paper, newsprint, wrapping paper, or on washable surface for mono-prints.

Finger Paint 2

1 cup dry laundry starch or 1 C. cornstarch
1 cup cold water
4 cup boiling water
1 cup soap flakes
1/4 cup talcum powder

Put the starch in a large saucepan. Add the cold water gradually, stirring until there are no lumps. Continue to stir while adding the boiling water, and cook over medium heat until clear, stirring constantly. When mix thickens, add the soap flakes and talcum powder. Remove from heat and beat with an eggbeater until smooth. The mixture should be thick. Store it in a plastic container in refrigerator or use while still warm.

Finger Paint 3

1 cup cornstarch
2 cup cold water
1/2 cup soap powder
2 quarts boiling water
Glycerin or oil of wintergreen
Liquid food coloring

Put cornstarch in a pitcher or bowl. Gradually add cold water, stirring until smooth. Pour this mixture slowly into two quarts of boiling water, stirring constantly. Cook until the mixture is clear and thick. Add the soap powder. Stir until smooth. Remove from heat and add a few drops of glycerin or wintergreen and food coloring.

Finger Paint 4

1 cup dry laundry starch
1/2 cup cold water
1 1/2 cup boiling water
3/4 cup powdered detergent

Put the dry starch in saucepan. Gradually add the cold water, stirring until smooth. Add the boiling water, stirring rapidly and continually. Add the detergent and stir again until smooth. There is no need to cook this recipe.

Finger Paint 5

1 cup dry laundry starch
1 cup cold water
3 cup soap flakes

Mix all ingredients together for a quick, no-cook finger-paint. The texture will not be as smooth and thick as the cooked kind.

Finger Paint 6

1 part liquid soap (NOT detergent)
4 parts liquid starch
Powdered tempera

Add soap to liquid starch and let the children use this mix on a smooth washable surface. Sprinkle tempera on the liquid to provide color.

Finger Paint 7

1 Tablespoon soap powder
1/4 cup liquid starch
1/3-1/2 cup water
1 one pound can powdered paint

Pour soap powder, starch, and water into blender. Gradually add powdered paint while machine is running. Blend until smooth. Use this recipe for extremely bright colors.

Finger Paint 8

1 cup flour
1 cup cold water
3 cup boiling water
Powdered tempera or food coloring

Mix the flour and water, stirring until smooth. When the mix is smooth, pour it gradually into the boiling water and bring to a boil, stirring constantly. Add the coloring.

Soap Flakes Finger Paint

1 1/2 cup dry laundry starch
1 1/2 cup soap flakes
1 quart boiling water
Water

Food coloring or tempera paint

Mix starch with enough cold water to make a paste. Add boiling water and stir until clear. Cool and add soap flakes and coloring. Store in a tightly sealed container.

Tempera and Starch Finger Paint 1

1/8 cup Liquid starch
1 Tablespoon Powdered tempera

Pour starch directly onto paper. Sprinkle the tempera over the starch. Mix the color in as you paint.

Tempera and Starch Finger Paint 2

2 cup powdered tempera
1 cup Liquid starch
Water

Mix tempera and starch until it is smooth and creamy. Slowly add water until the mixture has a good, thick consistency.

Finger Paint (Cooked)

2 cup flour
4 cup cold water
pinch of salt
Food coloring or dry tempera

Mix flour and water and cook over low heat until thick. Cool. Add a pinch of salt. Add dry tempera or food coloring, if desired. Store in covered jar in refrigerator.

Soap Finger Paint

Soap flakes
Food coloring or powder paint

Beat soap flakes in small amount of water until it reaches the consistency of whipped cream. Add color and mix well. Use smooth tabletop (it washes off easily), construction paper, or balloons, as well as on paper.

Simple Finger Paint

Clear liquid detergent
Dry tempera paint
Paper

Mark off the section of the table to be used with masking tape. (The same size as the paper) Squirt the detergent onto the table and add about a teaspoon of tempera paint. Allow your child to create their work of art. When they are finished, press the paper onto the paint, and lift carefully.

Finger Paint - Edible

Chocolate Pudding Finger Paint

Mix instant chocolate pudding according to the directions and paint on wax paper. Great for children who like to eat their art.

Kool-Aid Finger Paint

2 cup flour
2 packets un-sweetened Kool-Aid
1/2 cup salt
3 cup boiling water
3 Tablespoon Oil

Mix wet into dry. The kids love the color change. Then finger paint away.

Whipped Cream Finger Paint

1 cup whipped cream (the whip your own kind that comes in a carton)
Food coloring
Put whipped cream in a mixing bowl and mix with electric mixer. Add food coloring until you have the desired color. Paint and have fun!

Easy Quick Finger Paint

1 cup flour
1 cup water
One and a half teaspoons of salt
Food coloring

Mix well and put in plastic lids from coffee cans. The kids will enjoy this textured finger paint that sparkles when dry.

Scented Finger Paint

1/2 cup cornstarch
1 packet unflavored gelatin
1 packet unsweetened Kool-Aid
3 cup water

Mix 3/4-cup cold water with the cornstarch and Kool-Aid to make a paste. Soak gelatin in 1/4-cup cold water. Set it aside. Bring 2 cups of water to boil and slowly add the cornstarch mixture, stirring until the mixture is completely dissolved. Continue cooking over medium heat, stirring constantly until the mixture comes to a boil and clears. Remove from heat and stir in gelatin. Cool and store in an airtight container.

Jell-o Finger Paint

Any kind of flavored Jell-O
Enough boiling water to make it a good consistency for finger-paint.

Use your normal finger-painting material or glossy paper. Kids love the smell and the feel of it.

Washable Finger Paint

1 cup all-purpose Flour
4 cup Cold Water
Food Coloring

In large saucepan mix the flour with the 1-cup cold water. Stir until smooth. Then add the 3 cups cold water. Cook over medium heat, stirring until mixture thickens and bubbles. Reduce heat and simmer 1 minute more while still stirring. Divide into three heat-resistant bowls. Tint with food coloring. Cover and cool.

Salt and Flour Finger Paint

2 cup Flour
2 teaspoon Salt
3 cup Cold water
2 cup Hot water
Food coloring

Add salt to the flour in a saucepan. Pour in cold water gradually and beat the mixture with an eggbeater until smooth. Add the hot water and boil the mixture until it becomes glossy. Beat it until it is smooth. Mix in food coloring.

Pudding Finger Paint

1 package pudding mix
1 1/2 cup milk
Food Coloring

Mix the pudding with milk. Use different flavors of pudding for different colors of paint. (Vanilla may be tinted with food coloring.) "Paint" designs on wax paper, then eat. Finger-licking good!

Finger Licking Finger Paint

Finger printing paper
Corn syrup (thick)
Food coloring

Put a good size blob of syrup on each student's paper then add a drop or two of food coloring onto their syrup. Let them dig in! Be sure to let the painting dry for a day or so, you may want to outline the drawing with a black marker as well.

Flubber, Slime, Goop, Gak, and Silly Putty

Silly Putty

1 cup white glue
1 1/2 cup liquid starch

Mix glue and starch in a bowl. You may add a few drops of food coloring if you wish to color the putty. Cover bowl and let stand for a few hours. Pour off extra starch. Knead well, store in a covered container.

Flubber

1 teaspoon Metamucil or similar soluble fiber
8 oz water
microwave-safe bowl
microwave oven
food coloring (optional)

Mix 1 teaspoon of Metamucil with 1 cup (8 ounces) of water in a microwaveable bowl. You can add a drop or two of food coloring if you wish. Alternatively, you could add a little powdered drink mix or flavored gelatin to get color/flavor. Place bowl in the microwave and nuke on high for 4-5 minutes (actual time depends on microwave power) or until the goo is about to bubble out of the bowl. Turn off the microwave. Let the mixture cool slightly, then repeat step 3 (microwave until about to overflow). The more times this step is repeated the rubberier the substance will become. After 5-6 microwave runs, careful with handling it the mixture is hot pour the flubber onto a plate or cookie sheet. A spoon can be used to spread it out. Allow it to cool. What you have is a Non-stick flubber. A knife or cookie cutter may be used to cut the flubber into interesting shapes.

Homemade Kids Gooey Gak

Wire whisk
1 cup all-purpose white glue
3/4 cup water
Food coloring or 1 tablespoon tempera paint, your choice of color

Borax detergent

Mix with wire whisk the all-purpose glue, water, and food coloring/tempera paint. Mix separately 1/3 c. water and 1/2 tsp. Borax. Slowly pour Borax mix into glue mix. Let stand a few minutes, then knead. Pour off any remaining liquid. Store in plastic bags. Repeat in different colors. Tip: Avoid contact with hair or clothing, especially with small children. If the Gooey Gak happens to get caught in either substance, try using vegetable oil to break down the Gak.

Silly Putty

Plastic cup
Wooden craft stick
Zip lock Baggies
Food coloring 1 oz. Elmer's white glue
1 Tablespoon Borax
1 cup water

Mix the Borax with water. In the plastic cup, stir together 1 oz. glue with 1 oz. water with the wooden stick. Mix 1 oz. of the borax solution into the plastic cup. Add 1 drop of food coloring and mix as well as you can. Knead with your hands - store in plastic bags.

Clear Gak

2 cup Water
2 Tablespoon Borax
Glue

Heat water with borax until borax dissolves. Add this to a bowl of clear glue. Just play around till it feels right.

Funny Putty

2 Tablespoon white glue
1 Tablespoon liquid starch
Food coloring

Mix glue and desired food coloring. Pour starch over top. Swish so that all the glue is covered. Let sit 5 minutes. Squeeze off extra starch. Knead till mixed.

Silly Putty

Glue(wood glue works well but white glue will also work)
Epsom salts
Water
Measuring spoons
Plastic spoon
2 small cups
Waxed paper
Plastic bag (optional)

In one cup, put 1/2 tsp Epsom salt and 1/2 tsp water, stir to dissolve salt. (NOTE: It may not all dissolve.) In the other cup, put 1 tablespoon glue. Add the Epsom salt water to the glue and stir. Watch as your new material starts to form. Pull out the putty and put it on the waxed paper. You can experiment with it to find out more about its properties. You can store the new putty in a plastic bag. Store in a Ziploc bag in the refrigerator for maximum life. A few drops of Lysol can be added to recipes to minimize formation of mold and extend the lifetime. Wash hands before using slime to minimize mold growth as well. Keep off carpets and furniture as it can stain.

Homemade Hard Goop

1 cupcornstarch
1 cup baking soda
1/2 cup of water

Mix with your hands-they will get messy a bit and the "Liquid but Not" will harden– then soften –then drip while you form and play with it. It comes off with a little soap and water!

Edible Slime

1 can sweetened condensed milk

1 Tablespoon cornstarch
10-15 drops of red or green food coloring

Pour the can of SWEETENED condensed milk into a saucepan. Add the cornstarch and cook over a low heat, stirring constantly. When the mixture thickens remove it from the heat and then add the food coloring. Allow it to cool before playing or eating; it can also be used as a fun paper paint.

Great Goop

2 cup water
1/2 cup cornstarch
Food coloring

Boil water in saucepan - add cornstarch stirring until smooth. Add food coloring and stir. Remove from heat and cool. Child can play with the goop on any plastic covered surface. Using the boiling water makes a more stable "harder" substance that the Oobleck recipe.

Slime

1 box Ivory Soap flakes
1 Gallon Water
Food color

Beat with mixer - Makes 5-gallon bucket.

Flubber 1

Solution A:
1 1/2 cup Warm Water
2 cup Elmers Glue
Food Coloring

Solution B:
4 teaspoon Borax
1 1/3 cup Warm water

Mix solution A in one bowl, mix solution B in another bowl. Dissolve both well. Then just pour solution A into solution B, DO NOT MIX OR STIR! Just lift out flubber. It's neater than "Gak" or "slime". And it is also a safe chemical reaction for the kids to see. If you half the recipe, you only need to half the solution A and it will work the same.

Silly Putty

1 cup white glue
Food coloring
2 drops oil of cloves
Approximately 1/2 cup liquid starch

Mix glue with a few drops of food coloring until desired color is achieved. (Pastels work best; it's almost impossible to get brighter colors.) Stir in oil of cloves. Then begin adding liquid starch. Continue stirring in starch until mixture reaches a shapeable, stretchable consistency. You may need slightly less or more than one cup of starch, depending on humidity. Store in an airtight container.

Goop

1 Part Liquid starch
2 Part Elmer's Glue
Food Coloring (opt.)

Mix ingredients together until smooth. Enjoy! Try to make a ball with the mixture. Note how it kind of keeps its shape as long as you are working with it, but as soon as you stop, it "melts" through your fingers.

Oobleck or "Play Slime"

2 cup Water
1/2 cup Cornstarch
Food coloring (optional)

Put cornstarch in bowl. Add enough water to make a paste. If desired, you may also add food coloring. This makes a messy slime that goes from liquid to solid and is great fun to play with. The food coloring will stain so make sure you are not putting it down where you don't want to. You can change the consistency by changing how much water or cornstarch you add. This recipe (or green playdough) is especially fun to make after reading Bartholomew and the Oobleck by Dr. Seuss!

Silly Putty

1 part Liquid Starch
1 part Elmer's White Glue
Food coloring (optional)

Mix glue and starch together until it feels like a putty. If desired, add food coloring and mix thoroughly. When not in use, Silly Putty may be stored in an airtight container.
Important Note: Be sure to use Elmer's White Glue, NOT Elmer's "Washable" or "School Glue." Otherwise, you'll just get Gak!

Modeling "Goop"

2/3 cup water
2 cup salt
1/2 cup water
1 cup cornstarch

Beads, colored macaroni and other small objects

Add 2/3-cup water to the salt in a pan, stir and cook over med. heat, stirring 4-5 minutes until salt is dissolved. Remove mix from heat. Gradually mix 1/2 cup water with the cornstarch in a separate container. Stir until smooth. Add the cornstarch mixture to the salt mixture. Return to low heat and stir and cook until smooth. The goop will thicken quickly. Remove from heat and use for modeling objects. Objects made from this goop can also be hardened in the sun. This mix will not crumble when dry. Objects like macaroni, etc. can be added to the goop, and adhered to the models.

Flubber

1/2 cup white glue
1/3 cup warm water
Food coloring
1 teaspoon Borax
1/3 cup warm water
Zip lock baggie

Mix glue, 1/3 C. warm water and food coloring (this is the glue solution) in a small bowl. In a medium zip lock baggie, mix Borax and 1/3 C. warm water. (Borax solution) Pour glue solution into baggie with the Borax solution and gently knead (squash) together.

Silly Putty

Mix in one bowl:

3/4 cup water
1 cup glue

Dissolve in separate bowl:

1 cup water
1 teaspoon borax

Add both mixtures together and add any coloring you might want if any. You get a great shiny plastic like silly putty that is fun! Should be stored the same as playdough.

Glurch

1- 1/2 Tablespoon glue
1 teaspoon Borax solution (solution: a pinch of powdered Borax mixed with 6 Tablespoon plus 2 teaspoon water)
1 Tablespoon plus
1 teaspoon water

Put glue in the paper cup. Add water and stir well. Add food coloring, if desired. Add Borax solution and stir until mixture solidifies. Remove from cup and put in plastic wrap.

Silly Putty

1 1/2 cup water
2 cup white glue
A couple drops of food coloring (optional)
Mix these ingredients together.
In a separate bowl mix
1/2 cup warm water
1 Tablespoon Borax

Combine the two concoctions. Knead until smooth (about 10 minutes). As with the recipe above this will stain.

Sweet Smelling Glop

Flour
Glue
Thick Shampoo
Food Coloring

Mixthree parts flour, one part white glue, and one part thick shampoo. Add food coloring if desired. Makes a sweet-smelling mixture for modeling.

Drizzle Goo

1 cup Flour
1/4 cup Sugar
1/4 cup Salt
3/4 cup Water
Food coloring

Mix all together and put in squeeze bottle. Drizzle on paper.

Papier Mâché, Glue and Paste

Glitter Glue

White glue
Glitter
Powdered tempera paint (optional)

Combine 2 parts glue with 1 part glitter. Add powdered tempera paint if desired. Mix thoroughly. Store in airtight container.

Flour Papier Mâché Glue

Mix 1/2 cup all-purpose flour, and 2 cups cold water. Add that mixture to 2 cups boiling water and allow it to return to a boil. Remove from heat and add the sugar. Let the entire mix cool and thicken. Once the mixture cools it's ready to use.

Decoupage Glue

White glue
Warm water

Combine 3 parts glue with 1 part water. Mix thoroughly. Store in airtight container.

Papier Mâché with Starch

Liquid starch
Water
Newspaper strips

Mix equal parts of liquid starch and water. Stir until starch is dissolved. Soak newspaper strips in liquid mixture and pat into place.

Homemade Stickers

11 teaspoon flavored gelatin
2 teaspoon boiling water
Cut-outs to use as stickers

Place gelatin and boiling water in a small bowl. Stir until the gelatin is dissolved. Let mixture cool for 1 minute. While the sticker solution is warm, brush a thin coat on the back of each cut-out – use your finger or a small brush. When dry you can lick them and stick them on paper or glass just like a real stamp.

Paper Paste

1/3 cup non-self-rising wheat flour
2 Tablespoon sugar
1 cup water
1/4 teaspoon oil of cinnamon or other scent

Mix flour and sugar in a saucepan. Gradually add water, stirring vigorously to break up lumps. Cook over low heat until clear, stirring constantly. Remove from stove and add oil of cinnamon. Stir until well blended. Makes about 1 cup.

Spread paste with a brush or tongue depressor. Soft, smooth, thick and white, Paper Paste has a good spreading consistency and is especially appropriate for use with small children or for any paste-up work. This paste can be stored in a covered jar for several weeks without refrigeration.

Papier Mâché Paste

1 cup cold water
1/4 cup flour
5 cup boiling water

Mix the flour into cold water. Stir until lumps are dissolved. Gradually pour mixture into boiling water, stirring constantly. Boil for about 3 minutes, stirring constantly. Cool before using.

Thin Paste

1/4 cup sugar

1/4 cup non-self-rising flour
1/2 teaspoon powdered alum
1 3/4 cup water
1/4 teaspoon oil of cinnamon or other scent

In a medium-sized pan, mix sugar, flour and alum. Gradually add 1 cup water, stirring vigorously to break up lumps. Boil until clear and smooth stirring constantly. Add remaining water and oil of cinnamon. Stir until thoroughly mixed. Make one pint. How to use it: Spread paste with a brush or tongue depressor. Thin Paste is an excellent adhesive for scrapbooks, collages, and Strip Papier Mache'. This paste can be stored in a jar for several months without refrigeration.

Papier Mâché

Water
White flour (one part flour to one part water)
Strips of Newspaper, about 1" wide
Acrylic, tempera, or poster paints
Brushes

Mix flour and water in a large bowl (2 cups of each is a good amount with which to start) until it makes a smooth paste. Dip in the newspaper strips, one at a time, remove the excess paste from your fingers and lay the coated newspaper on the form. Smooth out the wrinkles and continue to place coated newspaper over the surface until completely covered. When the surface has totally dried, paint your own design using acrylic or poster paint, and decorate with craft supplies.

Papier Mâché with Flour

Place 2 or 3 Tablespoons plain flour in a bowl. Add a little bit of water. Stir to make a smooth paste. Gradually add more water until the paste is the consistency of thick cream. Apply paste with a brush or your fingers.

Simple Papier Mâché

For 1 to 1 1/2 cups Papier Mâché paste, mix one cup of flour with 1 cup water. Keep adding water (about 3 cups) and mix until all the lumps are gone. Bring to a boil in a saucepan and cool completely.

Transfer Solution

2 Tablespoon soap powder, like Ivory Snow (not detergent) or scrapings from a bar of soap
1/4 cup hot water
1 Tablespoon turpentine

Dissolve soap powder in hot water. Add turpentine. Use when cool.

This solution is used to transfer a picture to paper. To use, dip a brush into the ink and brush over the picture to be transferred, wait about ten seconds then place a piece of paper over the picture and rub the back of it with a spoon. The picture will be transferred to the paper. If the solution solidifies in its container, set the bottle in a pan of warm water to melt, then shake well before using.

Simple Modge Podge

1/4 cupsugar
1/4 cupall-purposeflour
1/2 teaspoon powderedalum
1 3/4 cupwater
1/4 teaspoon oil ofcinnamon

In a medium size pan, combine sugar, flour and alum. Gradually add 1 cup water, stirring vigorously to break all lumps. Boil until clear and smooth, stirring constantly. Remove from heat. Add remaining water and oil. Stir until thoroughly mixed. Store in glass container with airtight lid.

Crepe Paper Paste

Cut or tear 2 sheets crepe paper of a single color. The finer the paper is cut, the smoother the paste will be. Add 1/2 Tablespoon flour and 1/2 Tablespoon salt and enough water to make a paste. Stir and squash the mixture until it is as smooth as possible. Store in airtight container.

Papier Mâché Extra Soft

Paper Napkins, Cleansing Tissues or Toilet Tissue
Thin Paste or white glue

Crumple napkins or tissue and cover with paste. Model to desired shape. Use to add details such as noses, ears, eyebrows, and so forth to larger pieces. NOTE: This mixture does NOT keep and must be used immediately.

Stamp Glue

1 packet unflavored gelatin
2 Tablespoon boiling water
2 Tablespoon cold water
1/2 teaspoon white corn syrup
1/2 teaspoon almond extract

Dissolve gelatin in boiling water. Add cold water. Stir in corn syrup and flavoring.

Brush glue onto the back of stamps you've made. Allow it to dry. To stick stamps onto another paper product, just lick them.

Glue Paste

Dilute white glue with water 5 to 1.

Papier Mâché Paste

1/2 cup non-rising wheat flour
1/4 cup powdered resin glue (available at hobby shops)
1/2 cup warm water
1 1/2 cup hot water
4 drops oil of wintergreen

Mix the flour and resin glue in a saucepan. Slowly pour in the warm water. Then add the hot water and stir vigorously. Cook over low heat stirring until paste is smooth, thick and clear. Should be used in 2-3 days.

Stamp Gum

1 (1/4 ounce) package unflavored gelatin
1 Tablespoon cold water
3 Tablespoon boiling water
1/2 teaspoon corn syrup
1/2 teaspoon lemon or other flavored extract

In a small bowl, sprinkle the gelatin on the cold water. Let it sit 5 minutes to soften. Add the boiling water. Stir until the gelatin is dissolved. Add corn syrup and extract. Store in a small jar such as a baby food jar. Cut out pictures from magazines. Brush the picture on the back side with the gum. Let it dry, then moisten the gum with water or by licking and stick it to paper.

Wheat Paste

Wheat paste or wall paper paste
Warm water

You can get wheat paste at most hardware stores or art supply stores. Mix wheat paste and water until it is thick and creamy. Store in a container with a tight lid. Use it within 2-3 days.

Papier Mâché

1/3 cup White Glue
1/3 cup Water
Newspaper

Mix glue and water. Tear newspaper into one by 4-6" strips. Brush the glue on, and then put a paper strip. Smooth strip with fingers. Continue laying down 3-4 layers of strips. Let dry for 2-3 days.

Gum

1 packet of unflavored gelatin
1 Tablespoon cold water
3 Tablespoon boiling water
1/2 teaspoon white peppermint extract
2 drops boric acid solution

For stamps and paper labels. Sprinkle the gelatin into the cold water to soften. Pour into the boiling water, stirring until dissolved. Add the remaining ingredients and mix well.

Using glue, brush thinly onto the back of a stamp or some paper and let dry. When applying to paper, just moisten it a bit. To keep, store in a small jar or bottle with a lid. Warm in a pan to turn into a liquid again.

Papier Mâché from Glue

White glue
Water
Paper

Mix two parts of the white glue with one part of warm water. Stir well to produce the Papier Mâché paste. Adding Elmer glue to the above flour recipes will give it more strength.

Homemade Glue

3/4 cup water
2 Tablespoon corn syrup
1 teaspoon white vinegar
1/2 cup cornstarch
3/4 cup cold water

Mix water, syrup and vinegar in small saucepan. Bring to a rolling boil. In small bowl, mix cornstarch and cold water. Add this mixture slowly to the first mixture. Stir constantly. Let stand overnight before using.

Colored Salt Paste

2 parts salt
1 part flour
Powdered paint
Water

Mix salt and flour. Add powdered paint. Gradually stir in enough water to make a smooth, heavy paste. This mix can be used like regular paste. Store in airtight container.

Colored Glue

Empty glue into plastic bowl. Add food coloring. Return to glue container.

Papier Mâché

Flour
Water

Mix one cup of flour with 1 cup water. Keep adding water (about 3 cups) and mix until all the lumps are gone. Bring to a boil in a saucepan and cool completely.

Easy Glue

1 part flour
1 part water
A bowl and a wooden spoon for mixing

Mix well and add food coloring ... just for fun.

Homemade Paste

1/2 cup flour
Cold water

Add cold water to flour until a thick cream forms. Simmer on stove for 5 minutes. Add food coloring or flavoring if desired. This is a wet messy paint that takes a while to dry.

Papier Mâché Paste

3 cup water
1/2 cup flour
a drop or two of wintergreen

Mix the water and flour together in a large saucepan. Use your hands if you can stand it. Your hands are the best tools to break up the little lumps of flour. Heat the mixture over a medium heat stirring constantly. Add a couple drops of wintergreen.

Caution: wintergreen is toxic. It smells like yummy gum but don't be tempted to taste it. You use wintergreen to retard molding. If you are going to use your paste right away leave it out. Make sure your project is well ventilated while drying. After a while the paste will thicken. As soon as it thickens, remove it from the stove and let it cool.

Modge Podge Glaze

Glue
Water
Varnish

Mix 3 partswhite glue(any brand) to1 part water. Add water to get the desired texture and thickness. Add 2 Tbsp.varnish, for shine. Store in a glass container with airtight lid.

Papier Mâché

Flour
Water
2 Tablespoons Sugar

Mix 1/2 cup all-purpose flour, and 2 cups cold water. Add that mixture to 2 cups boiling water and allow it to return to a boil. Remove from heat and add the sugar. Let entire mix cool and thicken. Once the mixture cools its ready to use.

Rice and Pasta

Notes:
- Any of these recipes can be used for both rice and pasta.
- These recipes make the rice or pasta inedible use with caution when working with younger children.

Rice Dye

1 teaspoon rubbing alcohol
Food coloring
1 cup rice

Mix a few drops of food coloring with alcohol. Put rice in a sealable container. Pour liquid mixture over rice and shake until color is evenly distributed. Spread colored rice in a thin layer to dry. Store rice in dry airtight container.

Colored Pasta

Baggies
Food coloring
rubbing alcohol
Pasta

Pour 1/4-cup alcohol into a baggie. Add 10 drops (depending on shade you want) of food coloring to the alcohol. Add 1/2-cup pasta to the alcohol. Seal the baggie and allow the pasta to absorb the color for about 5 - 10 minutes. Turn the bag every couple minute to evenly coat the pasta. With a slotted spoon, scoop the pasta out of the baggie and allow to dry on a brown paper bag for about 1 hour. Rigatoni makes good beads for necklaces.

Sand and Salt

Sand Play

1 part white glue
2 parts flour
2 parts sand
2 parts water

Mix together to create a dough. You may need to add water or flour depending on the consistency.

Homemade Glitter

5-6 drops of food coloring
1/2 cup salt—stir well.

Mix and then cook in microwave for 1-2 minutes or spread out on a piece of waxed paper to air-dry. Store in an airtight container.

Colored Sand

Baggies
Dry tempera paint
Sand

Pour 1/4-cup sand into a baggie. Add tempera paint (depending on shade you want) to the sand. Seal the baggie and gently shake until the paint is evenly distributed throughout the sand.

Sand Play

Add sand to quick set cement and follow the instructions for mixing the cement. Use this recipe when you have a mold or have created a pattern in the sand.

Colored Salt

Baggies
Food coloring

Salt

Pour 1/4-cup salt into a baggie. Add 5 drops (depending on shade you want) of food coloring to the salt. Seal the baggie and gently shake until the food coloring is evenly distributed throughout the salt.

Homemade Moon Sand

1 1/2 cup water
3 cup corn starch
6 cup play sand
Optional: Add package of Kool-Aid if want it colored

Thoroughly mix the sand, cornstarch, and water. It will take a few minutes to get it smooth. Really work it in with your fingers...and then it's done! You may need to add a bit more water—but be careful and add just a small amount at a time; it could get goopy. When done, Place in an airtight container. Next time, revive it with 2-3 tablespoons of water. Just sprinkle it over and work it in.

Other Recipes

Rainbow Stew

1/3 cup sugar
1 cup cornstarch
4 cup cold water

Cook until thick. Put in bowls, add food coloring. Put in Ziplock baggies. Let the kids play with it while it is in the bags for a neat sensory experience or use it to mix colors.

Easy-Off Temporary Kids Tattoos

1 Tablespoon cold cream
2 Tablespoon cornstarch
1 Tablespoon water
Food coloring

Clean paint brush

Mix all ingredients together, stirring to mix well. Use a thin paintbrush to apply the tattoo.

Charcoal Garden

6 Charcoal briquettes
1/4 cup bluing (found in laundry area of stores)
1/4 cup salt
1/4 cup ammonia
Food coloring (red, yellow, blue, green)

Place 6 briquettes in an aluminum pie tin. Place food coloring drops on briquettes as follows (if you wish); One color on each of four briquettes, (1st Red, 2nd Blue, 3rd, Yellow, 4th Green) all 4 colors on the 5th briquette, and no colors on the 6th briquettes. Pour the combination of bluing, salt and ammonia over all the briquettes. In a day or so, colorful sprouts will form and soon you will have a garden! To keep the garden growing, pour a new mixture over the garden every 2 days.

Fruit Dyes

Provide several fruit juices that make dyes. Have the children drop the juices through an eyedropper onto coffee filters. Use juices such as grape, cranberry or apple juice.

Plain Old Mud

Just go outdoors and get a shovel full of dirt. Place it in a bowl and add a small amount of water. To dry the mud creations, just put creations out in the sun.

Homemade Soap Balls

Ivory Snow
Water
Bowl

Plastic trays
Food coloring optional
Fragrance optional (like perfume or cologne)

Moisten Ivory Snow with water in a bowl to the consistency of very stiff dough. Food coloring and fragrance may be added if desired. Have each child shape large spoonsful of soap into balls with their hands. Place shaped balls on plastic trays to harden- about 3 days.

Flower Preservative

1-part Powdered Borax
2 parts Cornmeal
Covered cardboard box (shoe or stationery box)
Fresh flowers

Thoroughly mix borax and cornmeal. Cover the bottom of the box with 3/4 of an inch of this mixture. Cut flower stems about 1 inch long. Lay the flowers face down in this mixture. Spread the petals and leaves so that they lie as flat as possible. Do not place flowers too close together. Cover the flowers with 3/4 of an inch of the mixture. Place the lid on the box and keep at room temperature for 3 to 4 weeks. This is an excellent way to preserve corsages or flowers from someone special. Try daisies, pansies, apple blossoms, asters, violets, and other flowers with this method. They will stay summer fresh indefinitely.

Rock Paperweight

Large, rounded rock
Tissue paper squares (various colors)
Wax paper
Diluted glue
Paintbrush

Spread a sheet of wax paper on top of the workspace. Lay a square of tissue paper on the rock and paint over it with diluted glue. Continue painting and placing until the rock is completely covered. Allow the glue to dry.

Salt Beads

2 parts table salt
1 part flour
Water

Mix the salt, flour and water into dough like consistency. For color, add dry pigment or food coloring. Break off small pieces and form into beads. Pierce with a toothpick and allow to dry, then string.

Squeeze Bottle Glitter

1 part flour
1 part salt
1 part water

Mix equal parts of flour, salt and water. Pour into plastic squeeze bottles, such as those used for ketchup and mustard. Add liquid coloring for variety. Squeeze onto heavy construction paper or cardboard. The salt gives the designs a glistening quality when dry.

Magic Garden Crystals

4 Tablespoon salt
4 Tablespoon water
1 Tablespoon ammonia
2 pieces charcoal, smashed into small chunks
Food coloring

Find a small disposable but waterproof container. Add the charcoal and spread out evenly. Combine the salt, water, and ammonia in a bowl, and pour over charcoal. Sprinkle a few drops of food coloring over the whole concoction. Place the container on a shelf low enough for children to see and let them watch it grow.

Felt

Remove the label from the jar, hot glue goodies (plastic flower, little toy, plastic fish, etc.) to inside of lid. Fill jar with water (leave room for water level to rise when the goodie lid is added) and add glitter, about a tablespoon. Put on lid checking water level, hot glue lid in place. Glue ribbon around the edge of the lid, tie in bow. Cut a circle of felt to fit the bottom (lid is the bottom) and glue in place. Shake and watch it sparkle!

Homemade Snow (It doesn't melt!)

Four bars of Ivory Soap
Twelve rolls of toilet paper
3 cup borax
Warm water
Large plastic tub with a tight lid.

Unroll and shred toilet paper into plastic tub. Add water until the paper is covered. Grate the soap into the soaking paper. Add the borax. If the mixture ends up too wet, drain over a fine screen or cheese
cloth. This will be kept for several weeks in an airtight container if no ingredients are added.

Slate Bag

Tempera Paint
Ziplock bag

Place paint in bag and smooth out bubbles. Make sure the bag is locked completely. Thick paint such as finger-paint works best. Allow children to press the bag with their fingers to make designs.

Clean Mud

Unroll 6 rolls of white bathroom tissue paper into a very large container. Generously add water until covered completely. Grate 2 bars of Ivory soap into mixture and add 1 1/2 C. of Borax. Mix well.

Bread Baubles

White loaf bread
Cookie cutters

Straws
Paintbrushes
Paints
Glue
Gold string
Glitter (optional)
Sequins, beads, etc. (optional)

Use a cookie cutter to cut shapes into white bread. Use the end of a straw to make a hole near the top of the shape. Leave shapes to harden overnight. Paint in bright colors using either poster paints or powder paints with a little household glue added. Leave ornaments to dry. After the ornaments have dried, turn them over and paint the other side. When dry, add beads, glitter etc. Loop gold string through the hole. Hang on Christmas tree.

Salt Art

Salt
Food Coloring

Place some salt in a bowl and add a few drops of food coloring. Mix well. Keep adding food coloring until the desired color is achieved. Make several colors. Take a small transparent empty jar with a lid or top on it. Baby food jars are good for this or try pickle relish jars. Take the label off. Pour different colored salt in layers into the jar using a toothpick or something like poke the salt down and make designs. Fill the jar all the way to the top. Put the lid on the jar and admire your creation.

Lick and Stick

Pour 2 Tablespoon cold water into a small bowl and sprinkle 1 pkg. of unflavored gelatin over it. With a fork, whisk in 3 Tablespoon boiling water and stir until dissolved. Add 1/2 teaspoon corn syrup and a few drops of flavored extract. Cut out any picture or paper and with a paintbrush apply a thin layer of the solution onto the back of the picture. Let dry. When ready, lick and stick! Note: This recipe will gel, return the mixture to a liquid for reuse, spoon into a jar and place jar in a bowl of hot water.

Fruity Lip Gloss

2 Tablespoon solid shortening
1 Tablespoon fruit-flavored powered drink mix
Food coloring
Small container

Mix shortening and drink together in a small microwave-safe container until smooth. Place container in the microwave on high for 30 seconds until mixture becomes a liquid. Pour the mixture into a plastic film container or any other type of small airtight container. Place the Fruity Lip-Gloss mixture in the refrigerator for 20-30 minutes or until firm.

Soap Crayons

1 3/4 cup Ivory (powder)
50 drops food coloring
1/4 cup water

Mix water & soap flakes together. Add food coloring & put mixture into an ice cube tray. Allow to harden. Break or cut into pieces. Fun to write with on the tub when bathing & face & hands.

Mud Pies

1 puddle
Plastic sand pails
Spoons
Cookie sheet

The "original" clay- dirt and water! Dig mud out of bottom of puddle and mix in sand pails. Spoon globs onto cookie sheets. Remove worms. Place in the sunshine until mud pies dry.

Flower Preservatives with Borax

Fresh Flowers (roses, pansies, violets, sweet peas, chrysanthemums, zinnias, marigolds, daisies, etc.)
Florist's wire
Airtight container such as -a coffee can
Plastic bag
Borax
Wire or string
Soft brush

Pick flowers at the peak of their bloom. Remove the stems. Make new stems with florist's wire. Run wire through the base of the flower and twist the two ends together. Line the coffee can with the plastic bag. Pour enough borax into the plastic bag to cover the bottom to a depth of 1 inch. Place flowers face down in the borax. Pour about 1 inch of borax over the top of the flower. Add more flowers and borax until the container is full. Gather the top of the bag, squeezing out all the air inside it. Fasten shut with wire or string. Place a lid on the can and set aside in a dry place for at least 4 weeks. Remove flowers from borax and carefully brush away all borax with a soft brush. Flowers preserved in this way make colorful "permanent" floral arrangements. Flowers picked at the peak of their bloom remain fresh looking indefinitely. Using the wire stems, make an attractive flower arrangement as you would a fresh-flower bouquet.

Snowflakes

Waxed paper
Thin white frosting
Disposable cake decorating bags
Silver cake decorations

Give each child a sheet of waxed paper and a disposable decorating bag filled with thin white frosting. Show children how to drizzle frosting onto paper in snowflake pattern. Add silver balls. Allow it to dry completely before eating.

Rubber – Kookie Creepies

1 envelope unflavored gelatin
2 Tablespoon hot water

2 Tablespoon white glue
1/2 Tablespoon liquid tempera paint
Assorted candy molds

Mix liquid tempera paint and white glue together in a bowl. In another small bowl, mix gelatin and hot water together until gelatin is completely dissolved. Add the gelatin/water mixture to the glue/paint mixture. Stir until the concoction begins to thicken. This can take as long as 6 to 7 minutes. When the mixture thickens, quickly pour it into a candy mold or cookie cutter. Place the mold in the freezer for 5 minutes or until firm. Carefully remove the Kookie Creepies from the candy molds or cookie cutters and allow them to dry for 1 hour on each side. Store in an airtight plastic zip bag. Play with Kookie Creepies just as you would any other kind of rubber-type creature. Allow Kookie Creepies to air-dry for 2-3 days and they will transform into hard plastic-like creatures.

Homemade Bath Salts

1 box Epsom's salts (2 qt)
Food coloring
Perfume or fragrance (sold in most craft stores)

Pour the salt in a large bowl, add food coloring to reach the color you want. Add fragrance if desired. You can decorate bottles to put the salt in. Makes a great gift for that special lady.

Simple Bath Bombs

10 Tablespoon baking soda
5 Tablespoon cornstarch
5 Tablespoon citric acid
1 1/2 Tablespoon safflower, sweet almond, or vegetable oil
1/2 Tablespoon water
Small amount of borax (1/2 tsp.)
1 Tablespoon fragrance oil or essential oil of your choice

Sieve all dry ingredients. Mix oil, water, borax, and scent in a jar - make sure to shake well. Drizzle this mixture onto the dry ingredients and then work it in with your hands. Press into a mold and then carefully pop them out. Let set for at least 24 hours to be totally hardened.

Holly Jolly Christmas Candies

4 cup corn flakes
2 cup marshmallows
1/2 cup margarine
1 teaspoon vanilla
Green food coloring
Heat source
Large mixing spoon
Waxed paper
Plastic spoons
Red hot candies

Melt together over low heat marshmallows and margarine. After mixture is melted, remove from heat and add vanilla and food coloring. Stir in corn flakes. Let children take turns dropping the mixture by spoonful onto waxed paper. Add three cinnamon "holly berries" to each candy. Allow it to dry before eating. Both pretty and delicious!

Materials for the Art Box and Sensory Play

(Keep in mind the ages of the children)

These are general ideas about what you can include in your art box/sensory play box that will help inspire you and your children to have hours of fun. There may be many more items that you could include that are not listed here. Please keep in mind the ages and abilities of the children as you select items.

A

Aluminum Foil
Animals
Apron

B

Baggies
Ball Bearings
Barrel Hoops
Basketry
Batik
Beads
Beading
Beans
Belts
Blueprints
Board
Books
Bottles
Bowls
Boxes
Bracelets
Braiding
Brass
Buckets
Buckles
Burlap
Buttons

C

Calculator
Candles
Cans
Canvas
Cardboard
Carpet
Cars
Cartons
Catalogs
Cellophane
Chains
Chalk
Chamois
Clay
Clamps
Clipboard
Cloth
Clothes Pins
Colander
Confetti
Construction Paper
Containers
Cookie Cutters
Copper Foil
Cord
Corn Husks
Corn Stalks
Costume Jewelry
Cotton Balls
Craft Kits
Crayon Pieces
Crochet
Cross Stitch
Crystals

D

Dirt and Worms
Dishes
Doilies
Drill
Drop Cloth

E

Embroidery Hoops
Emery Board
Eyelets

F

Fabric
Felt Squares
Flannel
Flashlight
Floor Covering
Frame
Funnels

G

Glass
Gloves
Glue
Golf Tees
Gourds

H

Hairpins
Hammer
Hard Hats
Hat Boxes
Hats
Hooks

I

Ice cubes
Inner tubes
Instant Potato Flakes

J

Jars
Jugs

K

Knitting

L

Lacing
Ladles
Lampshades
Leather
Level
Linoleum

M

Macaroni
Magazines
Magnets
Magnifying Glass
Marbles
Markers
Masonite
Measuring Cups
Measuring Spoons
Metal Foil
Mirrors
Molds
Muffin Tins
Muslin

N

Nail Practice Board

Nails
Napkins
Necklaces
Neckties
Needles
Newspaper
Noodles

O

Oilcloth
Ornaments

P

Packing Peanuts
Pails
Paint
Paint Brushes
Paint Rollers
Paint Tray
Pans
Paper
Paper Bags
Paper Clips
Paper Dishes
Paper Towels
Pasta
Patch Work
Patterns
Pebbles
Phonograph Records
Photographs
Picture Frames
Pinecones
Pencil
Pins

Pipe Cleaners
Plane
Potholder Loops

R

Rake
Reeds
Ribbon
Rice
Rings
Rocks
Rolling Pin
Rope
Rubber Bands
Rug Hooking
Ruler

S

Safety Goggles
Safety Pins
Sand
Sandpaper
Saw
Scale
Scoops
Screen
Screwdriver
Screws
Seashells
Seeds
Sewing Cards
Sewing Machine
Shaving Cream
Sheepskin
Shells

Shoe Polish
Shoelaces
Shovels
Sifters
Sieve
Soaps
Snaps
Snow
Sponges
Spools
Spoons
Staples
Sticks
Stockings
Strainer
Straws
Stuffing
Styrofoam Pieces

T

T-Square
Tacks
Tape
Tape Measurer
Thread
Tie Dye
Tiles
Tin Foil
Tissue Paper
Toilet Paper Tubes
Tongue Depressors
Toothpicks
Towels
Trucks
Tubes
Twine

V

Varnish
Vice Grip

W

Wallpaper
Wax
Weaving
Wiggle Eyes
Wire
Wire Hooks
Wire Mesh
Wood Glue
Wood Scraps
Wooden Beads
Wooden Blocks
Wool
Work Shirts
Wrapping Paper

Y

Yarn

Z

Zipper

Alternative Paint Brushes

There are many things that you can use for paintbrushes that make some interesting paintings. Try the different ideas below and try different types of paints. Please note if any of the below suggestions are editable if you do not use editable paint, you should not eat or allow the children to put it in their mouth as paint can be toxic and cause serious conditions.

Anything With Interesting Texture
Balloons
Balls
Bark
Bingo Dabbers/Markers
Body Parts (Hands, Fingers, Arms, Toes, Feet)
Bottle Caps
Branches
Brushes
Bubble Wrap
Candy "Peeps"
Combs
Corn Cobs
Cotton Balls
Eyedroppers
Feathers
Fly Swatters
Foods
Forks
Ice or Frozen Paint
Leaves
Jar Lids
Marbles
Pasta
Pipe Cleaners
Plastic Animals (Feet)

- Plastic Wrap or Plastic Grocery Bag (Crumpled)
- Q-tips
- Rag or Other Fabric
- Rocks
- Roll-on Deodorant Bottles
- Shells
- Shoe Polish Applicators
- Soap-less Scouring Pads
- Spaghetti Noodles (Cooked)
- Spoons
- Sponges
- Spray Bottles
- Squeeze Bottles
- Stamps
- String
- Tires
- Toothbrushes (Flick the Bristles)
- Toy Cars or Other Rolling Toys (roll the wheels through paint)
- Twigs
- Yarn

More Age-Appropriate Activities

Age 6-12 months Activities

Mirrors
Practice grasping-bean bag
Use own spoon
Busy box
Hide and seek w/blanket and toy
Ball-rolling
Wooden puzzle
Crib gym
Peek-a-boo games
Move toys up, down and around in front of baby's eyes
Rub baby's arms w/different kinds of cloth
Hang mobile
"Follow the Leader"-imitation game (blink eyes, clap hands, finger plays: Thumkin, pat-a-cake, This little piggy and others.)
Nursery rhymes
Blocks
Arm exercises
Leg exercises
Rhythm instruments
Let baby crawl after softball or bean bag
Puppets
Talk a lot to baby--use his/her name
Make happy, sad, mad, etc. faces
Telephone game
Pretend tea party w/baby and bear

Ages 12-18 months Activities

Blocks-try building towers
Drawing-large paper and crayons

Picture books
Puppets
Pull toys
Throw a ball
Pretend grocery shopping
Blowing and catching bubbles
Painting with water
Simple singing games and finger plays
Dancing with long scarves to music
Toys that rock
Work bench-hammer, etc. drum
Point to body parts
Feel different textures-flannel, silk, cotton, wool, tree bark, etc.
See-n-say

Age 18-24 months Activities

Spontaneous scribbling
Large pop beads
Simple puzzles
Play dough
Bead stringing
Ball bouncing
Sandbox
Water play

Age 24-30 months Activities

Fold paper
Trace shapes
Crayons and paper
Play dough
Nesting blocks
Puzzles
Sorting boxes
Finger plays-working on counting -ten little Indians, *One two buckle my shoe, etc

Follow the leader
Music
Teach colors
Bristle blocks
Large Legos
Books with tapes
Pegboard

Age 3-5 years Activities

Legos
Books
Color forms
Candyland
Chutes and Ladders
Hi Ho Cheery O!
Memory old maid
Books w/ tapes
Lacing cards
Pegboard
Puzzles
Beads
Painting
Finger-painting

Age 6-8 years Activities

Books
Memory
Sorry
Connect 4
Scrabble for Jr.
Dominos
Parchisi
Checkers
Pegboard
Legos

Puzzles
Lincoln logs
Tinker toys
Operation
Uno

Age 8 and up Activities

Sorry
Clue
Monopoly
Scrabble
Checkers
Parchisi
Operation
Uno
Chinese Checkers
Tri-Ominos
Concentration
Puzzles

Images to Stimulate Baby

Images are a great way for your baby to learn and to grow. Infants like high contrast images such as black and white it helps them focus on the image and see the contrasts and the shapes in the image.

The following images are just some examples you can create your own just remember to keep them simple so your baby can learn to focus on them better.

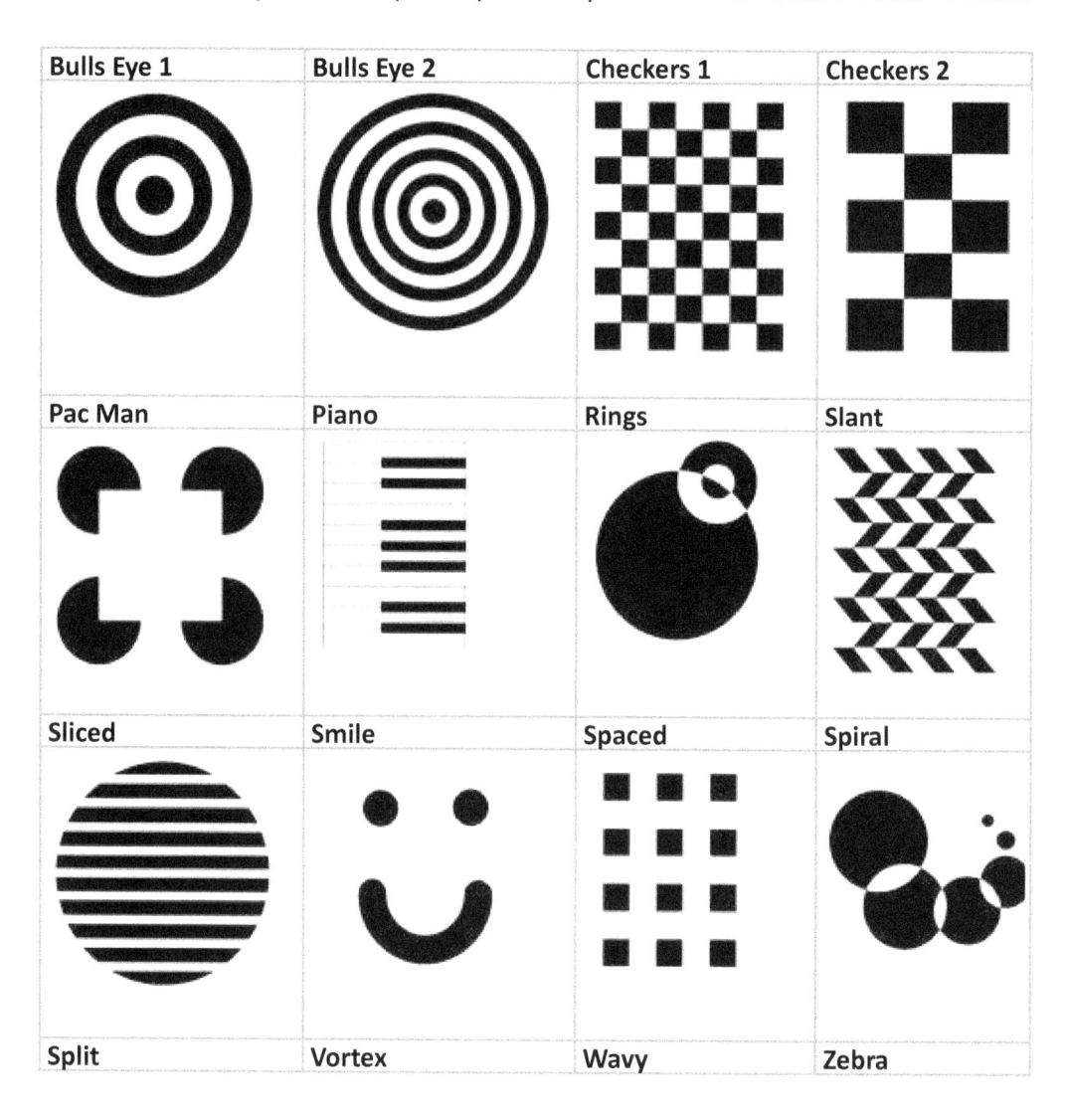

Bulls Eye 1	Bulls Eye 2	Checkers 1	Checkers 2
Pac Man	Piano	Rings	Slant
Sliced	Smile	Spaced	Spiral
Split	Vortex	Wavy	Zebra

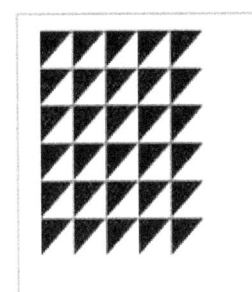

Bulls Eye 1

Bulls Eye 2

Checkers 1

Checkers 2

Pac Man

Piano

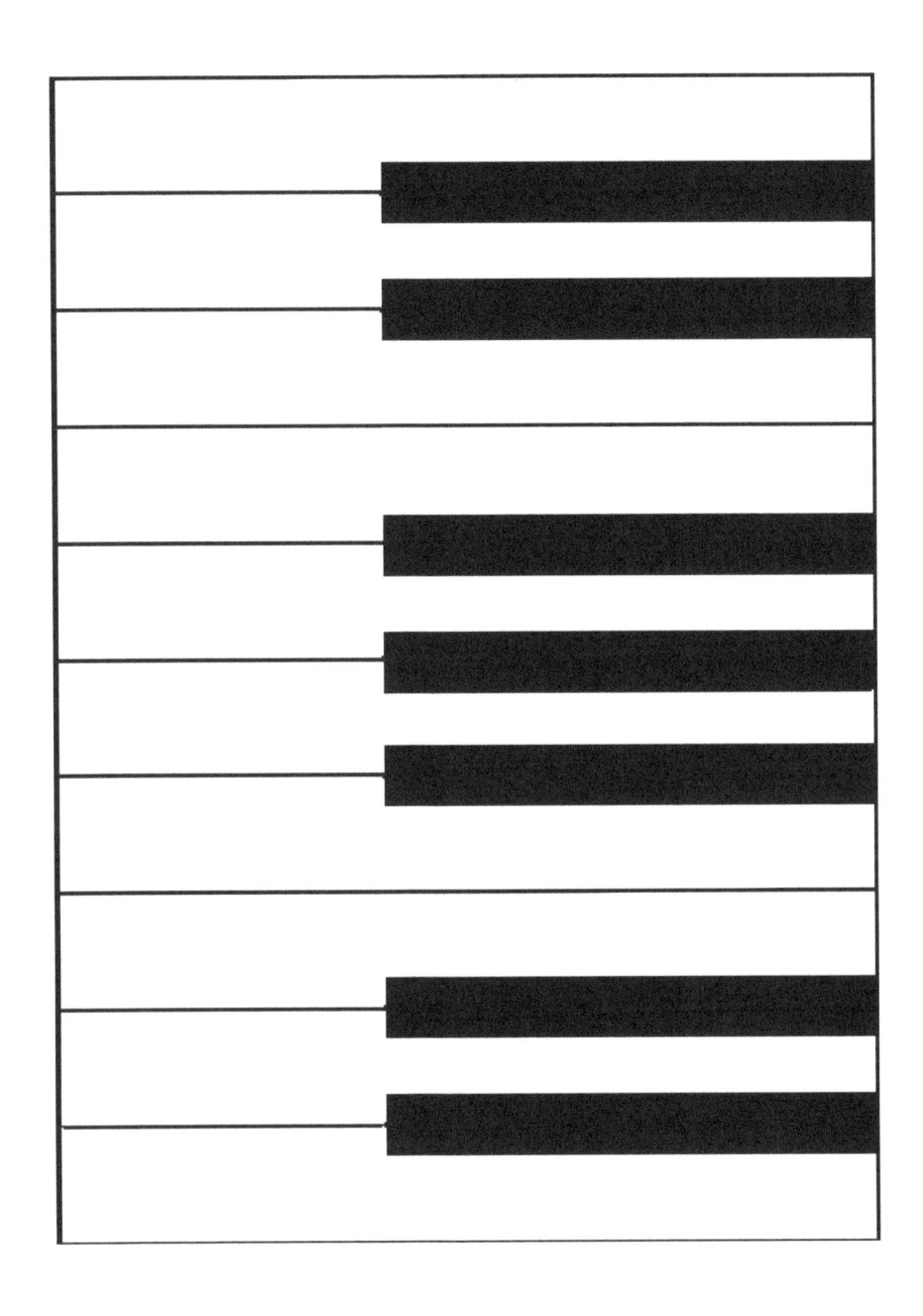

Rings

Zig Zag

Sliced

Smile

Spaced

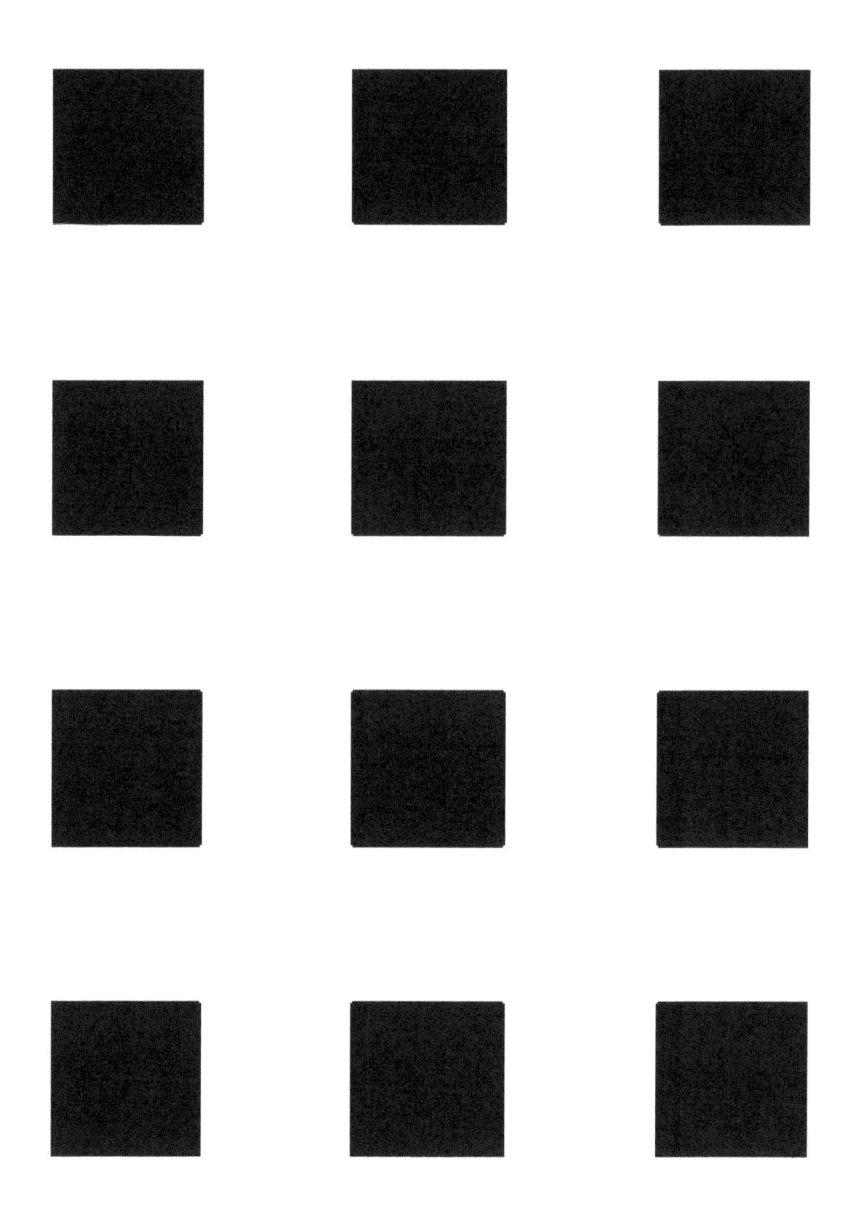

Spiral

Split

Vortex

Wavy

Zebra

Toddler Property Laws

I found this poem on the internet years ago and I have found it very true. I took my children to a church conference and my then two-year-old had a favorite blanket that she loved. I allowed her to have it in the car while we drove to the conference but because I did not want it accidentally lost or must keep track of it while keeping track of everything else, I made her leave it in the car. While on a break we were out in the hall, and she spotted "her blanket" wrapped around a little baby. It took a lot of convincing to get her to stop her tantrum and assure her that her blanket was waiting for her in the car. She was ready to fight the baby for what she deemed hers. So, enjoy this fun little poem and when you have a similar experience you will be able to think back to this and smile as you try to calm your irate toddler.

Toddler Property Laws

If I like it, it's mine.
If it's in my hand, it's mine.
If I can take it from you, it's mine.
If I had it a little while ago, it's mine.
If it's mine, it must never appear to be yours in any way.
If I'm doing or building something, all the pieces are mine.
If it looks just like mine, then it is mine.

Unknown